RESHAPING AUSTRALIA

RESHAPING AUSTRALIA

URBAN PROBLEMS AND POLICIES

Frank Stilwell

PLUTO PRESS
AUSTRALIA

First published in November 1993 by
Pluto Press Australia Limited,
PO Box 199, Leichhardt, NSW 2040

Cover design: Trevor Hood

Index: Neale Towart

Typeset, printed and bound by
Southwood Press, 80 Chapel Street, Marrickville, NSW 2204

Australian Cataloguing in Publication Data

Stilwell, Frank J.B.
Reshaping Australia.

Bibliography.
Includes index.
ISBN 1 86403 001 1.

1. Urban economics. 2. Urban policy — Australia.
3. Cities and towns — Australia. 4. City planning — Australia.
5. Regional planning — Australia. 6. Australia — Economic
conditions — 1990-   . I. Title.

307.140994

Contents

Preface

Australian society is principally urban. A higher proportion of the population lives in cities than in any other country, with the exception of tiny nations like Singapore and Hong Kong. The ideology of a rugged rural life style as the source of national identity lingers uncomfortably beside this dominant urban existence. The pattern of Australian urban development is also distinctive in combining a high degree of metropolitan dominance in each of the States with a low overall population density within those metropolitan areas. Suburbia is the norm.

These characteristics of urban Australia have important economic, social, political and cultural expressions. They constrain the possibilities for new patterns of regional development. They are linked with a range of problems in the big cities, including inadequate access to affordable housing, excessive traffic congestion and localised unemployment. Such problems do not impinge equally on all. However, some other problems are of growing significance for the society as a whole, such as the shortage of land for urban development and pressure on scarce environmental resources. These problems are not uniquely Australian, of course, being more or less evident in major cities worldwide. Their general origins and the specifically Australian features warrant careful attention.

It is also important to acknowledge the array of remedial policies that have been tried, often with a disappointing degree of success. There have been attempts to promote decentralisation, based on the assumption that excessive urban size or growth is the key problem. More recently urban consolidation policies have been in vogue, based on the assumption of the need for higher urban population densities. Specific policy measures have been used to tackle particular problems of land allocation, housing, transport, employment and environmental quality. A review of the experience with these policies can help to reveal the limits of reformism and to identify what else could be done.

Reshaping Australia: Urban Problems and Policies does not purport to provide a blueprint for resolving all the problems of Australian cities, let alone the socio-economic system in its entirety. Rather, its primary concern is to examine how Australian urban structure is shaped by capital, class and state. This involves examining the nature of the problems in the major cities, the experience of remedial public policies and the nature of urban conflicts. This type of analysis is a prerequisite for considering alternative urban futures.

The book is the companion volume to *Understanding Cities and Regions: Spatial Political Economy* (Pluto Press, 1992). The points made in the preface to that book about the objectives of the inquiry and the method of exposition apply equally to this volume. So do the acknowledgments, in particular the appreciation of the research assistance by Matthew Eaton, the word-processing by Lynne Harvey and Eleanor Armstrong and the personal support of Ann Grealis. Peter Murphy is to be thanked for his help in assembling Census data for this volume. The principal difference between the two books is the focus here on more down-to-earth urban problems and policy issues rather than theories of regional development. This should enhance the appeal of the present book to a broader readership. The recurrent reference in this volume to the particular features of Australian cities and urban policies is also distinctive.

The issues are analysed from the perspective of political economy. This recognises that, since urban problems often have their roots in general characteristics of the socio-economic system, they may not be soluble through policies of spatial regulation or redistribution alone. It is necessary to identify the structural basis of urban problems, exploring the relationship between general socio-economic processes and spatial form. Such a political economic approach requires the juxtaposition of theory, empirical research and engagement with practical issues in the pursuit of social progress. It is a challenging task.

Frank Stilwell
University of Sydney

1

Jobs

The owners and managers of capital are reshaping Australian cities. There is nothing particularly novel about this. Historically, there has been a close association between the growth of cities and the changing structure of production and employment. The development of commercial activities, industrial production and specialised service functions in cities has taken the form of overlapping waves. The emergence of patterns of uneven regional development has been closely linked with the changing structure of industries such as agriculture, mining, manufacturing and tourism. What is now of increasing concern is that recent structural changes are leading to the intensification of economic, social and environmental problems in the cities. In circumstances of economic recession the issue of jobs is of particularly pressing concern.

This chapter begins the process of unravelling the key issues affecting the economic base of our cities by:

- examining the broad patterns of boom, slump and restructuring of capital which shape employment conditions;
- considering how these structural economic changes impact on urban employment;
- analysing the patterns of unemployment, taking as a case study the impact of the recession in the early 1990s.

This involves moving from the general to the specific, from international and national economic trends to the local impacts on regional and urban employment. First, a little history is needed in order to put contemporary urban employment problems in a broader perspective.

BOOM, SLUMP AND RESTRUCTURING

The growth of urban employment opportunities in Australia, as in many other capitalist nations, was at its most impressive during the 'long boom' of economic growth in the 1950s and 1960s. With the benefit of hindsight we can see that this rested on a historically specific set of international political-economic conditions.

- The first of these was the second world war itself, causing widespread devastation, particularly in Europe and Japan, but leading to an energetic period of international post-war reconstruction.

- Governments' own expenditures grew rapidly throughout the capitalist nations, as provisions for public health, education, social security and other welfare provisions were added to the armourment expenditures associated with the cold-war. This 'welfare-warfare state' laid the foundation for the growing demand for goods and services.

- The rapid economic growth of the industrialised economies was facilitated by the extraction of cheap resources from what were then the poorer nations. Cheap oil fuelled the growth of industry and the transport system.

- There were stable financial conditions in the international economy, based on the Bretton Woods agreement which provided for the convertibility of US dollars to gold and for fixed rates of exchange between international currencies. This ensured predictability in the settlement of payments for international trade and thereby provided a further pre-condition for economic growth.

- There were stable political conditions, based on the accepted territorial division between the capitalist and 'communist' countries, and on the role of the USA as the self-appointed policeman of the former. This degree of political stability, albeit in the uncomfortable conditions of the cold-war, was also conducive to the expansion of international trade and investment.

The resulting long boom provided a solid base for sustained urban development in the major capitalist countries. The capital accumulation process was stimulated by the building of new factories and offices. Urban infrastructure, which had deteriorated through neglect in the years of the great depression and the second world war, was a focus for new construction. Housing development in the suburbs also proceeded rapidly, generating more jobs and incomes. This, in turn, enhanced the conditions for growth as the increased incomes flowed through into higher levels of consumption. Material living standards climbed. In Australia it meant a home of your own, a Holden car in the driveway, an electric refrigerator in the kitchen and a TV in the lounge ... That was the promise, and for many (but by no means all) the reality, of the long boom.

All these conditions changed in the 1970s.

- Post-war reconstruction had long since petered-out.
- The major role for the welfare state was under increasing attack as governments, spurred on by the influence of the 'new right', responded to the perceived difficulties of financing it through taxation. This heralded the emergence of the fiscal crisis of the state.

- The extraction of cheap resources was dramatically terminated when OPEC countries increased in the price of oil tenfold in the 1970s (albeit slipping back in the 1980s). Other third world countries joined together in proposals for a New International Economic Order and their opposition to economic and political domination continued to challenge the conditions on which the growth of the industrialised capitalist countries has been based.

- International financial stability was eroded when President Nixon ended the system of convertibility of US dollars for gold, leading to fluctuating currency exchange rates and all the attendant uncertainties about the financing of international trade.

- International political stability was also terminated with the defeat of the USA in Vietnam, compounded by an array of other political and military conflicts around the world. The hegemony of the United States was challenged by the economic ascendancy of Japan and West Germany. The American orchestration of the political-economic system became less effective.

Political-economic conditions in the international economy were no longer so conducive to the accumulation of capital. Capitalism moved from 'the age of growth' to what J.K. Galbraith (1977) called 'the age of uncertainty'.

The two decades since can be interpreted as a period during which *structural economic change* has transformed the employment situation. This has been true across the capitalist nations, affecting both urban and non-urban areas. It has been the subject of much research by contemporary political economists (e.g. Stilwell 1980, Henderson & Castells 1987, Knox & Agnew 1989, Storper & Walker 1989). In Australian cities, the overall growth of employment has continued, but it has become much more uneven and unreliable in character. Alternating booms and slumps have come to be accepted as a feature of urban housing, property and labour markets. Expectations of full employment and steadily rising incomes have been frustrated.

What are the structural changes which have moulded these different — and difficult — conditions? The first concerns *government policy*. In Australia, as in many of the industrial nations, governments have responded to these new economic conditions by major changes in the character of macroeconomic policy. The Keynesian approach to stabilisation, with full employment as the top priority, gave way to a more monetarist-oriented policy. This is not to say that Keynesian 'fine-tuning' had been consistently applied, still less that it had underpinned the long boom. Rather, the point is that the partial shift to monetarism abandoned the official full employment commitment in favour of accepting a 'natural rate of unemployment'. Its principal policy emphasis was on fighting inflation through restrictive monetary policies and cutting the growth of the public sector. The outcome was increased unemployment, of which the cities copped their share.

The most striking example of this policy approach was in the United Kingdom where Margaret Thatcher's policies, aimed in her own words at 'setting free the creative genius of the British people', were quickly accompanied by a rise in unemployment to three million, approximately 12 per cent of the work-force. In the United States, Reagonomics involved the same sort of approach to economic policy with much the same effects on the level of economic activity, registered unemployment climbing to 10 million by 1983.

After some years in which the Fraser government in Australia pursued a rather less consistent version of the monetarist approach to economic policy, the Hawke government sought to chart a different course with an emphasis on prices and incomes policy under the Accord (Stilwell 1986). Total employment grew between 1983 and 1990 by over 1.5 million jobs. However, the international conditions for sustained economic success were not auspicious. Falling terms of trade for Australia's primary exports in the mid 1980s and growing competition from the Newly Industrialising Countries of Southeast Asia further compounded the difficulties. The Federal Treasurer began to sound warnings of the nation becoming a 'banana republic', and economic policies became increasingly tailored to dealing with the balance of payments problem rather than domestic economic expansion. Although the dramatic international stock exchange crash of October 1987 did not result in a generalised recession at the time, it reminded us of the essential interdependence of the Australian economy with a volatile international economy. Moreover, by the late 1980s, a policy of tight money and high interest rates further undermined the conditions for a resurgence of economic growth. Recession set in sharply in 1990–2. In Australian cities the consequential unemployment was particularly evident, although very uneven in its spatial impacts, as noted later in this chapter.

Important structural economic changes have also taken place in the *disposition of the economic surplus*. The general tendency to economic instability has been fuelled by the tendency for capital to be directed into the pursuit of speculative gains rather than the expansion of productive capacity. Of course, speculation may generate considerable income for individuals, but for the society as a whole it involves redistribution rather than creation of wealth. It is a tendency which is evident on an international scale, being variously described as 'profits without production' (Melman 1983) and 'casino capitalism' (Strange 1986). Financial deregulation in Australia in the 1980s gave it particularly free reign. High interest rates, which generally attract funds into financial assets and curtail borrowing for purposes of investment in economically productive assets, were another factor. High interest rates also curtail consumer demand to the extent that they reduce the size of disposable income remaining after mortgage interest payments and other debt commitments are met. Much economic damage is done.

The combination of these factors compounds the tendency to economic recession by reducing the contribution of productive investment and/or consumption to the level of aggregate demand in the economy. More generally, it provides the preconditions for economic crisis in a speculation-oriented economy. Property speculation is a classic manifestation, rife in Australian cities and having adverse consequences for inflation, distributional inequities and urban planning. In the unstable economic conditions of recent years, such speculation has been much in evidence. This may be regarded as illustrative of the reswitching of capital between industrial purposes and investment in the built environment in the face of looming economic crisis (Harvey 1982).

Geographical restructuring of capital has also been much in evidence. In any period of economic instability or recession, it is usual for capital to be restructured in an attempt to renew the conditions for profitable capital accumulation. The 'weeding out' of inefficient industries tends to raise the rate of profit for capital as a whole. Relocation of economic activities has been a particularly important aspect of structural economic change in the 'age of uncertainty'. It has been manifest in the emergence of the 'new international division of labour' (Froebel, Heinricks & Kreye 1980). This involves the multinational corporations dividing the various stages of their operations between different countries, in order to take advantage of the differential cost of labour and resources and to minimise taxation through the practice of transfer pricing. In the Southeast Asia-Pacific region it has been described as the Pacific Rim strategy (Crough and Wheelwright 1982). For Australia (together with Canada and New Zealand) this has involved an increasing emphasis on its role as a supplier of foodstuffs and minerals and semi-processing activities, such as aluminium smelting and wood-chipping, which take advantage of abundant energy resources. The other side of the coin is a selective *deindustrialisation*, involving those relatively labour-intensive manufacturing activities such as clothing, textiles and footwear. This has been pushed along by the cuts in tariffs on imported goods.

This shift in the relative balance of the major economic sectors has been a striking dimension of structural change. Although the 'resources boom' of the late 1970s and early 1980s failed to materialise on the expected scale, mineral and agricultural production have continued to be Australia's leading export sectors, while manufacturing has declined in terms of employment levels. The failure to develop comprehensive industry policies has left Australian industry, and the urban work-force dependent on it for employment, in a vulnerable position.

A further dimension of structural change in political-economic conditions has been the increased application of *labour-displacing technology*. There is nothing new about this, in that jobs in various industries are recurrently displaced by the introduction of new technology. Nor is this necessarily a source of macro-economic employment problems because, while there is labour-displacement in particular industries, waves of technological progress create economic growth in other sectors. Historically, agricultural mechanisation, the development of capital-intensive mineral extraction and increased mechanisation of manufacture have all occurred without a long-run increase in the pool of technological unemployment. However, what is distinctive about the impact of new technology in the last couple of decades is that it also has the capacity to displace labour in the service sector, which historically has absorbed the labour displaced by technological change in other sectors of the economy. Computerisation, word processors, automatic banking and so on have thereby compounded the 'age of uncertainty' and led to growing concern

about the future of work (Butler 1983, Gorz 1985). New technologies also open up possibilities for urban restructuring, with
more flexibility in the location of workplaces (Stilwell 1992: ch.
12).

The *flexibility of labour* has become of increasing concern
in these circumstances. In part this reflects a 'new right' agenda,
as noted by Burgess and Macdonald (1991), requiring the
workforce to become more malleable to the dictates of capital.
More generally, it envisages the need for substantial adaptation
by labour to rapid structural economic change. This is not easily
done. It is impeded by the rigidities associated with existing
work-force skills, structures of employment and locational
preferences. Table 1.1 illustrates the point by looking at changing
patterns of occupational, industrial and locational mobility. In
each case there is some evidence of increased mobility but the
changes are very modest. This is understandable, particularly in
regard to location, since the human attachment to place is more
than a 'labour market rigidity'. It is the embodiment of social and
family connections and of regional identity.

TABLE 1.1   OCCUPATIONAL, INDUSTRIAL AND REGIONAL
             MOBILITY OF LABOUR

| | (average annual percentage change of total work-force) | | |
Year	Changing occupation	Changing industry	Changing location
1976	5.1	7.0	3.7
1982	4.9	7.0	3.7
1989	5.9	7.6	4.8

Source: ABS, *Labour Mobility*, AGPS, Canberra, 1990.

Overall, these are important structural changes — in government policy, in the balance between productive and speculative
investment, in the geographical pattern of capital accumulation,
its sectoral composition, the associated character of technology
and the pressures for more 'labour market flexibility'. Their
common element is the quest to re-create the conditions for
capital accumulation. The results have sometimes been quite
spectacularly successful, but not consistently so and without

comparable benefits for labour. In the Australian case, despite the quite impressive expansion in aggregate employment after the recession of 1982–3, employment conditions collapsed again in the recession of 1991–2. Capitalism again revealed its incapacity to provide for stability in employment, not only in Australia, but on a world scale. People are now questioning whether full employment can ever be achieved again. One political economist, characteristically the first to identify new trends, has argued that 'the age of uncertainty' is turning into an 'age of upheaval' (Wheelwright 1991).

REGIONAL EMPLOYMENT IMPACTS

The Australian economy, like all partially industrialised economies has been characterised by distinctive urban and regional economic specialisations. Diversified manufacturing cities (e.g. Sydney, Melbourne, Adelaide), specialised heavy industrial areas (e.g. Newcastle, Wollongong, Gladstone, Whyalla), mining areas (e.g. Broken Hill, Mt Isa, Kalgoorlie, the Pilbara), and agricultural-based regions (e.g. the Riverina, Barossa Valley) are some of the more obvious categories. The last decade has seen significant structural-spatial shifts, largely in response to the changes in the conditions for capital accumulation already surveyed in this chapter.

The most obvious dimension involves the *sectoral* distribution of industry and employment. By the 1970s Australia had developed a significant manufacturing sector to complement its traditional reliance on primary industries. This had been facilitated by a system of tariff protection and a large scale immigration programme, with the result that 25 per cent of the employed population was in the manufacturing sector in 1966. This percentage fell in the 1970s and by 1983 it had declined to 18 per cent, falling further to 13 per cent by 1991. Total employment in the manufacturing sector fell by 271,000 (or 20 per cent of the work-force) between 1973 and 1985, this being a particularly pronounced period of contraction. At the same time, natural resource extraction has grown but, since this is a very capital-intensive sector, direct employment generation has been minor. It amounted to only 27,000 persons (or 10 per cent of the number of jobs lost in the manufacturing sector) in the same period from 1973 to 1985. The mining sector still directly employs less than 2 per cent of the Australian work-force. Meanwhile employment in agriculture has been stagnant, the small farm sector having been particularly affected by a combination of tight market conditions and high interest rates, leading to what is widely perceived as a deep rural crisis (Lawrence 1987). Although employment in services has risen, this has not been sufficient to fill the gap between a continuous increase in the size of the potential work-force, resulting from immigration and increased female work-force participation, and the declining number of jobs in manufacturing industry.

The *spatial* impact of the sectoral changes in the patterns of capital accumulation and employment is reasonably clear. This is particularly true of the changes in the manufacturing sector, given its spatial concentration and the rapidity of its restructuring. Table 1.2 provides a general summary of the distribution of employment in the capital cities in 1991. The proportion of employment in manufacturing was highest in Melbourne at only just under 18 per cent. The State capitals as a whole provided 66 per cent of the nation's total manufacturing jobs — Sydney, Melbourne and Adelaide alone accounted for 61 per cent. Each of the State capitals sustained losses in the period 1981–91. The total decline in manufacturing jobs in the decade preceding 1991 was over 25 per cent in Sydney, 24 per cent in Melbourne and between 10 and 20 per cent in all the other State capitals except Perth which only had a 7 per cent decline. Adelaide's problems can be interpreted as a continuing legacy of 'an industrial structure highly concentrated on consumer durable goods and a location far removed from the home markets in which these goods are sold' (Robins 1981). Its peripheral position *vis à vis* the international economy is a further factor, although this did not prevent it becoming the site selected for the Multi Function Polis (a matter to which we return in chapter 13). On a smaller scale, but equally problematic, the urban economy of Hobart, and that of Tasmania in general, has suffered from the combined effects of a peripheral location and an inability to adapt its industrial structure to those sectors experiencing employment growth (Wilde 1981). Both Adelaide and Hobart did experience growth in employment in the services sector in the 70s and 80s but the rate of growth in both was significantly below that in all the other State capitals. There is some evidence that, in general, South Australia and Tasmania were less sensitive to the stimulatory effects of employment growth since the 1982–3 recession (Groenwold 1991). But in terms of the aggregate size of job losses consequent on structural change in manufacturing, Sydney and Melbourne have dominated the picture with over 80 per cent of the total losses.

TABLE 1.2   EMPLOYMENT IN STATE CAPITAL CITIES, 1991

	Primary Total	%	Manufacturing Total	%	Services Total	%	Total Employment	%
Sydney	14 366	0.9	219 016	14.0	1 329 719	85.1	1 563 101	100
Melbourne	12 278	0.9	233 898	17.7	1 071 834	81.3	1 318 010	100
Brisbane	3 419	1.0	37 101	11.0	295 606	87.9	336 126	100
Adelaide	5 489	1.2	67 618	15.3	369 172	83.4	442 279	100
Perth	12 932	2.7	53 573	11.2	413 921	86.2	480 426	100
Hobart	1 951	2.5	8 300	10.7	67 091	86.7	77 342	100
Australia	407 170	5.7	933 652	13.1	5 768 513	81.1	7 169 335	100

Source: Census of Population and Housing, 1986.

Together with the general changes involving the application of new technology and the restructuring of labour force requirements, this process of sectoral-spatial restructuring can be seen to have eroded the conditions under which sustained employment growth in urban Australia had previously taken place. There have been major problems of structural adjustment which have not been easily accommodated (Ohlsson 1984, Bureau of Industry Economics 1985, EPAC 1991). Regions have varied widely in their resilience and vulnerability to structural economic change (Office of Local Government 1991). This was evident back in the 1981–3 recession. In New South Wales, for example, the heavy industrial towns of Newcastle and Wollongong recorded 1983 unemployment rates of 14.5 per cent and 14 per cent respectively. The recession and the associated restructuring of the steel industry by the monopoly producer, the Broken Hill Proprietary Ltd and its affiliates, generated a chronic problem of localised unemployment in these steel-producing localities

(Schultz 1985). As in any recession, one expects industries producing capital goods to suffer greater relative declines than those producing consumer goods, but in these cases the local downward multiplier effects compounded the problem. The federal government's steel plan supposedly put the steel industry on a firmer footing in the 1980s but recovery of output levels was accompanied by further decreases in employment (Haughton 1990). When the 'great recession' hit in the early 1990s it had an impact at least comparable in severity to the previous recession. Registered unemployment in Newcastle and Wollongong rose to 13 per cent and 16 per cent respectively by the first quarter of 1992. The term 'rust-belt', previously coined to describe the situation in the north-eastern regions of the USA, has come to be widely applied in the Australian context with reference not only to the steel cities but more generally to the manufacturing-based urban economies of Melbourne and Adelaide. The local impacts on working-class communities in areas in the north and west of Melbourne and in Elizabeth to the north of Adelaide have been particularly pronounced.

By contrast some regions have remained relatively unaffected by the costs of economic restructuring. This is partly because some service industries, notably tourism and financial and business services, experienced rapid growth during the decade of the 1980s, although tempered in the latter case by the financial crash of 1987 and the subsequent shake-out in finance and business services. The relative prosperity of some areas also reflects the spatial separation between the residential locations of the owners of capital and the locations of industry and employment. Such spatial specialisation is possible because the part of profits which is not reinvested flows out of industrial regions into the more attractive areas where the recipients of income from capital tend to reside. The northern suburbs of Sydney are a case in point. The material living standards there have been much less affected by structural economic change during the 'age of uncertainty', and local unemployment rates have been not much higher than those prevailing nationally during the years of more rapid economic growth. This feature comes out clearly in the following case study.

URBAN UNEMPLOYMENT: SYDNEY IN RECESSION

The economic recession of the early 1990s had its origins in a range of economic and political elements. In part, it was a manifestation of the long-established cyclical character of the capitalist economy. In part, it was a response to growing international economic problems and financial instability, even ensnaring the former 'miracle' cases of Germany and Japan. These destabilising tendencies were compounded by particular structural problems in the Australian economy, manifest in the continuing problems of the current account deficit and foreign debt. Government policies, including tariff cuts and an emphasis on restrictionist monetary policies, exacerbated the problems. Indeed, this latter factor led Australia into the recession ahead of other countries. These causes of the recession are well known. What is more important in the present context are the distinctive local labour market manifestations.

The structural-spatial interactions in different segments of the labour market are complex, as always, but a case study of Sydney helps to illuminate the general forces at work. Table 1.3 shows the changes in unemployment rates for each of the Sydney statistical regions as the recession set in between April 1989 and April 1992. The various regions are grouped into two according to long established differences in their dominant socio-economic status and labour market conditions. The dualism is not sharply defined, since each of these regions has its relatively advantaged and disadvantaged localities, while gentrification in the inner-city areas has created greater socio-economic diversity within those localities (a matter to which we return in chapter 7). Nevertheless, it provides a general basis for studying the impact of recession.

On this basis we can see that rates of unemployment in early 1992 in the upper status areas (Group B) ranged between 4 per cent and 7 per cent of the work-force. The lower status areas (Group A) had unemployment rates in the range from 8 per cent to 17 per cent of the work-force. A little more disaggregation of the ABS statistics actually shows the unemployment rate for the Fairfield-Liverpool area at 18.6 per cent for April 1992, comprising 26,400 persons seeking work in that area alone. The

preceding column in Table 1.3 also gives the longer term picture.
In general, the regions with the highest rates of unemployment
in early 1992 were also those with sustained unemployment
problems reaching back into the 1980s. Fairfield-Liverpool and
the South-West, for example, averaged over 10 per cent for the
three year period from 1989 to 1982, while the three North Shore
areas (taken together to overcome possible statistical bias because
of the small numbers in each area) recorded only around 4 per
cent for the same period. So, while the onset of the recession
certainly had an effect across the board, the unemployment
situation in the upper status areas was still not as adverse *after* the
recession had set in as was the situation in the lower status
areas *before* the recession. Meanwhile, the latter areas had
unemployment levels of sufficient severity to start causing
significant secondary effects on the demand for local service
industries.

TABLE 1.3   UNEMPLOYMENT RATES: SYDNEY SUB-REGIONS

	Monthly average unemployment rate 1989–92	Unemployment rate (%) April 1992
Group A		
Inner Sydney & Inner Western Sydney	7.1	8.6
Canterbury Bankstown	9.6	12.2
Fairfield-Liverpool & the South-West	10.2	16.1
Central Western Sydney	9.0	11.9
Outer Western Sydney	5.4	7.6
Bankstown–Baulkham Hills	6.5	8.9
Group B		
Eastern Suburbs	5.0	4.7
St George–Sutherland	4.4	5.9
Lower Northern Sydney*	4.2	4.6
Hornsby–Kuring-gai*	3.4	4.2
Manly–Warringah*	3.9	6.7

Sources: ABS Regional Labour Force statistics.
Note: Regions marked with an * included some data which has a sampling
variability with a relative standard error greater than 25 per cent.

A thorough analysis of these variations would need to take
account of various factors causing regional imbalance in the

demand and supply of labour. As identified in an earlier study (Stilwell 1980) these form three clusters:

- the demographic characteristics of each region (sex, age and ethnicity);
- the structure of the work-force (occupational and industrial);
- the spatial functioning of the metropolitan labour market (including the extent to which the distribution of industry, transport facilities and spatial discrimination impede its functioning as a coherent entity).

Among demographic factors, age and ethnicity appear to be the most significant influences on the incidence of unemployment. The effect of age on variations in unemployment rates is striking. In the year to April 1992, the largest overall increase in aggregate unemployment rates was among the young, particularly in the 15–19 age group. By the middle of 1992 the overall national rate of youth unemployment had climbed to 38 per cent. This figure relates only to those seeking full-time employment and therefore excludes the young people in full-time education. Both aspects — education retention rates and youth unemployment rates — show significant regional variation. For example, official youth unemployment rates in February 1991 were over three times higher in the South-West, Fairfield-Liverpool and Blacktown–Baulkham Hills than in Manly-Warringah and the Eastern Suburbs.

Ethnicity also shows up clearly as an influential variable. Taking NSW figures for February 1991, there was only a minor difference (1.4 per cent) between unemployment rates for Australian-born and overseas-born persons. However, there was a big difference (5.7 per cent) between immigrants from English-speaking and non-English speaking countries. Similarly, there was a big variation according to length of time living in Australia: for those arrived since 1981 the average unemployment rate was 13.9 per cent. Interacting with the variations in the ethnic composition, this helps in explaining the high incidence of unemployment in suburbs like Fairfield, Liverpool and the South-West and in Inner Sydney and the Inner West.

The occupational and industrial structure of the work-force

also has a big impact. Aggregate employment trends for NSW reveal two categories which were the major casualties at the onset of the recession: tradespersons (8 per cent fall in employment in the year 1990–91) and labourers (2 per cent fall). On the other hand, aggregate employment levels were still rising solidly for professionals, managers and administrators. Looking at the last job held by those registered as unemployed, the outstanding categories were again tradespersons and labourers, with salespersons and clerks also well represented. These occupational trends interact with changes in the structure of employment by industry. Significant falls in employment levels during the same year were recorded in manufacturing (7 per cent), electricity, gas and water and mining (6 per cent), wholesale and retail trade (2 per cent). Even finance, property and business services fell, a clear barometer of changing conditions, given the claim of Sydney to have overtaken Melbourne as the financial centre of Australia. Employment in transport, storage and most other service industries continued to grow slowly. Because of the established spatial variations in the industrial and occupational composition of the work force in the upper and lower status areas, these trends flow through into distinctive patterns of urban unemployment.

The extent to which the metropolitan area functions as a coherent, unified labour market is a further consideration. It is commonplace to claim, as does the standard textbook by Werner Hirsch (1973), that urban labour markets work 'efficiently and speedily' because of good information about labour demand and supply. However, their capacity to do so is undermined by their sheer size and spatial form, including the dispersal of industry and inadequate transport facilities. These features are of long standing in Australian cities, although continued peripheral expansion unmatched by improvements in transport services intensifies the problems of access and the tendency for breakdown into sub-metropolitan labour markets. No doubt the failure to develop local employment opportunities comparable with the rate of population growth in a peripheral area like Campbelltown (in the south-western Sydney region) makes it particularly vulnerable in circumstances of general recession.

These spatial factors interact with the demographic and structural elements in creating conditions of relative disadvantage.

ECONOMIC POLICY: FROM PROBLEM TO SOLUTION?

The problem of unemployment is not fundamentally spatial. It is largely the product of more general contradictions within the structure of the capitalist economy, interacting with the socio-economic inequalities in cities and regions. The effects of government economic policy are also significant — for better or worse. Restrictionist monetary policy, together with policies to depress real wages and enforce austerity through the (ultimately unsuccessful) pursuit of a fiscal surplus, have undoubtedly been contributory factors to rising unemployment in the early 1990s. Tariff cuts accentuate the problems, at least in the short term, because they make imported goods relatively cheaper and hence further divert demand away from locally produced items. On the supply side, the failure to implement a comprehensive interventionist industry policy in the 1980s, and to establish a national investment fund for channelling superannuation funds and other savings into productive investment, left the economy with a legacy of outdated capital stock. The era of 'corporate cowboys' and 'paper entrepreneurs' ushered in by financial deregulation provided no basis for improved economic performance: rather it left behind a massive foreign debt and a productive capacity depleted by the diversion of funds into speculation in property development and financial assets (Heywood and Tamaschke 1991, Stilwell 1988). In all these respects, the prevailing economic policies have been part of the problem.

It is at that national economic level that solutions must initially be sought. That means a rejection of the dogmas of 'economic rationalism', a reassertion of the role of the public sector in job-creation, the application of strategic trade planning and policies for industrial development: see, for example, Flew (1991) and Rees, Rodley & Stilwell (1992). Only then can the problem of urban unemployment be brought under control. In the long term this also requires more consideration of measures to ensure the equitable distribution of employment opportunities. In an increasingly technologically sophisticated economy that could mean shorter working weeks, job-sharing and more flexibility in lifetime work patterns. It is a challenge which goes far beyond the urban labour market manifestations of structural change and economic recession.

This focus on changes to *national* economic policy is not to deny the need for *regionally* targeted employment policies. Local solutions certainly have some appealing features. Improvements in infrastructure through capital works projects provide an obvious means of simultaneously creating employment and improving the conditions in cities and regions. Plentiful opportunities exist for the improvement of transport infrastructure, schools, universities and technical colleges, child-care facilities, hospitals and so forth. Moreover, such programmes can be directed to the localities where the need is greatest. In that respect, selective employment-creation policies are more regionally sensitive that the use of heavy, blunt instruments like monetary policy. There is also typically little import-component in the products used in local job-creation infrastructure projects, so the potentially adverse impact of this kind of 'pump-priming' on the balance of payments current account is minimised. Indeed, to the extent that local employment-generation can be linked to an industry policy of import-replacement, it can make a positive contribution to the nation's trade balance.

The commitment to tackle the unemployment problem in these ways requires a significant involvement by State and federal governments. The experience of the recession in the early 1990s shows the necessity for such remedial action as a means of confronting the fundamental irrationality of having unemployed resources coexisting with unmet social needs. Whether this fundamental and recurrent aspect of capitalism can be ameliorated remains one of the key issues in political economy. Recognising the urban and regional dimension of the problem makes the issue just a little more sophisticated.

FURTHER READING

Massey and Meegan (1982): an exploratory analysis of regional job loss in the context of broader structural changes, with reference to the UK.

Bluestone & Harrison (1982): on a similar theme, with reference to the USA.

Rich (1986): a stock-taking of Australian industrial geography with a State-by-State description.

Vipond (1985): a brief review of alternative approaches to the analysis of urban unemployment.

2

Housing

Housing problems have been a dominant feature of discussion on urban issues, particularly in the biggest Australian cities where there has been recurrent talk of a 'housing crisis'. Housing is a very special commodity: it is a basic necessity but very expensive. As a government report puts it, 'housing is the most significant item of expenditure for most Australians over their lifetimes, and their most important asset' (National Housing Strategy 1991a). The problems of Australian housing affordability have been acute, partly because of the costs of land, partly because of the costs of house construction, and partly because of the interest rates which have had to be paid on housing loans. It is commonplace to note that the 'great Australian dream' of home-ownership has turned for many people into 'the great Australian nightmare' (Kemeny 1983, Yates 1988). The problems of home-ownership have been mirrored by difficulties in private rental, public rental and emergency accommodation. Each of these sectors has experienced chronic stresses. The consequences have included massive shifts in the distribution of income and wealth and mounting demands for reform of housing policy.

While we cannot do full justice to these complex issues in one chapter — they properly require a book to themselves — we can sketch out how housing problems relate to the broader aspects of urban political economy. This is attempted by discussing:

- the analysis of housing and the special characteristics of this commodity;
- the main dimensions of the housing crisis in Australia;

- the physical — spatial dimensions (e.g. metropolitan bias);
- the sectoral dimension (owner-occupation bias);
- the distributional dimension (class and life-cycle biases);
- alternative policy responses;
- whether housing is an economic drain or stimulus.

Two concerns underpin these explorations. One is the conundrum that the goal of decent and affordable housing for all should be so elusive in an 'affluent society' with a low ratio of population to land area and with so much of its total resources used for housing. The other centres on the interaction of the housing market with the labour market and the general economic conditions discussed in the preceding chapter; seeing this interaction as a 'scissors effect' which cuts sharply into the well-being of so many urban Australians.

ANALYSIS OF HOUSING

Housing problems may be analysed in a conventional demand-supply framework. Thus, one may identify the factors leading to a high *demand* — these are partly demographic (e.g. immigration, reduced average household size) and partly economic (e.g. rising *per capita* incomes, the purchase of real estate as a hedge against inflation or in pursuit of speculative gains). Similarly, one may identify the factors leading to a restricted *supply* (e.g. the tendency to exhaustion of land availability in existing metropolitan areas, the high cost of construction and provision of infrastructure for new housing).

However, this type of analysis needs to be extended in at least two ways. First it is important to recognise the impact of *macroeconomic* conditions (e.g. monetary policy, interest rates and the general conditions for capital accumulation) on the microeconomics of housing. Second, it is important to recognise the social, cultural and distributional factors which shape what happens in the housing market. Indeed, even the terminology 'housing market' suggests a rather restricted way of posing the issue. As with 'labour market', it conveys the impression that it is all a matter of exchange relationships — buying and selling — rather than an array of production relationships, distributional influences and institutional processes.

More generally, it is necessary to recognise that housing is a special commodity and deserving of a correspondingly special analysis. Certainly, housing in a capitalist economy is a commodity that exists primarily as private property which can be bought and sold. As such, housing can be analysed through the application of various economic theories of value or price. However, it is a very special commodity for various reasons. As David Harvey (1987) puts it, 'housing means more than just shelter from the elements. It defines a space of social reproduction that necessarily reflects gender, familial and other types of social relations.' The form of its provision has major economic, political and ideological implications.

Economically, it is typically the most expensive commodity people purchase in their lifetime. Considering housing expenditures as a flow (whether in the form of rent or repayments on a housing loan), they are characteristically the largest single item in the household budget. More generally, the magnitude of social resources involved in the provision, servicing, distribution and maintenance of housing exceeds that for any other commodity. Therein lies a particular contradiction for the capitalist economy because, while adequate housing (like health) is absolutely essential for the reproduction of the work-force, housing is typically so expensive that it cannot be bought outright. Hence the necessity for various institutional arrangements to bridge the gap, ranging from the mortgage finance to facilities for private rental and the provision of public housing.

Politically, the form of housing provision is important because it creates additional seams of social conflict. These run sometimes concordant but sometimes discordant to the seams of conflict associated with the process of economic production. Housing provision (or its inadequacies) may fuel class conflict between capital and labour. On the other hand it may deflect attention from that capital-labour conflict if, say, working-class owner-occupiers and working-class rental-tenants perceive themselves to have differing interests. One classic study of these tenure groups accorded them the status of 'housing classes' (Rex and

Moore 1967). More recently, it has been recognised that, while housing tenure is not the principal basis for identification of classes, it is a key element in generating social divisions and political conflicts. As Peter Saunders (1984) puts it, 'housing tenure, as one expression of the division between privatised and collectivised means of consumption ... is the single most pertinent factor in the determination of consumption sector cleavages'. More generally, in Harvey's (1987) words, 'the housing question remains a serious social and political issue in advanced capitalist cities and periodically becomes the focus of intense political struggles that sometimes touch at the very root of the capitalist form of urbanisation'. There is abundant evidence in the Australian case that the point has not been lost on the politicians themselves: witness the encouragement of owner-occupation as a 'bulwark against Bolshevism' (Kemeny 1983).

Ideologically, the form of housing provision is also important in that it shapes people's perceptions about the society in which they live and the social values they adopt. The relative importance placed on public and private spaces, the standards of their upkeep, even the internal layout of housing, all these can have profound ideological impact. It seems particularly significant for what young people accept as normal in the process of growing up. Commenting on the dominant Australian ideology of private home ownership in particular, Michael Berry (1983) contends that 'widespread owner-occupation has been instrumental in diffusing values favourable to private ownership in general and private ownership of land in particular'.

The foregoing reasoning suggests that a comprehensive view of housing needs to be based on the analysis of housing values and prices, financial institutions, the state, class and intra-class relationships, ideology and the conditions for social and economic reproduction. That is a tall order! The story becomes still more complicated when we note the special significance of housing from the viewpoint of *urban development*. The form of housing provision materially shapes spatial structure, interacting with the provision of transport and other elements of infrastructure. In the Australian case for example, the classic case of the detached dwelling on a quarter acre block has been associated with sprawling suburbanised metropolitan areas. This contrasts, for example, with more compact European cities featuring a much higher proportion of terraced housing and/or apartments. Yes, the form of housing is a key element shaping the pattern of urban development. This, in turn, is a major influence on the intensity of housing problems and the relationship of those problems to the urban system as a whole.

AN AUSTRALIAN HOUSING CRISIS?

These general propositions can be applied in the more specific context of the much-discussed Australian 'housing crisis'. The existence of such a crisis is a perplexing phenomenon. At first sight, it would appear that Australia should have no major housing problems, given the plentiful supply of land and the generally good physical condition of the housing stock by international standards. However, major problems of access and cost of housing in the major urban areas are all too evident. The goal of decent and affordable housing for all seems extraordinarily elusive. Of course, most people *do* find housing, albeit often not in their most preferred form or location. Indeed, one of the distinctive features of housing is that (almost) everyone does consume it, whether it be a mansion, a rented room, a squat or a bed in a hostel. For the most part, the allocation of the available housing stock amongst its various potential users takes place through a market process. The outcome may be inequitable but, being based primarily on 'ability to pay', no new principles are introduced which do not apply elsewhere in a capitalist economy.

So in what sense is there a crisis? The answer lies in terms of the earlier discussion of the economic, political and ideological significance of housing. If the problems of access to decent, affordable housing are such that the conditions for economic and social reproduction are threatened, there is indeed a potential crisis. So it is not just that affordability has become a chronic problem and that many people are being forced into less-preferred housing sectors. It is that the constellation of these effects impacts on the process of capital accumulation and the legitimacy of the existing social order. In this sense, there may properly be said to be the recurrent potential for a housing crisis.

Its main dimensions are physical-spatial, sectoral and distributional. We consider each in turn.

THE PHYSICAL-SPATIAL DIMENSION

One of the most important features of housing is the element of *inertia*. Its quantity, quality and spatial distribution cannot be quickly changed. Indeed, this is one of the general lessons of urban political economy — the extra immobility or 'stickiness' which the built environment imparts into the functioning of the economic system and society. One effect of this inertia is that changes in demand conditions are typically more volatile than changes in supply. This helps to explain why housing is subject to periodic booms and slumps.

The quality and spatial form of Australian housing is the product of a particular historical experience. To quote Max Neutze (1977) at length:

> ... at the end of the Second World War Australia was suffering from a housing shortage, after some fifteen years when there had been very little new construction and even maintenance had been neglected. There was over-crowding, especially in the poorer inner areas of the major cities, and many people were living in temporary accommodation. Many houses were shared by two or more households and others lived in dwellings without their own kitchens or bathrooms. Because of shortages of building materials it took some years for the building industry to pick up, but once the recovery got under way it began a period of sustained construction which, during the fifties and sixties, not only made up for the backlog of construction and maintenance during the thirties and forties but also raised housing standards to higher levels than ever before. With higher incomes most Australians could afford to be well housed. There was a decline in the number of shared houses, temporary and non-self-contained dwellings. The number of occupants per house or flat and per room declined so that overcrowding became less prevalent.

The number of structured dwellings more than doubled over the first 30 years after the war, while the total population increased by 68 per cent. To quote Neutze again:

> ... one of the reasons for the more rapid increase in structured dwellings was that a decreasing number of households either shared dwellings or lived in non-self-contained or temporary dwellings, the proportion falling dramatically from about 14 per cent in 1947 to 3 per cent in 1971. Among the structured dwellings the number of houses increased less rapidly than the number of flats. Most of the growth in the number of flats occurred after 1954 and during the 1960s alone the number doubled.

There was also a legacy of inadequate building standards: 33 per cent of housing in 1971 was unsewered, a figure which was reduced to 26 per cent by 1976 mainly as the result of the Whitlam government's programme for dealing with the 'sewerage backlog'.

More recently there have been surges in house construction which have gone a long way towards overcoming this historical legacy and generating a housing stock to match the growing demand, fuelled by continuing immigration and an increase in the ratio of households to total population. However, it is pertinent to remember that house construction in a capitalist society does not take place independently of conditions prevailing elsewhere in the economy. In the late 1970s, for example, there is evidence that the 'resources boom' sucked investable funds away from urban development (Australian Institute of Urban Studies 1980). On the other hand, the experience of the stock-exchange crash in 1987 led to a flight of capital into real estate, although fuelling inflation more than it did the construction of new homes. Then high interest rates throttled back the housing industry. These high interest rates in the late 1980s and 1990 were an instrument of macroeconomic policy, designed ostensibly to deal with the nation's persistent balance of payments problems. It is ironic that one of the main casualties of this policy was the housing sector, where the propensity to import is very low.

On average, only about 10 per cent of building materials are imported, so the curtailment of expansion in this sector, although generating great social costs, does little to resolve the current account deficit. It did add to macroeconomic difficulties in the early 1990s by provoking recession. That, in turn, undermined the conditions of profitability and buoyant demand which are the prerequisite for new house construction.

The physical housing stock also has an obvious *spatial* form, most obviously in the distribution between metropolitan and non-metropolitan areas. This has an obvious relationship to the population distribution, but the correlation is far from perfect. Indeed, this is partly why the housing crisis is not a generalised spatial phenomenon, except to the extent that new buyers are affected by the same interest rates on borrowed funds irrespective of location. The demand-supply balance for the housing stock, the price of housing and prevailing rents, all have a distinctive urban/rural pattern. In the country areas and smaller towns (with few exceptions) there is no comparable housing crisis. Its incidence also varies between the metropolitan areas: most obviously, it is more intense in Sydney than in other major Australian cities. One study of comparative housing costs in the 1980s indicated Sydney households spending on average about 13 per cent more on housing than Melbourne households, but on lower average quality housing than their counterparts in Melbourne (Nevile, Vipond and Warren 1984). The longer-term dimensions of inter-metropolitan inequalities are illustrated in Figure 2.1 which shows relative trends in house prices for all the capital cities for the period 1977 to 1990.

Then there is the issue of spatial form *within* the metropolitan areas. The high degree of metropolitan concentration has gone hand in hand with a low average density of housing in those areas. Much has been written about this dual characteristic of Australian housing. Part of the concern has focused on the social consequences and inadequate services associated with further metropolitan sprawl, particularly in the peripheral suburbs. Partly the concerns have come from feminists noting the association between this physical housing form and a particular sexual division of labour (stemming from the work of Game and

Pringle 1979). The problems and costs of servicing low-density suburbanised housing with adequate transport facilities have also long been acknowledged (e.g. Black 1977). Most generally, the psychological, social and cultural correlates of the suburban form ('suburban neurosis' and the 'great Australian ugliness') have been the subject of recurring concern, not to mention the comic caricature exemplified by Barry Humphries' characters Sandy Stone and Edna Everidge! This concern is not exclusively Australian: writing of the scene in the United States, political economist David Gordon (1977) long ago described the urban housing crisis as having a critical *non-physical dimension*:

> Increasingly in many urban areas, the *character* of housing and neighbourhoods is becoming hopelessly standardized. Housing tends more and more to appear in environments that serve the simple physical need for shelter but that ignore other important human needs — the need for variety; the need for pleasant surroundings; the need for various, unexpected, and intimate human contact. In the suburbs, tract homes proliferate, spreading conformity, homogeneity, and compartmentalized living. In the central cities, high-rise luxury apartments and huge prison-like public housing abound, replacing older, more varied environments. For many people the physical quality of housing has improved but the strength of community has been fractured.

Sounds familiar . . .

THE SECTORAL DIMENSION

Housing has four main tenure sectors: owner-occupation, private rental, public rental and emergency accommodation. Each is fraught with problems and the difficulties in any one usually flow on to the others. This can be illustrated by reference to contemporary housing trends in Australian cities.

The *owner-occupied* sector is overwhelmingly the largest, having grown from 53 per cent of households to 70 per cent between 1947 and 1961 and remained roughly constant ever since (Troy

1991). The major problem of housing in this sector is its cost. This is partly a legacy of the rapid price increases which have taken the form of successive waves in the late 1970s, early 1980s and late 1980s, driving house ownership beyond the reach of many new entrants to the market. Average Sydney house prices rose by 80 per cent in 1988–9 alone. High interest rates in the late 1980s and 1990 meant additional financial problems, not only for the new entrants in that period, but for existing purchasers, in meeting the necessary repayments.

FIGURE 2.1   MEDIAN HOUSE PRICES, CAPITAL CITIES, 1977 TO 1990

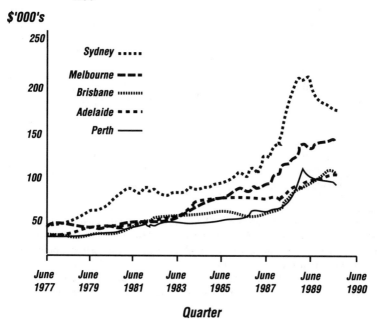

Source: Real Estate Institute of Australia, *Market Facts*, 1990.

From 1980 to 1992, according to the calculations of Bourassa & Hendershott (1993) real house asset prices in the major cities increased by an average of 40 per cent, ranging from 6 per cent in Perth and 16 per cent in Adelaide to 48 per cent in Sydney, 55 per cent in Brisbane and 69 per cent in Canberra. Table 2.1 shows the deterioration in housing affordability, taking the case of Sydney, as a result of trends in the relationship between house prices, the rate of interest on mortgage finance and average weekly earnings. Defining an 'affordable loan' as one whose repayments comprise 25 per cent of monthly income, the 'deposit gap' (the difference between the price of the house and the affordable loan) as a proportion of income rose from a low of 40 per cent in 1960 to a peak of 512 per cent in 1990. Falling interest rates in the early 1990s evidently caused some settling back, but the long term trend is clearly towards increasing financial difficulties of entry to this housing sector.

TABLE 2.1   ACCESS TO OWNER-OCCUPATION: SYDNEY, 1950–1992

June	median house price[a] $	rate of interest[b] %	average weekly earnings[c] $	affordable loan[d] $	deposit gap/ $	deposit gap income pa %
1950	4 670	3.9	19	3 650	1 020	103
1960	8 450	5.0	44	7 530	920	40
1970	17 610	8.3	76	9 640	7 970	202
1975	32 700	11.5	148	14 560	18 140	236
1980	64 500	10.5	248	26 270	38 230	296
1985	83 500	12.0	391	37 120	46 380	228
1990	187 000	17.0	556	39 000	148 000	512
1991	186 000	13.0	570	50 530	135 470	457
1992	183 000	10.5	600	66 080	116 920	375

Notes:
a. *Source:* 1950–1985 – BIS-Shrapnel house prices for established houses in Sydney; 1990–92 – Commonwealth Bank/HIA Housing Report, established house prices.
b. *Source:* Reserve Bank of Australia, Bulletins, various issues; upper limit on savings bank housing interest rates.
c. *Source:* ABS cat no 6302.0; average weekly earnings: all male employees.
d. Based on 25 year credit foncier loan with monthly repayments equal to average weekly earnings.

Source: Yates (1988) updated by the original author.

In the *private rental* sector the problems have been, if anything, more acute. The long term trend in average rents, adjusted for the general rate of inflation, has not climbed as rapidly as real house asset prices, averaging only 8 per cent from 1980 to 1992 with a range from 14 per cent rise in Sydney to a 16 per cent fall in Hobart (Bourassa & Hendershott 1993). But average incomes of people in the rental sector are lower. Private renters are more likely than house purchasers to be paying over a quarter of their income on housing. In 1988, just over 40 per cent of private renters were spending more than a quarter of their income on rent while 10 per cent were spending over half of their income on rent (National Housing Strategy 1991a). Private rental is also a problematic solution to housing needs because of the insecurity of tenure. For particular groups of people, such as the young who put a premium on mobility and the aged who wish to avoid the tasks of house maintenance, private rental is often attractive. Others may have expected lifetime incomes insufficient to contemplate tying up their limited wealth in such an illiquid form or they may be averse to the risks of capital loss (Yates 1989). However, the problem is that these groups have been joined by others whose preference *is* for owner-occupation but who cannot get access because of the difficulty of surmounting the deposit gap. These people add to the level of demand in what is already a very tight private rental housing market. 'Dutch auctions' involving bidding among potential tenants have become a periodic feature of the renting process.

The problem in the *public housing* sector is also one of excess demand, but here it is manifest primarily in terms of long queues rather than rapidly rising rents. Not that the latter tendency is absent — State government housing departments have moved more towards a policy of 'economic rents' which usually means higher housing costs unless tenants' incomes are deemed inadequate to pay. However, the policy of using public housing largely as welfare housing has meant that the allocative process has emphasised queueing more heavily than the market price mechanism. Access is determined by a combination of waiting time and tests of social need which determine one's priority in the queue. The underlying problem is the niggardly provision — a mere 5 per cent of the total housing stock. With such a limited stock, it is hard to make the case for using it for anything other than welfare purposes, despite the recurrent problems of social stigmatisation which accompany that policy. There are evidently severe financial constraints on expanding the public housing stock but there seems to have been little political will to give a higher priority to this sector. It is hard to escape the conclusion that, whereas home ownership has been officially regarded as a 'bulwark against Bolshevism', public housing has been regarded as a breeding-ground for it or, at best, a residual sector for the 'deserving poor'. The outcome has been growing waiting lists. The official queue in NSW was estimated as containing some 86,000 applicants by the start of the 1990s. A wait of over five years is common. The problem is less severe in other States but the total waiting list nationally is of the order of 200,000 households.

So people filter further down the hierarchy of housing 'options'. Sharing of houses, or young people continuing to live with their parents beyond the age at which they would normally have left home, are among the mechanisms of accommodation. So too, is caravan dwelling, home for an estimated 250–300,000 people — a preference for some but reluctant accommodation for many (Powell 1987). Squatting in vacant houses (discussed further in chapter 14) sometimes starts to look an attractive proposition. Acute housing access problems force others into the *emergency housing* category, including the women's and youth refuges and charity hostels for the homeless.

The strains on this emergency sector are acute. The combined effects of the rental crisis, unemployment and pensions below the poverty line has generated a rapid rise in the number of evictions from private rental housing. The problem of funding the initial bond payment is a further barrier for many seeking entry to the private sector. The refuges also have to cope with women driven from their homes by bashings and emotional distress or evicted because they cannot pay high rents. In the prevailing circumstances where the refuges and hostels do not have the capacity to cope with this influx, people sleep rough in parks, under bridges, at railway stations and in wrecked cars. Even where hostels are able to provide accommodation, it may involve families splitting up, with the men staying in hostels and their wives and children staying in women's refuges. The Burdekin report (1989) estimated some 20,000-25,000 young people to be homeless in 1988. An earlier consultants' study estimated some 40,000 Australians being forced to sleep out of doors with up to a further 60,000 on the verge of homelessness, dependent on voluntary services and without secure housing tenure (Lybrand, Cooper & Scott 1984). The definition of homelessness is contentious and culturally relative (Chamberlain & Mackenzie 1992), but it is an increasingly prominent issue at the tail-end of the housing situation.

The problems in the various housing sub-sectors are *interrelated* and *sequential*. People are squeezed out of their preferred options into less preferred options for which the supply is woefully inadequate. The key element in this story lies in the first sector: it is the dominance of home-ownership based on market provision which shapes the contours of the overall housing crisis. The focus on that form of housing provision has created a bias which, in circumstances of rising costs and difficulties of access, has thrown strains onto the other sectors beyond their capacity to cope. This is not to deny that home-ownership is the preferred option for many people: the security of tenure and the role of the housing asset as a store of accumulating wealth makes it widely attractive (Troy 1991). However, it is the inadequacy of the conditions in other housing tenure sectors — such as the insecurity of private tenancy and the niggardly provision of public housing — which reinforces the primacy of home-ownership.

Moreover, home-owners have received favourable treatment from governments through the taxation system: home-owners receive 'imputed rent' which is not subject to tax. This notion of imputed rent is quite important in understanding the bias towards owner-occupation. If you buy a house and rent it to someone else, you receive a rental income which is subject to income tax (less any expenses such as maintenance and mortgage interest). However, if you live in the house yourself, you effectively become your own tenant. A benefit is received — a flow of housing services — although no money exchanges hands. In some European countries this benefit, or imputed rent, is taxed. In Australia since the second world war it has not been taxed. So people are encouraged to invest in a home of their own rather than to undertake other kinds of investment (Bourassa & Hendershott 1992). Additionally, it should be noted that owner-occupied housing is exempt from capital gains tax, that home-purchasers benefited from grants totalling over $1.2 billion under the federal government's First Home Owners Scheme and that some State governments have provided concessional loans to people unable to afford private finance. Adding it all up, Flood and Yates (1987) estimated the total subsidy at an annual average of $1250 per household (compared with $1800 for public tenants through rent subsidies and $300 for private tenants through rent allowances).

THE DISTRIBUTIONAL DIMENSION

As Judy Yates (1989) notes, 'without any comprehensive information on the distribution and source of wealth in Australia and of the extent to which it is accumulated or passed on through inter-generational transfers, it is difficult to assess the relative importance of the factors which affect access to home ownership'. The same point applies to the distributional consequences of housing provision in general. Nevertheless, it is possible to identify some particular ways in which housing conditions interact with the main dimensions of economic and social inequality—class, gender and age.

The underlying contention is that, while there are certain deficiencies in the aggregate housing stock, the severity of the housing crisis is also a product of its inefficient and inequitable distribution. Take the issue of overcrowding/underutilisation. Some houses are physically overcrowded, albeit relatively few by international standards. Other houses are underutilised. On this basis, one may infer that a reallocation of the housing stock is warranted in the name of efficiency and equity. Of course, it must be conceded that people may have an attachment to a particular house for all sorts of reasons despite it being objectively 'too big' for them. They may, for example, be parents who have stayed on in the house where they raised children who have since moved on. They may be elderly people who have lived there with a partner who has since died. Compulsory relocation from the family home is not the issue here. The point is that, to the extent that housing allocation reflects class, gender and age inequalities, it may be made more efficient and equitable via measures which bear on those distributional factors.

Class provides a clear example. Relationship to the means of production and the associated socio-economic position is a crucial determinant of access to the housing market. Incidentally, it is also an influence on the spatial form of demand for housing, illustrated by the contrast between workers who must live in reasonable proximity to their work and shareholders whose ownership of capital generates income irrespective of their residential location. However, it is differential access to housing according to income which is the most striking element. The extreme case is access to home-ownership. Table 2.2 sums up the results of one study illustrating the point. Column 1 shows the income distribution of all income units (single person, single parent or married couple with or without children). Column 2 shows those who might be regarded as potential home-purchasers because they were not currently buying or did not own one. Column 3 shows the distribution according to income of those who actually did get access to housing finance in order to buy a first home. If we take $25,000 per annum income as a cut-off point (just above the average weekly annual earnings level of $23,500 prevailing at the time) we can contrast the differential access of upper and lower income categories. Thus, whereas 84 per cent of potential buyers had below average incomes, only 22 per cent of actual buyers were from that income category. On the other hand, whereas 16 per cent of potential buyers had above-average incomes, they amounted to 78 per cent of the actual buyers.

The effect of this inequality of access to owner-occupation is to force lower income groups into the other housing categories — private rental, public rental and emergency accommodation — irrespective of their preferences between categories of housing tenure. It also has the effect of ensuring that the capital appreciation associated with home-ownership, together with the subsidies arising from the non-taxation of imputed rents, accrue to the already relatively well-off. Economic and social inequalities associated with class positions thereby become perpetuated and intensified through the operation of the housing market.

The *gender* dimension in inequality in housing provision is less easy to analyse in this way. Nevertheless, there is evidence that a combination of factors, including income differentials in the labour market, lower ownership of capital, child-bearing responsibilities, the inadequacy of child care services and discriminatory practices by lending institutions have combined to put women at a systematic disadvantage in housing (Watson 1988). Certainly, women are disproportionately represented among the people officially defined as being subject to 'housing stress' (those with incomes in the lowest 40 per cent of the income distribution paying over 30 per cent of their income on housing). Older women, women who are sole parents and single women between the ages of 35 and 64 renting privately are the groups who stand out. About 50 per cent of single women, compared with 23 per cent of single men, are classified as subject to housing stress (National Housing Strategy 1991a).

TABLE 2.2   INCOME DISTRIBUTION BY INCOME UNIT, NSW, 1985–86

Income range $	1 income units: %	2 potential buyers: %	3 first home buyers: %
0–15 000	45	58	1
15 001–20 000	12	17	9
20 001–25 000	10	9	12
25 001–30 000	8	5	15
30 001–35 000	7	4	15
35 001–40 000	5	3	15
40 001–45 000	3	2	11
45 001–50 000	3	1	8
50 001–55 000	2	0	6
>55 000	4	1	8

Source: 1986 Income Distribution Survey, unit record data, adapted from Yates (1990).

Additionally, it should be noted that the general affordability crisis in housing impacts on gender relationships. Most obviously, for many young couples there is difficulty in buying a home and having children, since two incomes must be maintained in order to meet loan repayments. It is sometimes a choice between children *or* having a home of their own — a choice that has tended to increase the number of DINK (Double Income No Kids) households. As such, housing affordability also impacts on demographic trends. Demographic trends affect the demand for housing but the consequential problems of price and availability feed back onto average household size.

Age is a further consideration. One of the most striking features of data on housing is the high correlation between age and home-ownership (for married couples and singles but not single parents). A life-cycle effect is evident. This is not unexpected, of course, given the association between youth and mobility and, more generally, the simple fact that entrants to owner-occupation seldom leave that housing sector unless forced to do so by advanced age and/or ill-health. On the other hand, the evidence suggests that those who do not get into home-ownership by their forties are unlikely ever to do so. Overall, these age effects, together with gender inequalities, make the distributional aspects of housing more complex than class, income and wealth inequalities would otherwise determine. This further complicates the question of appropriate policy responses.

HOUSING POLICIES

Recent years have seen much debate about policy solutions for the housing crisis. The foregoing analysis indicates the need to address each of the three interrelated dimensions. Examples of such policies include:

- *physical-spatial:* decentralisation policies; urban consolidation;
- *sectoral:* subsidies for first home buyers; rent rebates; more finance for public housing and the community housing sector; emergency accommodation;
- *distributional:* tax reform (e.g. wealth taxes, estate duties); low-start loans; regulation of interest rates.

The first group focuses on housing problems as an *urban* phenomenon amenable to spatial solutions. Certainly, the problem of housing affordability is most acute in the cities, Sydney being the extreme case among Australian cities, as noted earlier. Within the metropolitan areas, there are major variations in housing costs as between the inner areas, established residential suburbs and new houses on the periphery. These mainly reflect the price differentials for the *land* on which the houses stand. It follows from this reasoning that policy solutions need to tackle the land price issue, as discussed later in chapter 4. Suffice to note here that this may involve attempts at price stabilisation through greater government intervention in the ownership, management and sale of land. It may also involve policies of spatial rearrangement, as where decentralisation policy leads to the use of cheaper land away from existing metropolitan areas. Alternatively, urban consolidation may involve reducing housing lot sizes in the hope of reducing housing costs in existing cities — a hope that may be undermined by the rising price of land per square metre once it becomes the norm to have those higher density settlements (Nicolades 1989). These issues are discussed further in the broader context of regional and urban policy in chapters 10 and 12.

The second group of policies seeks to target *particular sectors* of housing where the stresses are seen to be particularly chronic. The First Home Owners Scheme introduced by the Hawke government was an obvious case in point, targeted at the issue of access to the owner-occupied housing sector (Paris 1987). The small subsidy had a marginal impact in practice, certainly not sufficient to bridge the deposit gap for low and middle income earners identified earlier in this chapter. In any case, to the extent that such subsidies increase demand, they raise housing prices and are therefore self-defeating. Rent control and/or rent subsidies may involve similar problems. Controls tend to have the effect of restricting the supply, depending on their form and severity, whereas subsidies may have unintended distributional effects to the extent that they accrue eventually to the owners of the rented houses. Measures to increase finance for public housing and for the community housing sector are more efficacious, in that these directly increase the supply of housing and reduce the overall inflationary effects of excess demand. The federal Labor government committed itself in 1983 to doubling the proportion of public housing in Australia over the following decade but, in practice, the proportion actually fell. There seems little prospect of this trend being reversed in the 1990s despite the role which construction of public housing can play in simultaneously providing jobs and affordable homes. This issue of provision of funds for public housing is at the root of the housing crisis.

The third group of policies focuses on *distributional* aspects of housing. They can include various macroeconomic and social policies which have a bearing on the distribution of income. Taxation reform and incomes policies are the two most obvious elements, since both bear directly on distribution and hence ability to pay for housing. Taxation reforms can even be tailored directly to deal with housing policy. This is the case, for example, with taxes on imputed rents or the removal of exemptions of owner-occupied houses from capital gains tax to overcome the bias towards owner-occupation. (I hasten to add that these issues are usually considered to be political dynamite and hence not discussed in polite circles!) The introduction of an annual tax on wealth would have a major distributional effect, since about one third of national wealth in Australia comprises ownership of houses. Inheritance taxes would hit directly at inter-generational transfers. All such policies affect both the distribution of income and wealth and the relative economic attractiveness of different housing tenure sectors. Particular changes to the provision of housing finance such as 'low-start loans' and 'reverse annuity loans' can also help tackle the inequalities associated with age and the life cycle (Yates 1988).

More generally, it must be recognised that various government economic policies bear heavily on housing market conditions. An obvious case in point is the financial deregulation and monetary policies pursued by the federal government in Australia in the 1980s. By removing interest rate ceilings and the requirements regarding the proportion of funds to be allocated by banks for home loans, the government changed the patterns of access to owner-occupation. Borrowers suddenly had ready access to funds but at an inflated price. Rob Carter (1987) noted the emerging trends: 'With the financial system deregulated, the competition for a share of more lucrative markets — especially in commercial loans — has become intense. Housing now has to compete for funds from a far less privileged position than in the past. Traditional home finance institutions such as building societies are under pressure to diversify their services away from housing and compete with the banks for lucrative commercial customers.' With the benefit of hindsight, one can see that this led to more high-risk lending and banking bad debts. It was also accompanied by a widening of the margins between financial institutions' borrowing and lending rates of interest (Singh 1989). The restrictionist monetary policy of the late 1980s sent interest rates higher still. Not only did that impose greater difficulty in repayment of home loans, causing default in many cases and further restricting access for new home-buyers, but it also generated further inequality in the distribution of income and wealth. High interest rates redistribute income from borrowers to lenders — broadly speaking from poor to rich — and hence compound the distributional inequalities underlying the housing crisis (and, incidentally, also worsen the current account problem). As such, financial deregulation and restrictionist monetary policies can be considered a key component of the housing crisis. Even the substantial falls in interest rates in the early 1990s could not reverse this situation, coinciding as they did with the onset of recession and the correspondingly reduced incomes of many potential home-buyers.

HOUSING-DRAIN OR STIMULUS?

One question remains — would it be desirable for more resources to be allocated to housing? On the one hand, there is the view that spending on housing absorbs national savings and, to the extent that it 'crowds out' other forms of investment, it fuels the build-up of the foreign debt. Looked at as a zero-sum game, savings used to finance housing are funds not available for the expansion and modernisation of Australian industries and infrastructure. This is a considerable 'opportunity cost', given the impact of outdated capital stock on poor aggregate economic performance. However, the economy does *not* operate according to the principles of a zero-sum game. In a dynamic setting, as Hugh Stretton (1974, 1987) has recurrently stressed, improved housing conditions can improve the overall performance of the economy.

First, house building gives a stimulus to economic growth, leading to more savings. Second, this sort of demand stimulus has only a small import component, as previously noted, because about 90 per cent of material inputs for housing construction are locally produced. True, this is not investment in the tradeable goods sector, so one cannot anticipate a direct boost to exports, at least not without conscious policy strategies to that end (e.g. export of modular housing). Third, improved housing creates the milieu for improved productivity, especially because so much production actually occurs in the household, characteristically but not exclusively done by women. Stretton (1987) has estimated that this domestic production comprises some 35–45 per cent of total value added in the economy. From this viewpoint, investment in housing is not a social luxury so much as a prerequisite for improved economic functioning. Fourth, investment in housing may yield external benefits, such as better neighbourhoods. That depends crucially on its social and spatial distribution: over-investment in housing may have the contrary effect of intensifying 'urban sprawl'. Finally, as Bourassa and Hendershott (1992) note in their study for the National Housing Strategy, the distributional element is also relevant. Indeed, it is not unreasonable to posit the tendency to 'too much investment in housing at high incomes but not enough for those with low incomes'.

This is not to say that there are no trade-offs between alternative uses of funds for investment. Nor is it to gainsay the need to develop means of financing housing which are more efficient and equitable. The mobilisation of superannuation funds for this purpose is one obvious example, drawing on the striking experience of this sort of scheme adopted in Singapore. Indeed, the development of a National Development Fund, as advocated by the ACTU/TDC (1987) report *Australia Reconstructed*, could provide a means of striking a systematic balance between housing and alternative uses of funds for investment. Of course, there are opportunity costs of investment in housing — the goods and services foregone by using resources in this way rather than for other purposes. Unfortunately though, in Australia the alternative use of the investment funds has typically been speculative outlays by 'paper entrepreneurs' and 'corporate cowboys' (Flew 1991). The coexistence in the 1990s of a crisis of over-supply of office-space in Australian cities and a continuing crisis of inadequate housing clearly illustrates the social cost of this imbalance.

HOUSING: AN URBAN PROBLEM?

The general physical standard of Australian housing is good by international standards. However, housing problems are acute in the large metropolitan areas, particularly in Sydney. There is a spatial imbalance in the demand and supply which is not easily corrected, given the inherent immobility of capital in housing. However, the roots of the housing problems lie in a more general constellation of economic, social and political factors. As set out in this chapter, such factors include the historical legacy of a particular housing stock, the distinctive bias towards home-ownership and the negligent provision of public housing, the overall inequality in the distribution of income and wealth and the effect of macroeconomic policies. This conclusion reflects the general theme that what appears as an urban problem is sympto-matic of more general features of the socio-economic system. The housing problem is not an aberration which can easily be tidied up through localised policies. Its resolution requires a broad approach to transforming its causes. Urban policies — and hous-ing policies in particular — can have a role to play in this process, but only work effectively in conjunction with strategies for more general economic stabilisation and social redistribution.

FURTHER READING

Yates and Vipond (1991): an introduction to housing inequalities and urban economic issues.

Kemeny (1983): a critique of the home-ownership bias in Australian housing.

Watson (1988): a feminist perspective on the problems of access to housing.

National Housing Strategy (1991a, 1991b, 1992): reports from the federal govern-ment's major housing policy review.

3

Transport

The problems of urban transport are evident enough: congested streets, long journeys to work, inadequate infrastructure, deficient public services and inefficient usage of scarce energy resources. As such, transport problems rival housing and employment problems as visible manifestations of the contemporary 'urban crisis'. Indeed, they are more striking manifestations in that their connection with the spatial form of the cities is more obvious. Whether the problems are soluble within the existing urban forms, or whether they require the comprehensive reshaping of urban development, continues to be a matter of debate. As with the housing crisis, there is no shortage of proposed solutions, ranging from the construction of further urban freeway networks to more strict regulation or pricing of vehicle use, and from the provision of more public transport in existing urban areas to the construction of new cities which would generate more modest transport demands.

This chapter does not seek to resolve all these issues. Its more limited objectives are to:

- identify the nature of the demand for transport;
- consider the social costs arising from the imbalance between public and private provision;
- discuss some alternative policy responses.

Thus, we set out to examine the pressures generating urban transport problems, exploring the connection between the dominant mode of transport, the underlying mode of production and the collective irrationalities associated with 'market-based solutions' to urban transport problems. This is the story of cars, capital and congestion.

THE DEMAND FOR TRANSPORT

Transport is a rather special commodity. It is the means by which we reconcile our attachment to place with our need for space. It is the means of 'getting around' and thereby widening our array of economic, social, cultural and recreational opportunities. The efficiency and equity of its provision has a major bearing on the quality of urban life.

Like housing, transport has distinctive economic, political and ideological features which distinguish it from more run-of-the-mill commodities. It is important *economically* because it consumes a high proportion of resources for the society as a whole. It is necessary for the reproduction of the economic system (e.g. getting the workers to work); yet the form of urban development continually threatens to impair that function. It is important *politically* in that the state is centrally involved in attempting to reconcile such contradictions and to ensure that this item of 'collective consumption' is adequately provided. Meanwhile, the industries involved in the provision of transport goods (vehicles, insurance, accessories, fuel, highways and so forth) seek to influence transport policy through the operation of the 'roads lobby'. Transport is important *ideologically* in that it determines our mobility and hence the range of our experiences. It affects the form of social interaction, e.g. the individualism of the private car versus the 'collectivism' of a crowded bus. It is integrally linked with the form of urban development. Sprawling suburbia based on the car as the dominant mode of transport contrasts with more compact settlements which can be more readily serviced by public transport provision, cycling or (heaven forbid!) by walking.

For all these reasons, it is important to understand how transport demands are generated, channelled and met. The *overall* demand which is generated depends on the whole social-spatial structure. It is partly determined by the spatial relationships between work-places, residences, retail, social, cultural and recreational facilities—how compact or how distant? It is also influenced by the complexity of economic and social life which shapes, for example, how many activities are performed outside the home and how much movement of goods occurs between different firms. Elizabeth Harman's (1983) analysis of the increased role of the non-residential sphere of consumption is relevant in this context. So too are the prospects of the 'informational city' in which computer-based informational communications partially substitute for physical travel (Stilwell 1992: ch. 12).

How are the total transport demands channelled and met? What modes of transport are used? Table 3.1 presents some figures to show the situation in major Australian cities, focusing on information about the mode of travel to work taken from the latest Census. In 1991, just under 57 per cent of journeys in Sydney were by car (either as driver or passenger), rising to 62 per cent in Brisbane, 63 per cent in Adelaide, 65 per cent in Melbourne and 69 per cent in Perth.

TABLE 3.1   METHOD OF TRAVEL TO WORK: MAJOR AUSTRALIAN CITIES, 1991

	Sydney (%)	Melbourne (%)	Brisbane (%)	Adelaide (%)	Perth (%)
Train	12.5	7.7	6.4	2.0	1.6
Bus	8.1	2.8	7.4	7.0	6.3
Ferry/tram	0.5	2.8	0.3	0.3	0.1
Taxi	0.6	0.4	0.6	0.4	0.2
Car as driver	49.2	57.7	53.9	58.4	61.1
Car as passenger	7.7	7.4	8.4	8.3	7.6
Motorbike	0.5	0.4	0.9	0.8	0.9
Bicycle	0.6	0.9	1.2	1.6	1.3
Walked	3.9	3.0	3.6	2.7	2.1
Other	1.1	0.9	0.9	1.0	1.1
Worked at home	3.4	3.4	3.7	2.9	3.6
Did not go to work	7.9	8.3	9.0	10.0	10.1
Not stated	4.0	4.3	3.7	4.6	4.1

Source: Census of Population & Housing, 1991.

Why has the car become so dominant? One obvious response is that it is an inherently desirable and superior form of transport which more people have gained the opportunity to use as *per capita* incomes have risen. As one American writer put it many years ago, the car 'offers individual personal, and flexible mobility, as nothing before it has ever done, and as nothing else now available can do ... [Moreover] the road and car together have an enormous capacity for promoting economic growth, raising standards of living and creating a good society' (Rae 1971). It is a view which has become, if anything, still more widespread. It involves the familiar 'consumer sovereignty' argument of neoclassical microeconomics, hitched up to a macroeconomic view about the demand for cars as a key element in creating the conditions for material progress. However, it is a view which sits uneasily alongside the evidence in Figure 3.1 on significant national and international variations for places of comparable material standard of living. According to this evidence, travellers in each of the Australian mainland capital cities use public transport at between one-fifth (Perth) and just over one-half (Sydney) the rate at which it is used on average in European cities. Consumer sovereignty is evidently contingent on factors such as the availability of attractive public transport alternatives.

The consumer sovereignty view also sits uneasily alongside observations of the effect of increased car use in large urban areas. It is over a quarter of a century since Lewis Mumford (1964) noted that 'every metropolis that has encouraged the wholesale invasion of the automobile can bear testimony to its disintegrating effects, expanding every year with the expansion of the motor-car and petroleum industries: stalled traffic, personal confusion and frustration, excessive noise, poisoned air, increased necessity to spend an undue portion of the day in performing scattered functions that were once more adequately carried on without the aid of wheeled vehicles in a compact urban area'. Today it is little exaggeration to say that the car is killing the ambience of many of the major cities of the world — cities as diverse as London and Athens, Bangkok and Cairo, Rome and Caracas. Meanwhile, cities which have developed around reliance on the car as the principal means of transport — ranging from planned cities like Canberra to formless free market sprawls like Phoenix, Arizona — lack the character associated with more compact urban places in which human interaction is not automobile-dependent.

FIGURE 3.1   PUBLIC TRANSPORT USE IN AUSTRALIAN, AMERICAN
                      AND EUROPEAN CITIES

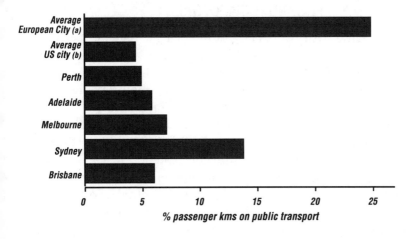

Notes: (a)   Averaged from Hamburg, Frankfurt, Zurich, Stockholm, Brussels,
                Paris, London, Munich, West Berlin, Copenhagen, Vienna and
                Amsterdam.
          (b)   Averaged from Houston, Phoenix, Detroit, Denver, Los Angeles, San
                Francisco, Washington, Chicago and New York.
Source: Newman and Kenworthy (1989).

The standard explanation of this incongruity between an individualistic automobile consumer sovereignty and the adverse
consequences for the quality of urban life lies in the theory of
'externalities'. E.J. Mishan (1967) made much of this in his
pioneering broadside against the role of the car in a deteriorating
urban environment and it has recently re-emerged in official
assessments of urban policy options (EPAC 1991). The essential
argument is simple. Motorists incur costs for car-use, comprising petrol, depreciation of the vehicle, repairs, registration
and insurance, but other costs fall on the community at large.
These are the social costs of congestion, pollution, hazards to
pedestrians, and so forth. Because these negative externalities are
not reflected in the private costs of motoring, the volume of
motoring is not adequately regulated by the price mechanism.
Too much occurs. The problems of urban congestion and a

deteriorating urban environment thereby reflect an imbalance between private and social costs.

PRIVATE BENEFITS AND SOCIAL COSTS

The NRMA, Australia's largest motoring association, estimated average motoring costs at $136 per week for a Toyota Corolla 1.3 litre to $184 for a Holden Commodore in 1992. These estimates were based solely on private costs to the motorists themselves, hefty enough without taking account of the costs of publicly provided infrastructure and other social costs. Updating another calculation previously suggested by E.F. Schumacher (1979), the guru of the 'small is beautiful' movement, we can relate the typical transport usage of a car to the time involved in achieving that transport usage. The average annual number of kilometres travelled by a motorist is about 15,000. Adding up the time spent in working to pay for the car, the fuel, insurance, repairs and other motoring costs, the time spent driving, looking for a parking space, repairs and maintenance, we get a total of approximately 1600 hours. That is a big total, comprising some 30 hours per week, but it is explicable in circumstances where the average weekly cost of running a Commodore, as estimated by the NRMA, is over 35 per cent of the average adult weekly wage. The overall result of the calculation is clear enough—1600 hours to travel 15,000 kilometres. That works out at an average speed of less than 10 kilometres an hour. In other words, the overall efficiency of motoring has declined to a level not substantially greater than rapid walking or jogging!

This does not mean it would be just as efficient to travel on foot (although it could be more healthy). The use of a car is often indispensable, not only for driving in rural areas where there is often no alternative, but also in metropolitan areas where the low-density form of sprawling suburban development, coupled with poor provision of public transport, makes the car all-but-essential for many. The lack of convenient local shopping and other service facilities compounds the problem. Yes, the car is a convenient and flexible mode of transport, capable of carrying small loads which are otherwise difficult to transport, not to mention its role as a status symbol, even a partial compensation for sexual inadequacies! However, all this is bought at a very high social cost.

The dominance of the car results from the very limited context within which 'consumer sovereignty' is allowed to operate in transport. Henry Ford once made the famous statement that his customers could have their [Model T Ford] car any colour they wanted as long as it was black. Modern consumers can now have multiple models in almost any colour of the rainbow, but other constraints on choice have come to bite more sharply. In effect, a dialectical (some would say diabolical) process is at work. The more people have the capacity to become motorists, the more flexible spatial arrangements for economic and social activity can become. Low-density urban development with substantial distances from home to work becomes a feasible urban form. So too does concentration of shopping facilities in suburban complexes (replacing the traditional corner shop), together with fast-food provision, banking and other services based on drive-in systems.

The quite remarkable 'job sprawl' evident in the last couple of decades is particularly pertinent in this context. For example, Sydney's central business district (CBD) boasted some 225,000 jobs in 1971, comprising 23 per cent of the metropolitan work-force: by 1986, the absolute number had been slimmed down to 188,000 and the relative proportion to just 12.6 per cent. This has important implications not just for the total number of transport journeys, but also for trip lengths and, given the generally radial character of the public transport network, for the balance between public and private transport usage. To the extent that the decentralisation of jobs is to sub-regional centres well-served by public transport, it does not inevitably lead to more car usage, but it has tended to do so because of the proliferation of complex criss-cross journeys within the metropolitan area. Then, as the total dependence on private motoring grows, the tendency towards congestion reasserts itself and becomes more wide-spread, with disastrous consequences for pollution and energy usage, not to mention physical and mental well-being. In other words, the freedom of choice between transport modes is highly constrained and contradictory.

There are many examples of how individual transport decisions take place in a macro-environment which limits choices in a socially adverse manner. The classic case is the destruction of the public transport system in Los Angeles. It is an extreme example of corporate capitalist interests having operated at the expense of society as a whole — of private benefits, not to transport users but to the producers of transport goods, coupled with enormous social costs. People normally think of L.A. as a city constructed around the use of private cars — the ultimate freeway city. In fact, L.A. developed around an extensive rail transit system covering the Southern California region which permitted the development of a series of interlinked communities. Those rail systems were bought up by a holding company set up by General Motors in conjunction with Firestone Tyres and Standard Oil of California. To cut a long and well-documented story short, the holding company destroyed the railways, ripping up the last of the lines in 1961, because it judged that it could make more profits out of providing the goods for a road-based transport system (cars, tyres, petrol) than out of continuing to provide public rail services. Thus, it imposed automobile-dependence.

Rising incomes would surely have led to growing car-use anyway, but the people had little other choice. The result is well known — the development of 'smog city' with millions of cars pumping thousands of tonnes of pollutants into the air daily, where 'red alerts' periodically arise due to exhaust emissions, and where gunfights have occurred in petrol stations during periods of petrol restrictions. The motor manufacturing, oil and tyre producing interests that effectively engineered this outcome were found guilty by a US court of conspiracy against the public interest and fined $5000! (Snell 1974). That much is history. Now, three decades later, a new rail transit system is being re-constructed over substantially the same routes as the system which had been destroyed.

It may be objected that such a situation could not happen in a country like Australia where private monopoly interests have not been allowed to figure so prominently in transport provision. However, the activities of the 'roads lobby' have generated similar, if less dramatic, outcomes. Certainly, there has been a massive subsidisation of roads by public funds. Recent years have seen an enormous disparity between federal funding for road and rail infrastructure, the latter falling to zero in fiscal year 1990, and averaging only one twentieth of the former over the previous decade. To take one specific instance, $730 million was allocated to upgrading the Hume highway between 1983 and 1990 but nothing was allocated for upgrading the rail mainline between Sydney and Melbourne. Yet an estimated $335–530 million could reduce current XPT rail passenger transport time between the two cities by 40 per cent to 7.5 hours and rail freight time by 36 per cent to 9 hours (Ferris 1990). The costs of this imbalance in capital spending on road and rail have become a source of major controversy, particularly because of the high incidence of road casualties. Some critics argue for policies to redirect bulky traffic to rail transport, while others argue for still more expenditure on the upgrading of the road system. The construction interests continue to be a prominent influence on the policy outcome, favouring road transport. In February 1992, the federal govern-ment, concerned to fund transport infrastructure projects as part of a 'pump-priming' exercise to combat the recession, did set out to redress the neglect of capital works in the railways, but even then the increased funding announced for road improvements was more substantial.

The imbalance in the transport system, favouring road trans-port and the private car, partly reflects a focus on profitability to the exclusion of broader public interests. However, the foregoing illustrations also suggest that the public sector is part of the problem, particularly because of its tendency to accommodate the pattern of existing transport demands. Clive Beed (1981) has noted the in-built bias associated with 'trend planning' based on the extrapolation of existing transport demands. It arises in part because of the limitations of transport modelling techniques. More fundamentally, it reflects a restricted view of how transport demands are generated and changed. A memorable, albeit rather personal, example goes back to the Sydney Area Transpor-tation Study of the 1970s. The study's director, Dr Nielson, was speaking at a meeting convened by Sydney University's Planning

Research Centre. During the discussion the audience was critical of the over-reliance on freeway development because it encouraged more car use. Dr Nielson requested a show of hands by those who had driven to the meeting. The majority had done so, and Dr Nielson promptly concluded his presentation, contented at having demonstrated the audience's hypocrisy. The underlying fallacy is not hard to discern. It is that the reliance on the car is partly due to the failure of transport planners to provide adequate alternative modes of transport!

The legacy of transport planning which accommodates to the extrapolation of current trends, and thereby accentuates them, lives on. The relentless expansion of inner-city car parks is an obvious case in point — for example the massive parking facility for 1200 cars associated with the proposed tunnel under the Sydney CBD. However, there are also indications that transport planners are becoming more conscious of externality problems. Applications of cost-benefit analysis have become more widespread in transport decisions, which is welcome although such studies rarely give unambiguous conclusions where different modes of transport are at issue, as distinct from different routes for a single transport mode. There is also a growing recognition of the imperative to address broader questions such as long-run depletion of energy resources. Reliance on the car, or on other major users of fossil fuels, is a major element in the mounting environmental crisis. It is estimated that, on average in OECD countries, vehicles contribute 75 per cent of carbon monoxide emissions, 48 per cent of nitrogen oxides and 40 per cent of hydrocarbons. Washington's Worldwatch Institute estimates that the world's 400 million cars pump more than 500 million tonnes of carbon into the atmosphere every year (Ellwood 1989). Even the development of electric cars provides no solution, to the extent that electricity is produced by the combustion of fossil fuels, leading to resource depletion, atmospheric pollution and global warming.

The environmental crisis is the most obvious pressure for radical reappraisal of transport policy. However, it can be regarded as one manifestation of a common dichotomy — between individual rationality and collective irrationality. Yes, each individual can be expected to make rational decisions about choice of transportation modes. But the aggregation of those decisions can be collectively irrational and wasteful of society's resources. Indeed, the aggregate outcome usually negates the individual motivations which began the process—the quest for speed, cheapness and convenience. The earlier calculations suggested by Schumacher are an illustration of this problem. Certainly, a decentralised market system has some attractive features but it generates a recurrent tendency for collectively irrational outcomes. Negative externalities are so pervasive in a capitalist market economy. The point is of particular significance in an era when the doctrines of economic rationalism, user pays, and privatisation have been in the ascendency. In this sense, the transport problem is also a problem of economic ideology.

TRANSPORT POLICIES

Given the biases in the transport system arising from vested interests, prevailing ideologies and the historical legacy of past transport infrastructive investments, it may seem that there is little scope for solutions. However, the intensity of transport problems in the urban areas means that issues of transport policy are continuously under public scrutiny. The state, for all its limitations and complicity, is subject to recurrent demand for remedial policies. Four principal currents can be identified in the resulting proliferation of policy proposals. One concerns the provision of more and better roads. The second advocates more effective pricing and/or regulation of alternative transport modes. The third concerns changes in the form of public transport provision. The fourth involves spatial solutions such as those associated with urban consolidation. Of course, these do not exhaust all the possibilities. As with the discussion of housing policy in chapter 2, we cannot do justice here to a range of issues that warrant a book to themselves. However, we can usefully identify some aspects of these four approaches to transport policy that fit in with more general consideration of Australian urban development.

The provision of *more and better roads* is the most direct response to the increased ownership and usage of cars and the corresponding increase in the intensity of urban congestion. It is reflected in the construction of urban freeways and major projects like Sydney's harbour tunnel which began operation in 1992. The costs are considerable, both in terms of direct building costs and the expense of acquiring the necessary land. Moreover, this approach is, at best, a stop-gap measure. While temporary relief may be generated in particular parts of the urban road system by new road construction or road widening, the usual effect is to relocate congestion bottle-necks elsewhere. Then, when they are remedied by new road works, the overall volume of traffic grows to occupy the expanded facilities. This was evident with the opening of Sydney's harbour tunnel which immediately encouraged more people to drive downtown — an extra 13,500 car journeys a day being made across the harbour within days of the tunnel opening. It is as if supply creates its own demand. As Blunden and Black (1984) demonstrate, car usage is actually stimulated by increased road capacity. This is not to deny that improvements are possible through road construction. Rather it is to stress that the combination of an indefinitely growing demand for and supply of road space in a finite urban setting involves an inherent contradiction. *Reductio ad absurdum*, the equilibrium is where the city is dominated by roads and associated facilities for car — in the words of Jonie Mitchell's song 'Pave paradise and put up a parking lot'.

Road pricing is a frequently posited alternative. Recognising the inherently finite supply of urban space for transport facilities, the task is to ration its use. The pricing system is advocated because of its alleged sensitivity to consumer preferences. This may involve direct tolls, as on new freeways and on Sydney's harbour bridge and tunnel. Alternatively, it may involve more complex systems, as in Hong Kong where a computer-based system tracks car movements into the downtown core, clocking up charges for motorists according to the time of day and the type of streets through which their vehicle is driven. 'Getting the car off welfare', to use the American catch-cry, is one way of expressing this concern to ensure full recovery of economic and social costs. It is an approach which is evidently compatible with the prevailing 'user-pays' approach to public policy. However, it is bedevilled by problems of inequity. Urban road use tends to become the privilege of the wealthy. Where car-use is indispensable as a means of getting to work, because of the absence of public transport alternatives, particular problems arise for the lowly-paid. In the extreme, road-pricing can involve the denial of access to work, unless the funds generated are used to finance improved public transport.

Direct *regulation* is another alternative. This may involve the banning of vehicles altogether from city centres. It may involve restrictions on car use such as requiring three or more occupants per vehicle using peak-hour transit lanes (or, as in Singapore, requiring drivers to pay a special periodic fee for the right of access to the restricted downtown area — a mixture of pricing and regulation). In conjunction with the provision of adequate public transport alternatives, regulation can result in considerable diversion of transport demand to more collectively efficient modes. 'Traffic calming', through the application of street closures, speed-humps and other impediments to rapid car movement may, paradoxically, also contribute substantially to a solution to urban transport problems (Engwicht 1992). However, as with road pricing, all these measures require the provision of appropriate alternatives to car use as the dominant urban transport mode.

It is this availability of *public transport*, in the right places in appropriate forms and at the right price, which is the key. Public transport facilities have typically been inadequate and have suffered from deterioration as the vicious circle of declining demand — rising price — declining supply has operated. The revealed preference for private car transport is not surprising in these circumstances. However, there is no inexorable logic in this process. With adequate commitment by public authorities, efficient and comfortable public transport systems can attract widespread patronage. The forms can vary enormously — from train to bus, light rail, minibus on phone-call, jeepney and ferry.

Take public rail transport as a case in point. It has an economic justification in that rail per person typically represents a cheaper individual subsidy than that for private car users. It takes up less space and is the cheapest way of catering for mass peak-hour demands. It also has a welfare justification, catering for the people who do not have access to a car, including children and many pensioners whose mobility is otherwise restricted. It has a land-use justification: it can work in conjunction with the objectives of urban consolidation and the reorientation of the job sprawl towards metropolitan sub-regional centres. It also has a significant environmental justification, to the extent that the electricity generation required for rail emits less greenhouse gases on a passenger per kilometre basis than do car emissions. This is not to say that rail provides a universal solution, either in its conventional or light rail forms. Its effectiveness depends equally on its accessibility, attractiveness, personal safety and its coordination with other transport modes.

Successful transport policies must, above all, take account of *urban form*. As with the employment and housing policies discussed in the preceding chapters, a judicious mix of national and local policy measures is required. In the case of transport the spatial dimension is particularly important. Newman and Kenworthy (1989, 1992), for example, put a strong case for a solution which involves light rail and traffic calming, but stress that this must be combined with a refocusing of housing in 'urban villages'. Earlier proposals for the restructuring of Melbourne and a more recent argument for redesigning cities on ecological principles also envisage a stronger neighbourhood focus for urban economic and social activities (Socialist Alternative Melbourne Collective 1985, Engwicht 1992). More generally still, the argument of this chapter suggests that transport problems are inextricably linked with patterns of urban development, the provision of housing, the location of industry, energy pricing and public control of corporate interests. A solution necessarily involves a simultaneous reconstruction of policy towards these various issues. To simply accommodate to existing demands is to perpetuate them, serving particular private interests but at enormous social cost.

FURTHER READING

Rimmer (1988a): a short survey of Australian transport geography.

Beed and Moriarty (1988a, 1992): discussions of private-public transport im-
    balance and means of dealing with the unsustainable growth of car usage.

Manning (1991): an analysis of the history and politics of automobile dominance in
    Australian cities.

Newman, Kenworthy and Robinson (1992): advocacy of an approach to planning of
    transport and urban development based on light rail, traffic calming and urban
    villages.

4

Land

A study of the functioning of cities must include, as a central feature, an analysis of *land*. Land is an essentially scarce resource in urban areas. Its ownership, control and disposition affects the *efficiency* of the urban economy, the *distribution* of wealth (especially through the effects of land speculation) and the form of urban *growth*. Locational factors are important too, since the position and accessibility of urban land is crucial in determining its market price and the use to which it is put. Other urban problems, such as those explored in the preceding three chapters are integrally linked with the allocation of urban land.

In Australian cities, the issues of land ownership, price and use are of particular significance. Unequal ownership of land is an important dimension of socio-economic inequality. Rising land prices have been a major component in the housing affordability crisis. Incompatible land uses are a significant element in the intensification of environmental problems; as for example, where intra-urban airports add to problems of noise, dirt and danger for urban residents, or where industries produce, store or discharge toxic chemicals in proximity to residential areas. The regulation of land uses continues to be one of the most problematic issues facing local and State governments.

While an understanding of the factors shaping the availability, distribution, price and use of urban land is necessary, it is not easily achieved. This is an aspect of economic analysis which has proved to be particularly troublesome. For this reason it is necessary to review some aspects of the theory of land rent before we turn to practical problems associated with land in Australian cities. Accordingly, the principal sections of this chapter are ordered as follows:

- theories of urban land use and rents;
- urban land cost variations;
- urban development interests;
- land speculation;
- public policy.

The general objective is not to examine detailed land-use patterns but to identify the nature of the underlying allocative mechanisms and to evaluate whose interests are served in the process.

URBAN LAND USE AND RENT

How is scarce urban land allocated between competing uses? In a capitalist economy where land is privately owned its allocation primarily occurs through the price system. The use which may be made of any particular parcel of land may be constrained by government regulations pertaining to zoning of acceptable land uses and by detailed development approval requirements. The imposition of taxes on land ownership and land transactions (stamp duties) also involves a degree of government intervention. Subject to these constraints, land use is shaped by market processes.

What determines the price of land? Economists have sought to answer this question through developing theories of *rent*. Rent here is not to be confused with the more common use of the term to refer to the rent of housing, which is the price of hiring particular housing services (although the price of the land on which the housing sits will usually affect housing rents). Rent in this context is land (or ground) rent. It is paid for the use of a particular area of land for a particular period. That earning capacity determines the market price of the land when it is bought and sold. When the land is built on the rent is capitalised into the price of the total package of the land and the commercial, residential or industrial property which stands on it.

Thus, the question of land price resolves into an analysis of the determinants of rent. So far so good; but how is rent to be analysed? Here we come up against the existence of competing paradigms in economics. One approach draws on neoclassical economics, seeking to theorise the relationship between rent and the various competing demands for urban land. The core of this analysis visualises the market system allocating the land according to the 'bid rents' of alternative commercial, industrial, residential and agricultural users (Stilwell 1992: ch. 9). Market-clearing prices are automatically established through this process of competitive bidding. Exponents of this theory may concede that the market outcome can be distributionally inequitable: those with the ability to pay will command the most attractive and advantageous sites, while the poor get the less preferred sites. Moreover, it may involve land rent payments being made to land-owners who derive large incomes by 'virtue' of their property rights rather than any directly productive contribution to the economy. However, the land-use outcome is held to be efficient in the narrow sense that any reallocation of the land would lead to some land going to less preferred uses, measured in terms of ability to pay.

Neoclassical economists have developed the analysis with 'any number of rococo twists' (Leitner and Sheppard 1989), adding modifications to take account of multi-centred cities, the ageing of buildings, and the existence of competing income groups. They also acknowledge that externalities may impede the attainment of efficient allocative outcomes through free-market processes. This latter problem may arise in urban areas where the use made of one land area, for example by industrial activities generating atmospheric pollution, impacts negatively on the well-being of neighbours. The pervasive character of these externalities in practice is a principal justification for the state using zoning to minimise problems arising from incompatible land uses. In these circumstances, the role of neoclassical theory as a buttress for *laissez-faire* ideology looks a little shaky.

On an analytical level, the neoclassical orthodoxy has also been challenged by the reformulation of rent theory developed in classical political economy by Ricardo and Marx (e.g. Harvey 1973, Walker 1974, Bruegel 1975, Edel 1976, Ball 1985, Harvey

1989a). The key proposition is that 'it is through production that a surplus is made in the space-economy, and it is from this profit that rents must be paid to the owners of land' (Leitner & Sheppard 1989). There are various elements in this alternative conception. One element is differential rent, which has a resemblance to the neoclassical notion of rent in that it varies according to the productive use made of the land. This theory of differential rent arising from the different attributes of locations is supplemented by Marx's notions of monopoly rent and class-monopoly rent, focusing on the power of land-owners as a *class*. This gives us a view of urban rents and land uses which does not deny the role of competition and markets, on which the neoclassical theory is based, but which integrates it with the analysis of capitalism as a system based on particular class relationships.

Differential rent is that part of the economic surplus appropriated by the owners of land according to its productivity in different uses. This is most evident where the land-use is one involving capitalist commodity production e.g. the premises of an industrial firm. To the extent that location influences the profits generated by the firm in a competitive market situation (e.g. because of spatial variations in labour or transport costs), there is a differential capacity of land-owners to charge rent to the firm for the use of their land. These differential rents apply equally to alternative uses of urban land which compete with industrial uses, such as use for residential purposes. If the differential rents are highest in the CBD, the broad pattern of rents and land uses will mirror that in the neoclassical theory, with rents decreasing in a gradient from the centre to the outer suburbs. However, an extra variable now impinges on differential rents — the general rate of profit prevailing in the economy (Sheppard and Barnes 1986). This means that there is not complete convergence between the neoclassical theory of land prices and the theory of differential rent.

The dichotomy becomes more marked when the categories of *monopoly* and *class-monopoly* rent are superimposed on differential rent. The former is the additional rent payment which a land-owner can extract when her/his land is rented by a firm earning large profits because of its monopoly in the sale of its products. In effect, the land-owner is using her/his control over land to extract part of the profits generated by their industrial or commercial tenant. Any firms with market power, whether they are in a situation of monopoly, oligopoly or monopolistic competition, can have a part of their profits siphoned off in this way. Class-monopoly rent, by contrast, results from the collective power of land-owners over the supply of land. To the extent that they can combine to restrict the supply of land, possibly in conjunction with the capitalist state, they can raise market rents above the level that would otherwise pertain. This may occur across-the-board or may have a more localised impact in particular parts of the city. The classic case is where financial institutions 'red-line' districts within which they will not provide funds for housing loans, leading to artificial scarcities and the potential for higher rents (Harvey 1974, Bassett and Short 1980).

The usefulness of these analytical categories for the decomposition of land rent into its component parts continues to be a matter of debate. To put this debate into perspective, it is pertinent to ask about the capacity of the competing theories to explain observable patterns of urban rent. The simplest case, already noted, is that of an intra-metropolitan pattern with highest rents downtown and a falling rent gradient as one moves out through the suburbs to the outer-metropolitan fringe. This is the general situation in Australian cities, as in other major cities, albeit subject to diverse local variations according to topographical factors and the effects of suburban commercial centres on rent patterns. It is generally consistent with the predictions of the neo-classical rent theory. It is also consistent with the theory of differential rent to the extent that there is a positive relationship between centrality of location and the capacity to generate surplus value through the production of goods and services. Monopoly rents may generate some local variations, but would not normally change the general rent-distance gradient unless there was a tendency for firms with monopoly in the product market to be more (or less) centralised than firms in competitive markets. Class-monopoly rents would certainly make a difference in that the whole rent-distance gradient would be shifted upwards to the extent that the land-owning class uses its collective monopoly over land to raise urban rents as a whole. However, there would be no reason to expect a change in the slope of the rent gradient. This being so, it is difficult to differentiate between the neoclassical theory and the Marxian analysis in terms of their capacity to explain the characteristic metropolitan rent patterns.

The difference lies more in what the theories tell us about the capitalist system and its mechanisms of *income redistribution*. The neoclassical theory takes distribution as given and asks how the existing land resources will be allocated. The Marxist-oriented theory, on the other hand, illuminates the mechanisms by which income is redistributed to the land-owning class. Probably the least interesting case is that of monopoly rent, where the redistribution is from industrial capitalist to land-owner. In a modern capitalist economy, where the ownership of land and other forms of capital are intertwined, the distinction is less important than at the time of Marx when a land-owning class was distinct from the owners of the means of production. In modern conditions, the industrial capitalist and land-owner are frequently the same institution, in which case no redistribution is observable.

More interesting is the situation where the redistribution is between workers paying rents for urban land (on which their houses stand) and a property-owning class seeking to maximise its returns via the mechanisms of class-monopoly rent. However, where the workers have become partly land-owning (as in the case of Australian owner-occupiers) the redistributions through rent have a more inter-generational dimension *within* the class. This is not to say that owner-occupation eliminates inter-class income redistribution. In circumstances where land and housing prices are very high (as in major Australian cities), owner-occupation is typically attainable only with mortgage finance which means massive redistributions occur via the interest charges payable to financial institutions. This issue underlies the housing crisis analysed in chapter 2 of this book. So, complex as these theoretical issues are, they give us a basis for understanding how the urban land market interacts with other urban problems through the mechanisms of income distribution.

URBAN LAND COST VARIATIONS

A general indication of spatial variations in land rent in the Australian context is provided by Table 4.1. This shows the land rentals for comparable small industrial sites in various metropolitan and non-metropolitan locations in New South Wales. The city-country variation is striking enough, with the industrial cities of Newcastle and Wollongong occupying inter-mediate positions. Within the metropolitan area the variation between the cost of outer-western locations and more centrally located sites averages nearly 1:4 for equivalent sized sites and over 1:5 for the west compared with the northern suburbs. Sydney's prices are generally higher than for other State capitals, not only for industrial sites but also for residential land. Of course, all such prices are subject to considerable flux, but still higher prices are inevitable eventually because of the physical shortage of supply of land for urban development.

The federal government's Indicative Planning Council predicts an intensification of a serious land supply problem comparable to that which fed into the acute housing crisis in the late 1980s. In part this is because of the high cost of providing infrastructure to service new land for urban development. The federal government's Department of Industry, Technology and Commerce has estimated that it costs $11,000 per average housing block to provide roads and stormwater drains in Sydney compared with $7700 in Melbourne and $9800 in Brisbane. It costs $9000 per block to develop sewerage in Sydney compared with $3500 in Melbourne and just over $2000 in Brisbane. Installing water in Sydney costs more than $5000 a block compared with $1300 in Melbourne and $2200 in Brisbane. In these circumstances, it is not surprising that there has been mounting concern about increasing the efficiency of the de-velopment process for urban land. It is not merely a technical matter of providing the necessary services more cheaply for new land releases, or even a managerial matter of coordinating the urban land release process more effectively. It is also a political matter of dealing with the various interest groups and the processes which fuel inflation in land prices throughout the urban economy.

TABLE 4.1   LAND VALUES FOR SMALL INDUSTRIAL SITES, NSW, 1992

Area	$ per square metre
Sydney: Central (5–10 km from CBD)	285
Inner West	122
South and South West	203
Northern	418
West	78
Gosford	72
Wollongong	64
Newcastle	52
Country NSW	
Albury	31
Armidale	31
Bathurst	20
Bomaderry	27
Coffs Harbour	66
Dubbo	13
Goulburn	27
Griffith	18
Lismore	28
Moree	7
Muswellbrook	9
Murwillumbah	26
Queanbeyan	37
Tamworth	17
Taree	40
Wagga Wagga	33
Average	27

Source: NSW Valuer General's Department, *NSW Real Estate Market*, values as of 30 June 1992.

URBAN DEVELOPMENT INTERESTS

Various interest groups are involved in the urban land market. The users of urban land obviously have a general interest in readily available alternatives at reasonable prices; and there is a general 'public interest' in ensuring that these requirements are met efficiently and equitably. However, there are also sectional interests involved, including investors, developers, financial institutions and real estate agents. To some extent their interests are divergent, though they all have a common interest in the growth of the market. *Investors* in the ownership of urban land have an obvious interest in capital appreciation and rising rents and, to that extent, can be expected to favour restrictions on supply of land. *Developers*, by contrast, have a shorter time-horizon and usually favour a rapid increase in the supply of land for conversion to new urban uses and/or restructuring of existing urban uses with bigger buildings on smaller spaces. *Finance companies* have an interest in the rapid expansion of the funds borrowed for purchase of land for residential, commercial and industrial uses, especially when high interest rates prevail. *Real estate agents* can be expected to favour the most rapid turnover of properties in the market, on which their sales commissions are based.

There is enormous scope for conflict between these 'fractions of capital' and there is no general reason to expect that the resulting management of urban land development will be effectively coordinated in that elusive 'public interest'. As Maurie Daly (1982) notes, in practice the activities of these competing interests in Australia have been manifest in a roller-coaster ride of urban land and property development characterised by alternating booms and busts.

Ostensibly, *the state* exists as a mediator and regulator of these competing interests. As Martin Boddy (1982) puts it, 'the basis of land use planning might conventionally be characterised as state intervention in the private land market'. As in other countries, the state is often called on to mediate in urban land-use conflicts which 'tend to form in geographic, sectoral and racial terms: local versus regional or national interests; consumer interests versus producers; whites versus non-whites' (Plotkin 1987). The orderly release of state-owned land for urban development and the application of zoning to avoid inappropriate land uses are instruments which the state can use for these purposes. We consider the success of such measures in chapter 11. Suffice for the moment to note that, far from preventing speculation in land markets, they have tended to become part of the process. To understand why requires a consideration of the nature of the speculative process.

LAND SPECULATION

Land is the focus of much speculative activity, comparable in some respects to gold, antique furniture and art-works. Its appeal in this respect is partly because both the demand and supply of land are subject to substantial changes which cause variability in its prices. The demand depends upon population growth, income levels and changing preferences for different locations. The supply, although fixed in an absolute sense, is subject to variations according to public policy, such as the rate at which state-owned land is released and changes in zoning. More generally, there is a general public perception that its price inevitably rises in the long run, especially in and around urban areas. This gives land speculation a seemingly attractive dual feature — general prospects of steady capital appreciation plus the possibility of particularly rapid price surges as the result of land being rezoned from rural to urban uses.

Land speculation in Australia has been described by Leonie Sandercock (1979) as the 'national hobby'. In her words, 'one of the most sensational themes in the history of Australian cities has been the story of land speculation and the corrupt behaviour of politicians and public officials in high and low places associated with that speculation'. She traces the saga through from the 1830s, with particular reference to Melbourne. Three notorious cases in one year alone — 1977 — are described as follows:

- The first episode to draw the attention of the press involved land at Mt Ridley owned by Lensworth Finance (Vic) Pty Ltd (a company also involved in transactions with the Housing Commission). In January 1977 it was announced that plans to develop this land as a satellite city had been approved by Cabinet, despite the fact that, in the Board of Works plan for the metropolitan area, all the land at Mt Ridley was zoned as non-urban (i.e. not available for any kind of urban development). Lensworth stood to make $9.2m if and when the land was rezoned. They were to sell it to T & G Mutual Life Society Ltd, the company which put up the development proposal to Cabinet.

- The second episode came to light only two months later.

'Magnate strikes gold in the hills' ran the headline in the *Age* on 21 March 1977. 'Government clears the path for Dandenongs subdivision'. Once again State Cabinet had overridden the decision of the planning authority, which had zoned the area at Kilsyth South as rural, to clear the way for American developers Kaiser Aetna Australia Properties Ltd to subdivide 111 acres into 400 suburban lots.

- The third episode came to the public attention on 5 April under the *Age* headlines 'Land owners stand to make millions', 'Geelong: why a growth centre became stunted'. Under legislation introduced in December 1976 landowners in the Geelong region stood to make millions of dollars because land needed for the growth centre was to be rezoned from rural to urban before the Geelong Regional Planning Authority acquired it. The landowners dominated the Liberal Party in the Geelong area.

The centrality of the state in creating the conditions for this type of land speculation speaks for itself. However, the adverse consequences of the land speculation process feed back via the state onto many sections of urban society. The planning process itself is undermined. Plans drawn up by metropolitan authorities are treated as 'form guides for the speculation stakes', and pressures are brought to bear for the modification of plans for urban growth corridors. Land on the suburban fringe is bought up, particularly by large insurance, finance and development companies, anticipating its eventual rezoning. This raises its price and thereby undermines the capacity of public authorities to provide the necessary public services at reasonable costs. More generally, the speculative process fuels inflation, redistributes income regressively, and impedes public control over the urban development process.

It is in these various ways that speculation in land has particularly problematic effects. Of course, speculation pervades many aspects of economic activity, and orthodox economic theorists claim that it helps to ensure the liquidity of the economy and the process of market-clearing. However, it can also have a significant role in undermining the productive capacity of the economy by diverting funds from more productive purposes (Stilwell

1988b). In the urban development process its effects are little short of diabolical. To quote Sandercock (1979) again:

> If I gamble on a horse I don't do much damage to other people's lives — except perhaps my family's if I lose my week's pay. But if I gamble on land in the expectation that its price will rise and then hang on to it till I can sell it at a profit, my behaviour has a very considerable effect on the sort of city we live in. When one person, or hundreds of thousands of people, engage in the hobby — or business — of speculating on land prices, then they make it damn near impossible for governments to plan decent cities for us to live in.

PUBLIC POLICY

The allocation and use of land is crucial to the goals of economic efficiency, social equity and environmental sustainability. However, the land market in practice is pervaded by competing interests and speculative processes which recurrently pervert these ideals. In these circumstances it is not surprising that a more interventionist role for the state is frequently mooted, ranging from land nationalisation and land rent taxation to the more widespread use of leasehold tenure. Sandercock (1979) discusses the local application of these options, and they have been considered more generally in an international context by Massey & Catalano (1978) and Boddy (1982).

The policy debates reflect long-standing concerns dating back at least to the powerful propositions of Henry George (1879). George's own vision was of a single tax on land which would ensure that land was put to productive use and which would minimise the inequities associated with its private disposition. Such a tax would force landowners to use their land productively in order to generate the revenue to pay the tax. However, they would receive no personal income from the surplus which would be effectively appropriated for the common purposes of the society. George argued that the use of a land tax to replace all other taxes would simultaneously remove disincentives to productive use of labour and capital. These ideas were very influential in Australia a century ago but vested interests in the land question have since proved to be more durable.

In any case, it is not clear that any one policy can resolve the problems of land speculation and inefficient allocation. The Georgist solution of land rent taxation tackles inequities and inefficiencies associated with the relationship of people to land while leaving unchallenged the general form of the capital-labour relationship. It sets ownership of land aside from the ownership of capital. Certainly, as Michael Chisholm (1983) argues, 'a tax based on the site value of the land ... would provide a powerful incentive to the owners of vacant urban land to ensure that it is brought into productive use at the earliest opportunity'. Agreed, but note the need to safeguard 'vacant' land which has significant environmental value while it remains in its natural state. That said, there is no reason why private monopoly of natural resources and land should be allowed to generate the private appropriation of 'unearned' site revenues when these could be captured by the state through taxes on annual rental value. Local government rates as a form of land tax and State government land taxes do capture part of that surplus; but this relatively small land rent component in the current system of taxation falls well short of Henry George's own vision for a single tax on land in place of all other taxes.

The introduction in Australia of capital gains taxation has been one step towards reducing the incentive to hold land for speculative gain, but the policy excludes land associated with owner-occupied housing and it allows indexation of asset values to inflation (which is exacerbated by the overall effects of land speculation!). The more targeted policies, involving changes in the system of land tenure, even nationalisation, retain at most a shadowy presence in public debates, because their radical character cuts across existing interests and modes of thinking about the issues. In any case, land nationalisation is no panacea for the problems of inefficiency and equity in capitalist cities. As Massey and Catalano (1978) point out, 'its primary effect will not be to end the struggle over land related issues, but to change the conditions of that struggle ... "The land problem", though once again changed in form, would still result from the continuing problem of systems of land ownership within a capitalist social formation.'

ANALYSIS AND PRAYER

As demonstrated in the first half of this chapter, theories of urban rent can provide a basis for understanding spatial variations in urban land prices and uses. In this context, both neoclassical and Marxian theories have the potential to explain the general gradients of rents for land at varying distance from the CBD. However, the reformulation of the Marxian approach, recognising the various components in rent, is better able to yield insights into the overall level of rents and the associated redistribution of income. As noted later in this chapter, we can also gain important insights into the problems of urban land use through the identification of the interest groups involved. This approach illuminates the role of speculation in the process of land price inflation and the associated problems for urban planning. The focus thereby shifts from the purely *spatial* aspects of land use and rent to the *temporal* dimensions of changes in land use and urban development. It also provides us with a clearer picture of the constraints placed by vested interests on policies to restrict 'the land racket'. Evidently, the difficulties of analysing urban land uses and prices are minor in relation to the difficulties of securing more efficient and equitable land uses in the real world.

Shall we pray? In the difficult circumstances just described it seems appropriate to conclude this chapter with a prayer. This one was delivered in Melbourne at a national congress of urban developers:

> O Almighty God who has given us this earth and commanded us to develop new estates to house the peoples of all colours, class and creed . . . we ask Thy blessing upon these men. Fill them with a sense of accomplishment, not just for the estates developed, but for the homes created for the nurturing and propagation of Thy flock and the greater joys which their new developments make available to mankind. Bless these, our nation's developers, and their friends and associates. Amen.

FURTHER READING

Sandercock (1979): an analysis of the adverse effects of land speculation on Australian cities.

Daly (1982): a detailed description of the interest groups involved in the urban land and property development process.

Harvey (1989a): chapter 3 presents reflections on the theory of urban rent.

Leitner and Sheppard (1989): setting land rent theory and property development in the broader context of production and location theory.

5

Environment

Environmental concerns have become increasingly intense in recent years. Urban transport systems which cause congestion and pollution are a major contributory factor. More generally, there is growing recognition of the ecologically unsustainable impacts of various production and consumption activities. Indeed, there is a growing recognition that many of these economic activities are, in the broader sense, uneconomic! The seemingly relentless production of goods with built-in obsolescence, the proliferation of trivial product differentiation, the use of non-renewable raw materials and energy sources, the inadequate facilities for recycling and waste disposal — these environmentally degrading aspects of modern industrial society are all too evident.

The environmental problems impact at various scales — global, national, local and individual. The urban dimensions are particularly important, as this chapter sets out to demonstrate. The most well-known environmental struggles have concerned 'wilderness' issues, e.g. clearance of native forests, damming of rivers, preservation of threatened plant and animal species. However, urban environmental issues are at least equally important, as Australian environmental activist Jack Mundey has repeatedly emphasised. The size and form of our cities intensifies the general tendency to environmental decay. Each city consumes energy and other resources and produces, together with an array of more-or-less useful goods and services, sundry by-products of polluted air, sewage and other non-recycled

garbage. From an ecological perspective it is not a pretty picture
nor a sustainable process.

This chapter explores the connection between urban development and environmental problems by:

- giving an 'urban twist' to analyses of the sources of environmental decay;
- considering the relationship between energy use and urban
  form;
- examining how pollution interacts with urban congestion.

Although couched in general terms, the discussion is particularly pertinent to Australian cities. Generally speaking, Australia
has many natural advantages from the environmental viewpoint,
including its physical size, small population and relative isolation
from other heavily polluting nations. On the other hand, it has
certain socio-economic characteristics which result in severe
environmental stresses. Most immediately obvious of these are
the emphasis on private motor transport, the low-density form of
housing, the sub-standard facilities for waste disposal and the
inadequacy of controls on industrial effluent. In Sydney alone, it
is estimated that every year the city's sewers dump in the ocean
106,000 tonnes of suspended solids and 24,000 tonnes of oils and
greases (Brown 1990). The sprawl of urban development to the
west is also causing severe environmental damage in the Nepean-
Hawkesbury river basin. One key factor is the effect on the
environment of the spatial distribution of population and
economic activities. It is in this respect that Australia provides a
striking example of adverse urban environmental impacts. As
John Minnery (1992) puts it in summary, 'Australian cities rely
mainly on private transport, have poorly serviced fringe areas
and very uneven patterns of social facility provision. They
consume too much land and have detrimental effects on the
environment.'

ENVIRONMENTAL DECAY: AN 'URBAN TWIST'

Environmental problems can be regarded as the result of two
types of interaction between the economic system and the bio-
physical system, as illustrated in Figure 5.1. Depletion occurs

FIGURE 5.1   ECONOMY–ENVIRONMENT INTERACTIONS

(a) A "throughput" economy

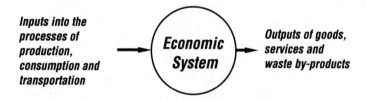

(b) Dual impact of a "throughput" economy on the environment

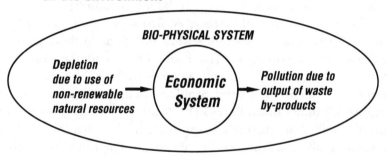

(c) A "spaceship" economy more in harmony with the environment

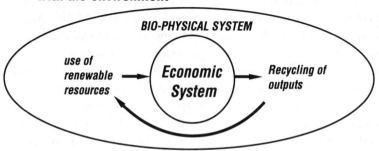

where the economic system uses non-renewable resources in the production of goods and services (e.g. fossil fuels for energy) or uses renewable resources at a faster rate than they are renewed (leading to degradation of arable land, desertification and deforestation). Pollution occurs where the economic system generates particular outputs, in the form of effluents, waste by-products or non biodegradable products. These twin dimensions of the environmental problem are illustrated in the latter parts of this chapter through the analysis of energy usage and pollution in cities. They are general problems of the 'throughput' type of economy, as distinct from a 'spaceship' economy in which the emphasis is on renewable resources and sustainability. Precisely what changes are necessary in order to achieve that more sustainable economy is the focus of much recent debate among environmentalists (e.g. Pearce *et al* 1989, Jacobs 1991).

How do cities enter this story? At first sight, matters of urban development may appear somewhat marginal to these general environmental concerns. The claim here is to the contrary, that they should be integral to any analysis of causes and remedies for environmental problems. The point is not novel: Figure 5.2 shows Brian Berry's (1974) attempt to suggest some of the linkages. The distinctive approach in this chapter involves reviewing six contributory factors to the environmental crisis and showing how each is accentuated by particular features of urban development. This is what is meant by giving the analysis of environmental decay an 'urban twist'.

First, we note the association between environmental problems and particular instances of 'market failure'. Yes, it is that issue of *externalities* again. The neoclassical economic theory of environmental decay recognises that economic activities may have consequences for people other than those directly involved in the decision to undertake them. An industrialist may pollute the atmosphere or water as a by-product of making goods and services. A motorist may foul the air and increase hazards to pedestrians as a side-effect of his/her decision to drive. Market failure arises in these cases because not all relevant consequences of the action are taken into account through the workings of the price system. So far this is familiar territory. What is the 'urban twist'? Simply, that these sorts of activities are more common in cities. The geographical proximity of different economic and social activities increases the impact of the spillover effects or externalities. In cities we live cheek-by-jowl in each other's mess. Thus, spatial interdependence compounds the externalities problem which arises in a market system where the use of environmental goods remains unregulated by the price mechanism.

FIGURE 5.2   LINKS BETWEEN URBAN ECONOMY, LAND USE AND ENVIRONMENTAL POLLUTION

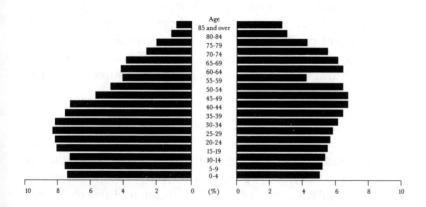

Source: Berry (1974).

Other analysts, most notably Paul Ehrlich, have emphasised *population growth* as a key ingredient in the mounting problem of environmental decay. On a global scale the pressure on physical resources, such as arable land, is an obvious manifestation of this. However, the resource demands of different geographical population segments are strikingly different. It is commonly noted that a baby born in the USA is likely to generate over twenty times as many natural resource demands over its lifetime as one born in India. The urban/rural balance is likewise significant, and therein lies the 'urban twist' to this particular type of analysis. As the Director of the WorldWatch Institute (Brown

1977) has noted, where population growth is concentrated in cities resource usage is increased in three ways:

- Urbanisation reduces the proportion of rural to urban population, so that the feeding of the population requires more mechanised methods of production. The agricultural production process itself becomes more energy-intensive, while the production of agricultural machinery compounds energy use and resource depletion.
- The agricultural products have to be transported to the cities, involving the use of further energy resources, plus the energy and resources in producing the transport equipment.
- The problem of effluent disposal in the cities typically involves using pumping systems which are energy-using. In an agricultural setting, or where there is closer integration of urban and rural activities in a more spatially decentralised system, those effluents may be used as fertilizer to enhance agricultural productivity or as an energy source for heating and lighting.

Third, what about *economic growth*? Ever since the pioneering projections by the Club of Rome (Meadows *et al* 1972) showed the impossibility of sustaining contemporary trends in industrial production, it has been argued that the rate of economic growth is the key contributory factor to environmental decay. Indeed, in some parts of the Green movement, being anti-economic growth is *de rigeur*. Actually, the general correlation between economic growth and environmental decay needs serious qualification, as we will see when we turn to the issues of technology and inequality. However, to the extent that a general relationship exists, urbanisation is a compounding element or catalyst. Historically, the growth of industrial production has gone hand-in-hand with urbanisation, the latter generating the labour pools necessary for the former. Many sectors of industry have been prominent polluters — chemicals, textiles, metal processing, engineering and paper manufacturing being obvious examples. When such industries are spatially concentrated in urban areas, three particular environmental consequences follow:

- Pollution tends to exceed acceptable threshold levels. Greater proximity of industrial production activities (and waste disposal from consumption too) increases the environmental problem by pushing pollution beyond levels with which the natural waste disposal mechanisms in ecological systems can cope. Irreversible changes in ecological systems are precipitated which would not occur with less spatial concentration of the polluting activities.
- Concentration of residuals intensifies. The occurrence of public exposure to high residuals concentrations in the environment increases the more rapid is the discharge of such residuals. This is because the exposure tends to be log-normally distributed; and with this sort of distribution, extreme concentrations grow faster than the increase in average concentrations.
- Interaction of contaminants exacerbates these problems by causing a 'cocktail effect'. While the air or water may be able to cope with limited quantities of individual pollutants reasonably well, a complex of them may interact in such a way as to cause irreversible ecological changes. In these circumstances, the total damaging effect is greater than the sum of the partial effects.

Fourth, there is the influence of *technology*. In general terms, technology governs the relationship between inputs and outputs in an economic system. The form of technology influences how resource-depleting or pollution-generating will be the production of any given set of economic outputs. That is one reason why the crude association between economic growth and environmental decay needs to be qualified. The use of inter-mediate technology and of renewable energy sources (e.g. solar, wind or wave power) can ameliorate environmental decay without major sacrifice of economic living standards. So too can the recycling of used products as inputs into further rounds of production. Where is the 'urban twist' here? It is partly in the difficulty of transforming the nature of technology used in the large cities. The form of transport technology is the most obvious case in point. Cities offer enormous potential to utilise relatively energy-efficient public transport systems. However, once they

become constructed around the 'flexibility' of the private car, as
in the case of suburbanised Australian cities, the conversion
process becomes extraordinarily difficult. In new towns, the
potential to construct the transport system around energy-
efficient modes is much greater than for an equivalent population grafted onto the periphery of an existing metropolitan
area. Prospects of using renewable energy resources are typically
greater in relatively smaller settlements, although there is no
general reason why the potential for recycling should be
negatively associated with urban size.

Next is the issue of socio-economic *inequality*. Although not so
obviously linked to environmental decay as the preceding factors,
its importance as an obstacle to more sound environmental
outcomes is becoming increasingly recognised. The earlier
observation about the differential resource demands of populations in rich and poor countries is a case in point. Also on an
international scale, it is evident that economic inequalities
between nations impede international agreements about
environmental standards. This was illustrated at the United
Nations Conference on the Global Environment in Rio de
Janiero in 1992. On a more local scale, socio-economic inequality also may explain why some regional populations are
more willing to tolerate economic growth at almost any environmental cost, especially if the economic benefits are more localised
than the environmental damages. The urban dimension is
important in this context too. Consider a city such as Sydney.
The business executives responsible for managing pollution-
generating businesses in industrial areas like Alexandria, Botany
and Granville-Clyde usually live on the north shore or in the
breezy eastern suburbs well away from the industrial pollution.
So they need not suffer the full environmental consequences of
their decisions. As such, a mechanism which might otherwise
provide some check on environmental decay is diminished.

Finally, there is the association between environmental decay
and particular ideologies. The causal role of 'materialistic' values
and the absence of social responsibility is a recurring theme in
contemporary environmental debate. Ken Boulding (1970)
neatly captured one element of this concern in his proposition

that 'the presence of pollution is symptomatic of the absence of community'. It is also reflected in the argument of Ted Wheelwright (1974), tracing the roots of environmental problems to the ascendancy of a particular set of human-centred beliefs associated with the Judeo-Christian ethic. The 'urban twist' to these concerns is not so immediately evident, except to the extent that there is a broad historical association between the spread of these ideologies and the development of urban industrial society. In principle, the spatial proximity associated with city living should be conducive to the development of communitarian values—a recognition of the continuous inter-dependence of the material well-being of all. However, the continuous promise of anonymity in 'the urban crowd' seems to work in quite the opposite direction in big cities. This is part of the appeal of cities for many people, contrasting with the situation in rural areas and country towns where 'everybody knows everybody else's business'. One outcome is a cultural milieu in cities in which a shared awareness of environmental concerns is generally absent. To the extent that big city living is integral to the generation and reproduction of individualistic and commercial values, it is an obstacle to the development of a widespread environmental consciousness. Paradoxically, a more localised neighbourhood focus may be more conducive to coping with environmental problems which are ultimately global in character.

DEPLETION: ENERGY AND URBAN FORM

The constraints on urban development imposed by *energy* conditions raise increasingly difficult concerns. Urbanisation raises energy requirements on various fronts, as noted in the preceding section of this chapter—energy for food production, transportation and waste disposal. Thus, increments to metro-politan population normally require more energy than an equivalent population growth in non-metropolitan areas. The structure of the cities compounds the tendency. Australian cities developed in the context of energy conditions which no longer apply. As noted in chapter 3, the transport system is orientated towards the use of the private car which is a relatively inefficient user of energy. The relative location of places of residence and employment is associated with long journeys to work. The suburbanised form of urban living frequently necessitates long journeys for recreational purposes too. Energy consumption *per capita*, especially in these oil-using forms, is insensitive to the requirements for sustainability.

This could be construed as a case for decentralisation. If it is urban scale and the internal structure of the existing cities that create the need for long and energy-intensive transport movements, then a solution to these aspects of the urban environmental crisis may be sought through slowing urban growth and redirecting it to smaller towns where congestion problems are typically less severe and average journey times substantially less. The more generalised case for decentralisation is considered further in chapter 10. However, it is worth noting four qualifications here which are particularly relevant to the implications for energy use arising from different urban forms.

First, it is not city size, but the *spatial relationship* between homes and work-places, shopping centres and places of leisure and recreation which determines transport journey lengths. Much energy-saving could be accomplished through spatial rearrangements within the urban areas. Of course, there are major constraints imposed by the existing structure of the cities, but changes are possible, especially when spurred on by the disincentives associated with high travel costs and growing congestion. The movement of upper income groups into inner-city areas can be interpreted in this light, though this 'gentrification' process (to be further analysed in chapter 7) was already under way before the energy crisis. More generally, the re-focusing of metropolitan areas on a 'neighbourhood' structure of urban villages has prospects of cutting demands for transport, as noted in chapter 3. Figure 5.3 illustrates this by comparing fuel use in Australian cities with more compact European cities and more low-density car-oriented American cities.

Second, the *mode of transport* is as important as journey lengths in determining the energy impact of journeys to work and other travel. Decentralisation policy is likely to have less impact on energy usage than a policy to increase the usage of public rather than private transport. Energy-consumption requirements vary sharply between different transport modes (Hall & Schou 1980). Cars rank below helicopters in terms of their energy usage per passenger mile but (depending on their size and efficiency) alongside aeroplanes and well above trains and buses (not to mention cycling and walking). Herein lies a big problem. As noted in chapter 3, the increased use of private cars, and the suburban sprawl which it has facilitated, partly reflects the economic and political dominance of the car, oil and tyre companies. What this suggests is that the fundamental problem is not the cities *per se* or even their low-density form but the structure of vested interests which ensures the dominance of high energy-consuming modes of transport.

FIGURE 5.3   FUEL USE IN AUSTRALIAN CAPITAL CITIES AND IN 'AVERAGE' CITIES IN THE UNITED STATES AND EUROPE

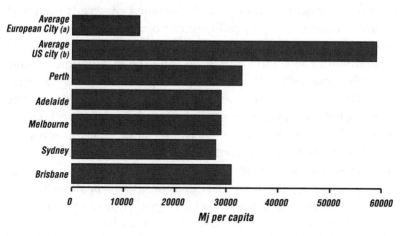

Notes: (a) Averaged from Hamburg, Frankfurt, Zurich, Stockholm, Brussels, Paris, London, Munich, West Berlin, Copenhagen, Vienna and Amsterdam.

(b) Averaged from Houston, Phoenix, Detroit, Denver, Los Angeles, San Francisco, Washington, Chicago and New York.

Source: Newman and Kenworthy (1989).

Third, there is a special problem which brings together the considerations of space and transport modes. It is that the dependence on private motoring, the heaviest user of energy resources in transport, is normally greater in smaller towns where the public transport system is less well developed. On the other hand, energy wastage due to cars idling in heavy traffic is uncommon. On balance, it may be that the immediate effect of decentralisation, given the *existing structure of transport alternatives*, is to increase energy demands. In the longer term, decentralisation offers the prospect for constructing more integrated transport systems in which this problem is overcome. Meanwhile, it would seem that, while energy problems are of increasing importance, they provide less of a case for decentralisation policy than for a broader range of policies to reduce the dominance of the private car. Given the political influence of the 'roads lobby' this becomes an essentially political process rather than a technical matter of spatial reorganisation.

Finally, the energy implications of alternative forms of urban *housing* deserve attention. Individual housing can be more or less energy-efficient, depending on the building materials used and facilities installed. The profligate use of air-conditioning is an obvious case in point. The use of double-glazing for windows, the insulation of roofs and cavity-walls, and the installation of solar water-heating — all have substantial impacts on energy saving. Equally important, the layout of housing can be more-or-less energy-efficient. To take an obvious case, terraced town housing is typically superior because there are fewer external walls for heat-loss than in a detached house or cottage. The balance between different housing forms (detached cottages, home units, terraced housing) therefore warrants consideration alongside the other questions of urban size and transport policy in the framing of strategies for a more ecologically sustainable society. These issues evidently bear on debates about the case for more vigorous policies of urban consolidation (to be considered in chapter 12).

Overall, the available evidence suggests that, despite methodological difficulties in relating energy consumption to spatial structure, the existing structure of the big cities is incompatible with the requirements for energy-efficiency and conservation. To quote Owens (1984), 'there is a certain degree of consensus that higher densities and clustering of land uses result in lower energy consumption, for both transport (due to shorter and fewer trips) and for space heating (because of more efficient built forms)'. On this basis it appears that the most energy-efficient spatial pattern is likely to consist of more small to medium sized settlement clusters. Reshaping Australian cities towards this ideal is a tall order.

POLLUTION AND CONGESTION

Turning from depletion to pollution, we need to take further account of the role of urban congestion in compounding environmental problems. This brings together the considerations of urban size and form. Congestion is a general characteristic of cities, being most spatially concentrated where the urban form focuses on a CBD which is the centre for employment, services and entertainment activities. However, congestion is also characteristic of cities where these activities are widely scattered through the metropolis, making for complex travel demands which are difficult to serve by public transport, as noted in chapter 3. In this latter case congestion is more widespread and typically more difficult to resolve. In addition to the heavy energy consumption generated in these circumstances, the output of effluents, particularly exhaust gases from slow-moving vehicles, is pronounced. Congestion generates pollution.

Mainstream economists regard congestion as a classic example of a problem which arises because the market economy does not internalise all the costs. As noted in chapter 3, the marginal private cost of motoring is less than the social cost, with the result that too much of this activity occurs and congestion rises to socially undesirable levels. Similarly, as noted earlier in this chapter in relation to pollution, the failure of the market economy to internalise all the costs leads to a non-optimal outcome (even by the restricted standards of the neoclassical theory of a capitalist economy). Congestion and pollution appear as symmetrical phenomena. However, what this analysis does not recognise is the *interaction* between congestion and pollution which exacerbates the environmental problem. Put simply, while congestion increases pollution, pollution does not decrease congestion. It is this asymmetry of the relationship which is crucial in explaining the cumulative tendency to environmental deterioration. This is important to emphasise because, among other things, it sets severe limits on the 'environmental fine-tuning' which economists like David Pearce *et al* (1989) advocate.

It is not difficult to demonstrate the link between the size and structure of cities and the tendency to *congestion*. With expansion of urban scale comes an increasing set of demands on transportation networks such that, even with heavy expenditure on new transportation facilities, there is a tendency for average journey times to increase. Average journey times are significantly shorter in the smaller cities of Brisbane, Adelaide and Perth than in metropolitan Sydney and Melbourne. Following the pioneering study of the costs of urban congestion by Max Neutze (1965), it is recognised that increments to population growth in the big cities generate more vehicle miles than the same increment in smaller towns and regional centre. Congestion in metropolitan areas is not only costly of itself, but it also makes problems of pollution worse than they would otherwise be. As noted in the first section of this chapter, the spatial proximity of the various polluting activities leads to irreversible traversing of threshold levels, high concentrations of residuals, more interaction among pollutants and therefore a more intense pollution problem than would exist if the same activities were more widely dispersed.

High pollution levels are both aesthetically offensive and medically dangerous. There are relatively minor problems such as eye irritation associated with petro-chemical smog, but respiratory problems are the most catastrophic consequence of such pollution. Emissions of particulates, sulphur dioxide, carbon monoxide, and hydro-carbons in Australian cities are comparable to the USA on a *per capita* basis. Emissions of particulates associated mainly with heavy industrial processes have been notably higher *per capita* in Australia than in the United States. Measurement of the carbon monoxide content in the atmosphere of the major metropolitan areas frequently reveals levels higher than the World Health Organisation's recommended limits.

Does the intensity of these problems in the big cities put a natural brake on their further growth? Were it so, the cause for concern would be diminished because there would be an in-built equilibrating mechanism. Certainly there are some individuals who translate their distaste of the physical environment of the large cities into evasive action—Nimbin lives! There is also growing evidence of population shifts to localities outside the metropolitan areas, strictly defined, but still within an accessible range for commuting or other interactions. However, excluding migration patterns associated with retirement from work, there are many obstacles to a larger decentralist response. One is the inadequate opportunities for employment in non-metropolitan areas. Related to this is the problem of interdependence. While it may be rational for large groups to relocate from the polluted cities to a more pleasant environment, it is less likely that any one individual will be able to do so without a significant decline in material standard of living. Moreover, as noted earlier in this chapter, many persons responsible for the cause of pollution do not live in their own mess. This applies particularly to industrial effluent but also, to some extent, to transport movements where commuting to environmentally attractive suburbs fouls the environment of those living in the inner cities and near the transport routes. Finally, one must consider the effect of adaptive expectations. Individuals accommodate to their environment, such that previous experience (especially that of previous generations) is relegated as higher levels of congestion and pollution come to be accepted as the norm.

Overall, if one set out to design an urban form most conducive to environmental degradation through the interaction of congestion and pollution, it could well end up looking like an Australian metropolis! The combination of metropolitan primacy and low density suburban sprawl interacts with the forms of housing and transport provision to cause cumulative problems. The asymmetry in the relationship between congestion and pollution means that there is no 'natural' tendency towards an environmentally optimal city size or form. On the contrary, the evidence suggests that environmental constraints have played a small role in putting a brake on the process of urbanisation. Nevertheless, the growing awareness of environmental concerns does generate the potential for a stronger check through the political process. Regional and urban policy is particularly relevant in this context because it can be tailored to deal with environmental problems. Also, at the grass-roots level environmentally conscious urban social movements are on the rise: campaigns against urban freeway developments, urban airport extensions and environmentally insensitive projects of various kinds are the essence of modern urban politics. The significance of these regional policies and of urban social movements is considered later in this book. Meanwhile, it is also important to stress that environmental problems, like urban problems in general, tend to have a markedly uneven incidence on different socio-economic groups. It is to these patterns of inequality in cities that we turn before more systematically confronting the political responses.

FURTHER READING

Bookchin (1980): essays from an anarchist/ecological perspective, including a critique of urban planning.

Beder (1989): an analysis of water pollution in Australia.

Engwicht (1992): proposals for the design and development of 'eco-cities'.

Rees, Rodley & Stilwell (1993): chapters by Rosewarne and Eckersley provide critiques of the 'economic rationalist' influence on environmental analysis and policy.

6

Social Inequality

The preceding five chapters have examined various urban problems associated with jobs, housing, land, transport and the environment. These problems interact in a way which does not impinge equally on all urban residents. There are winners and losers. This issue of urban inequality has a particular and long-standing resonance 'down under'. As pointed out by David Donnison (1974): 'to the British, urban problems mean, first and foremost, unemployment, bad housing and the decay of old industrial cities. To the Americans, they mean drugs, crime and conflict ... But to Australians, urban problems are a matter of access and distribution of opportunities.' In the last two decades the concerns with unemployment, drugs, crime and urban conflict have intensified 'down under' too, but the centrality of the equity issue remains distinctive.

Most Australian cities have a fairly evident division between 'rich', 'middle' and 'poor' areas. Various books on Australian cities have sought to capture this feature in their titles, ranging from *The Urban Mosaic* (Timms 1971) to *Unfairly Structured Cities* (Badcock 1984). The status differences are often caricatured, especially in youth culture, as in the distinctions between Sydney's working-class 'westies' and North Shore 'snobs'. Popular academic writings confirm the general contrast. To quote Miller & Fuhr (1983): 'Sydney is geographically divided according to class. With some exceptions, the rich have the north and the poor the west.' Similar characterisations are often made of the other metropolitan areas. In all major Australian cities the class/area association is usually held to be so strong that the question 'where do you live?' has come to be an effective substitute for the more traditional 'what do you do?' as a means of social pigeon-holing.

This general perception of the association between residential location and socio-economic position calls for a more systematic analysis, posing questions such as:

- How can socio-economic inequalities be measured?
- What are the main contours of urban socio-economic inequality in practice?
- What causes the territorial segmentation? Is it greater in big cities than smaller urban areas and has it been increasing over time?
- So what?

The following discussion embraces these themes, with particular examples drawn from a case study of Sydney.

MEASURING URBAN INEQUALITIES

Measurement of urban inequalities involves a choice between *subjective* and *objective* indicators of socio-economic position. For example, one may classify the socio-economic status of urban localities according to the general subjective perceptions of the public, using questionnaire/interview techniques. The classic study of Sydney by Athol Congalton (1969) was a case in point, based on interviews with 143 people, including 56 real estate agents who were deemed to have a particularly good understanding of suburb status rankings. (Incidentally, Congalton's results provide a fascinating basis for a comparison of perceived status rankings 'then and now': currently fashionable suburbs like Paddington, Balmain and Glebe all ranked in the bottom 20 out of a total of 368 suburbs!)

Alternatively, one can measure 'objective' indicators of socio-economic conditions, such as average *per capita* incomes, the proportion of employers, managers and administrators in the population, the ratio of white collar to blue collar employees or a wide array of measures of health, housing or education standards (e.g. Murphy 1990, NSW Planning and Environment Commission 1978). These are never perfectly correlated: hence the need for some choice of which indicators to use. Urban analysts have devoted much energy to the compilation of composite indices, using principal components analyses, social mapping and other devices to capture the essence of the multidimensional urban socio-economic inequalities (Smith, D.M. 1979; Stimson 1982). The methodological presumption is that insights into urban functioning will be generated through the production and distillation of vast quantities of statistical information about the social composition of the population in urban sub-areas.

But which sub-areas? This is the next measurement decision. Do local government areas (LGAs) provide a sufficient degree of spatial disaggregation to illuminate the principal dimensions of intra-urban inequality? Or are smaller census collectors districts more appropriate? Again, this is a matter on which there can quite properly be disagreement because there is a trade-off between the relative availability and tractability of data for LGAs and the greater detail revealed in more disaggregated data (where it is available). For most purposes, LGA data gives an adequate picture of the broad dimensions of socio-economic inequality in the metropolitan areas, although there is often considerable internal diversity within those sub-areas (Forrest 1985).

INEQUALITY IN PRACTICE: SYDNEY

Taking Australia's largest metropolitan area as a case study we can use data from the 1981 and 1991 Censuses in order to sketch out the main contours of spatial inequalities. General background information on the structure of LGAs is shown in Figure 6.1. Data on *population trends* is shown in Figure 6.2. The heavily shaded areas are those of the most rapid population growth. Three outer-metropolitan LGAs dominate the picture: Campbelltown (46,000 growth), Penrith (41,000 growth) and Fairfield (46,000 growth). These three accounted for over half of the metropolitan population increase. Within the inner metropolitan areas, the general picture is of stability or slight decline in total numbers. The result is what has been called a 'doughnut effect' (Jay 1978), although the pattern stops a long way short of a hollowed centre.

FIGURE 6.1   LOCAL GOVERNMENT AREAS IN SYDNEY

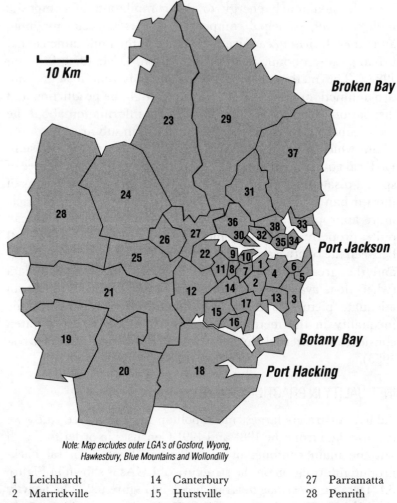

Note: Map excludes outer LGA's of Gosford, Wyong,
Hawkesbury, Blue Mountains and Wollondilly

1	Leichhardt	14	Canterbury	27	Parramatta
2	Marrickville	15	Hurstville	28	Penrith
3	Randwick	16	Kogarah	29	Hornsby
4	Sydney	17	Rockdale	30	Hunters Hill
5	Waverley	18	Sutherland	31	Kuring-gai
6	Woollahra	19	Camden	32	Lane Cove
7	Ashfield	20	Campbelltown	33	Manly
8	Burwood	21	Liverpool	34	Mosman
9	Concord	22	Auburn	35	North Sydney
10	Drummoyne	23	Baulkham Hills	36	Ryde
11	Strathfield	24	Blacktown	37	Warringah
12	Bankstown	25	Fairfield	38	Willoughby
13	Botany	26	Holroyd		

FIGURE 6.2   POPULATION CHANGE IN SYDNEY 1981–91

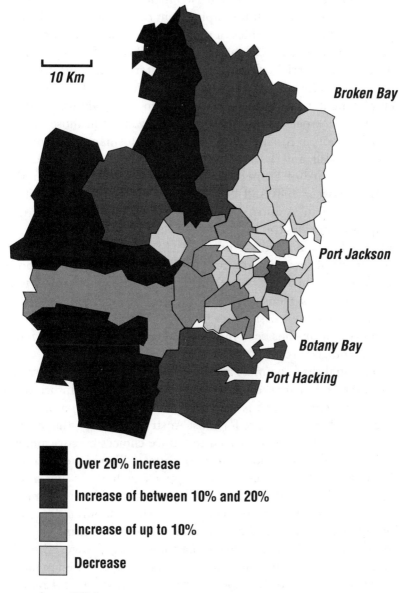

Source: 1991 Census.

What of the economic base on which these people depend? One indicator is *unemployment*. As Figure 6.3 shows, there has been considerable variation between the LGAs in the rate of unemployment. In 1981 unemployment rates ranged from 2 to 10 per cent. The highest rates of unemployment were concentrated in two areas — inner-city areas like the City of Sydney, Leichhardt and Marrickville and outer western and south-western areas like Blacktown, Fairfield and Liverpool. By 1991 unemployment rates were much higher in all localities, ranging from 5 to 22 per cent. The lowest rates were stilll those on the North Shore — Kuring-gai, Hornsby, Mosman, Warringah, Hunters Hill and Lane Cove, with Baulkham Hills and the southern shire of Sutherland in the same company. Over the period between 1981 and 1986, the most rapid deterioration had taken place in Auburn, Bankstown and Fairfield (where unemployment rates trebled), with Canterbury close behind. These LGAs all saw an extra 8 per cent (Bankstown) to 14 per cent (Fairfield) of their population out of work. In the North Shore suburbs, the corresponding figures were in the range from 2 to 3 per cent. This Census data confirms the analysis presented earlier in chapter 1, showing that the deterioration of employment conditions has been most concentrated in the already most disadvantaged areas.

The analysis of winners and losers can be extended by turning from the labour market to the housing market. One indicator is the *levels of home-ownership*. As noted in chapter 2, this has been the preferred housing tenure for most Australians, given the limited options and the bias imparted to tenure choices by government policies. Figure 6.4 shows the 1991 pattern. The highest rates of home-ownership are seen on the upper North Shore and in the southern shire of Sutherland, the lower rates being in the inner-city and eastern suburbs, with the western suburbs generally occupying an intermediate position. However, comparing the 1981 and 1991 Census shows some interesting changes. Significant decrease in home-ownership levels was experienced in many areas, most notably Holroyd, Parramatta, Kogarah and Bankstown. These are 'middle' suburbs where the great Australian dream is becoming less-and-less a reality. On the other hand,

FIGURE 6.3 UNEMPLOYMENT RATES IN SYDNEY 1991

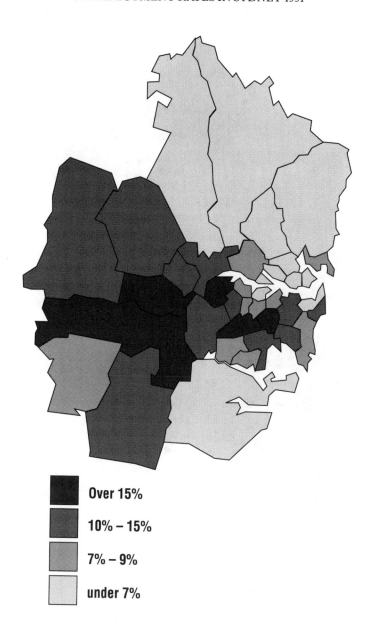

Over 15%

10% – 15%

7% – 9%

under 7%

Source: 1991 Census.

FIGURE 6.4   PERCENTAGE OF DWELLINGS OWNER-OCCUPIED,
SYDNEY 1991

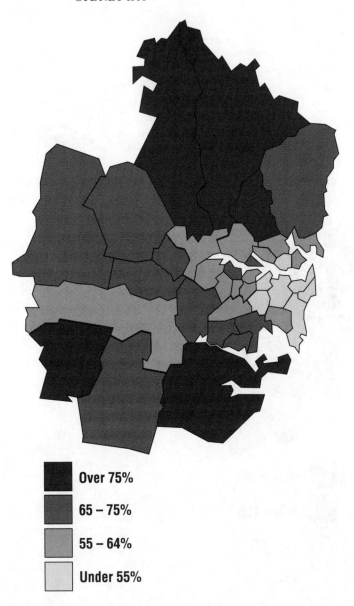

Note: Includes both home owners and those purchasing their home.
Source: 1991 Census.

increases in home ownership levels occurred in inner areas like the City of Sydney, Marrickville, Waverley, Woollahra and Ashfield — areas where the 'gentrification' phenomenon has been apparent.

The interaction of these characteristics of the housing market with the characteristics of the labour market results in a 'scissors effect'. Increased unemployment and falling average real wages, coupled with rising prices for housing and displacement by gentrification, is a recipe for economic hardship among the victims of structural economic change. On the other hand, the scissors effect is less relevant to those with more secure employment, rising incomes and the capacity to make capital gains from the ownership of houses. These disadvantaged and advantaged groups evidently have distinctive spatial concentrations.

The most readily accessible general indicator of inequality in living standards is the level of *per capita incomes*. Mapping this can provide an indication of how the winners and losers are spatially distributed. The territorial segregation of different income groups is well established, as shown in Figure 6.5. The lower average income households in Sydney have been concentrated in the inner areas south to Botany Bay and west to Auburn. Below average incomes also feature in a broad band of outer suburbs from Blacktown, through Fairfield and Liverpool to Campbelltown. The highest average incomes are on the North Shore and in the affluent eastern suburb of Woollahra. But the *change* between 1981 and 1991 reveals a significant pattern, with the most rapid increases in the gentrifying inner-city areas like Leichhardt and North Sydney. Table 6.1 shows the league table of major winners and losers.

The situation in western Sydney is particularly problematic. This is not a ghetto in the usual sense of that term, not being dominated by any one ethnic group (although there are particular local concentrations like the Vietnamese in Cabramatta) and being physically pleasant in comparison with areas inhabited by the urban disadvantaged in many countries. However, on the evidence shown here, the tendency has been for the western region's relative economic position to deteriorate. Most of the residents of the higher status suburbs such as those on the North

FIGURE 6.5   MEDIAN HOUSEHOLDS INCOME IN SYDNEY 1991

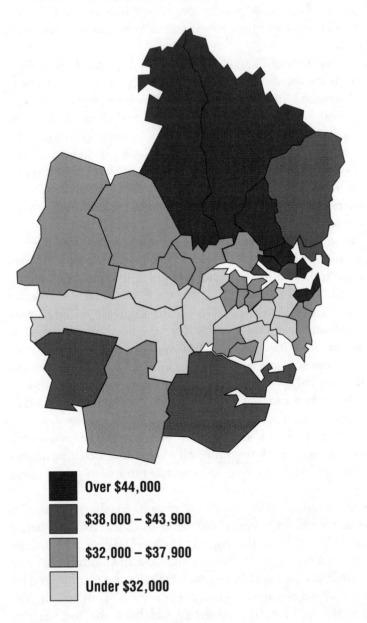

- Over $44,000
- $38,000 – $43,900
- $32,000 – $37,900
- Under $32,000

Source: 1991 Census.

TABLE 6.1   CHANGE IN MEDIAN INCOMES 1981–91: SYDNEY LGAs

Significant median income rise	Significant median income decline
North Sydney	Bankstown
Leichhardt	Liverpool
Mosman	Botany
Marrickville	Fairfield
Woollahra	Holroyd
Manly	Hurstville
Sydney	Parramatta
Baulkham Hills	Auburn

Note: Significant rise denotes 1991 median income ÷ 1981 median income (both in current dollar values) in excess of 228%. Significant decline denotes a corresponding figure of below 200%.
Source: Census 1981, 1991.

Shore, by contrast, have continued to enjoy material living standards largely unaffected by the changing conditions in labour and housing markets. At the time of the 1991 Census, 46 per cent of households in Kuring-gai recorded an annual income of over $50,000, compared with less than 20 per cent in Canterbury, Fairfield, Botany and Liverpool. It is worth repeating the general caution that analysis of local government areas doesn't reveal the full range of spatial variation: even on Sydney's North Shore there are some relatively disadvantaged population pockets. It is also pertinent to note that the recession of the early 1990s had a generalised impact, as noted in chapter 1. However, the overall picture seems to be one of increased spatial inequalities between the residents of the more affluent and less affluent suburbs.

ROOTS OF URBAN INEQUALITY

The next question is that of causation. The association of inequality with *urban size* and/or *growth* has been recurrently claimed. It underpinned the major urban public policy initiatives of the federal government led by Gough Whitlam in the period 1972–5. The underlying proposition, in Hugh Stretton's (1970) oft-quoted words, is that 'very big cities are both physical and psychological devices for quietly shifting resources from poorer to richer, and for excusing or concealing—with a baffled but complacent air—the increasing deprivation of the poor'. Chapter 10 considers this type of justification for decentralisation policy more fully. Some supporting evidence was generated during the Whitlam years (e.g. Stilwell and Hardwick 1973), but the empirical requirements for both cross-sectional and time-series statistical tests of the proposition seem to have eluded researchers since then. More fundamentally, there is the conceptual problem of abstracting from all the variables other than urban size and/or growth which, operating simultaneously, bear on socio-economic inequality. For example, the increase in spatial inequalities in Sydney described in this chapter went hand-in-hand with the growth of population but a lot of other demographic, social and economic changes were occurring concurrently. To attribute the widening spatial inequalities to urban growth alone would be simplistic.

Indeed, the more plausible explanation of changes in urban socio-economic inequality, already introduced in the discussion of the Sydney case-study, is that the extent of inequality is determined primarily by the *interaction of the labour and housing markets*. Some people's economic position is as employers or as recipients of income from capital; others derive wage or salary incomes from the sale of their labour power; while others lie either temporarily or permanently outside the labour market, relying primarily on welfare payments for their livelihood. This generates the familiar class inequalities in the distribution of income and wealth. This, in turn, creates differential access to the housing market. Any urban area normally contains suburbs of differential environmental quality, accessibility and housing standards. Since the housing in those various suburbs is allocated primarily through a market system, it is distributed according to ability to pay. Spatial segregation of socio-economic groups is a predictable outcome in these circumstances. Homel and Burns (1985) put the point simply as follows: 'People with money buy houses in desirable areas. People without money find cheap accommodation where they can. As a result area of residence is correlated with income.'

On this reasoning, the changes in the form and intensity of

urban socio-economic inequalities are mainly attributable to changes in labour market and housing market conditions. These have been such as to strengthen the spatially segregating forces. The two key elements in this process are increased *inequality in the distribution of income* and an *increased ratio of housing costs to income*. There is growing documentation of the general trend to increased income inequality in Australian society (e.g. Gregory 1992, Raskall 1992, Stilwell 1993b). It partly reflects a polarisation in the pattern of wage incomes associated with changes in the structure of employment. It also reflects the change in the functional distribution of income — the relative shares of labour (in the form of wages and salaries) and capital (in the form of profit, interest and rent). In the 1980s labour's share fell from 73 per cent to 63 per cent, while capital's share rose from 27 per cent to 37 per cent. This meant that 10 per cent of the national income was effectively switched from wages and salaries to profit, interest and rent. The latter incomes from capital are disproportionately concentrated in the hands of those living in the more well-to-do suburbs.

Reduced marginal rates of income taxes on upper income levels have further fuelled the gap between the capacities of rich and poor to secure the most attractive housing. The high interest rates prevailing throughout Australia later in the 1980s through into 1990 were another important factor, bearing both on the costs of funds for house purchase and on general economic conditions as the economy was driven into recession. Meanwhile, the ratio of average house prices to average annual earnings has risen in the metropolitan areas; e.g. in Sydney from around 5:1 at the start of the 1980s to nearly 7:1 by the end of the decade. The higher this ratio, the more effective is the housing market as a segregator of different income groups into those localities where housing is most expensive and those where it is relatively less expensive. Put the two trends together — growing inequality in the distribution of income and a rising share of housing costs in total household expenditure — and you have a sure-fire recipe for growing intra-urban spatial inequality.

This chain of reasoning suggests that it is not urban size or growth *per se* which generates territorial segregation of socio-economic groups. Rather, it is the outcome of structural economic changes, operating both through labour and housing markets, interacting with an urban spatial form which is systematically stratified by class position. The city acts as a medium through which class inequalities work in a spatial form. However, urban form acts not as a *passive* intervening variable, but as an *intensifying* factor. It does so to varying degrees depending on:

- the extent to which the structure of the city exacerbates inflationary problems in the housing market;
- the extent to which urban form reinforces inequality to access of employment opportunities;
- the extent to which functioning of the city impedes social mobility.

These considerations lead us into a more general analysis of the consequences of urban socio-economic segmentation.

SO WHAT?

Why does the spatial differentiation of socio-economic groups matter anyway? What is wrong with a situation where people of similar economic position inhabit particular areas? They do not do so in Australian cities as a result of official segregation, as has been the case under the apartheid system in South Africa. Rather, is it not the case that they choose suitable localities in the light of their personal circumstances and preferences? From this perspective, the spatial differentiation may be regarded not as a problem but as a solution to the allocative process in an economically unequal society. If there is inequality in the distribution of income and wealth, and if there are variations in the attractiveness of living in different suburbs, then spatial segregation is a reflection of how the people 'sort themselves out' in the marketplace.

Some would also claim that the distributional inequality is justified in terms of the need to maintain incentives, including the incentive to move to a better house in a more 'classy' suburb. In other words, territorial inequality reproduces incentives for the social mobility characteristic of a free society. This is a comfortable chain of reasoning with distinctively *laissez-faire* connotations. It needs to be set against some more disturbing aspects of urban spatial differentiation which impede the liberal ideal in practice.

First, there is a tendency for spatial segmentation, once established, to become intensified. This is partly due to activities of the state, such as *zoning* of land use which typically reinforces existing inter-suburban differentials in environmental quality. Differences in the character of *educational institutions* between rich and poor suburbs also tend to increase the appeal of the former areas to those with the capacity to pay, with the result that inter-generational mobility is further restricted. In these circumstances 'choice' starts to look an inappropriate term for describing the allocation process between suburbs. Rather, the situation is more in accord with David Harvey's (1973) proposition that 'the rich command space while the poor are trapped in it'.

Locational inequalities are further entrenched to the extent that services are financed by *local governments*. The tax-base for local government finance in poorer areas is typically quite inadequate to provide services of comparable quality to those in wealthier suburbs. So, to the extent that child-care facilities, libraries, recreational facilities and other services are locally provided, the inequalities in their provision reinforce social inequality (Mowbray 1982). The situation in Sydney's western suburbs illustrates this tendency, although ameliorated by the State government's commitment to give priority funding for service provision in those rapidly expanding areas (Gardiner 1987).

The *attitudinal* aspect is important too. Growing up in socially segmented cities reduces exposure to 'how the other half lives'. It thereby impedes perceptions of a wider world of possibilities. In the extreme, a 'culture of poverty' may develop, inhibiting upward social mobility. On the other hand, an atmosphere of high expectations for youth in the more affluent suburbs tends to be self-fulfilling. Teachers often, but not invariably, reinforce these different expectations. The police are also well known for their inconsistent treatment of young offenders in rich and poor neighbourhoods — maybe a few words with the parents in the former case and official court proceedings in the latter.

Further *spatial discrimination* may also result from urban socio-economic segmentation, as in the case where employers give preference to job applicants from more high-status suburbs. This reinforces the original basis of the economic inequalities. Where urban socio-economic segmentation has a distinctive relationship to ethnicity (as illustrated by Jupp *et al* 1990) the likelihood of such discrimination is further enhanced. For their part, the inhabitants of the poorer suburbs tend to localise their responses to economic difficulties. Denied good jobs, or any work at all, one possible response is crime, the victims of which are typically local — witness the generally higher incidence of robberies, both household break-ins and car thefts, in the poorer suburbs. White collar crime is more prevalent in the better suburbs but the victims are not typically the neighbours in quite such a direct sense!

The *electoral process* is also much influenced by the territorial segmentation of socio-economic groups, given that electorates are geographically defined. A spatially segmented city will have relatively few marginal seats, to the extent that the rich tend to vote for the Liberal Party while the lower-income groups tend to favour Labor. The point is crudely put, but consistent with the evidence from studies of electoral outcomes. The blue ribbon Liberal seats are characteristically in the wealthy suburbs whereas the predominantly lower-income districts provide the safest Labor seats. If the rich and poor were more spatially mixed, more seats would be marginal. Whether this would be desirable is a matter of opinion: the point is that the current situation gives considerable stability to the electoral process and is a partial bulwark against radical change.

Finally, there is the broader political question of *class consciousness*. The residential concentration of people of similar class position may be conducive to their social interaction and may also facilitate collective political organisation. On the other hand, it is often associated with the development of a regional rather than a class consciousness. For example, people in the western suburbs of Sydney and Melbourne often interpret their relative socio-economic disadvantage in terms of spatial factors ('discrimination against the west'). The recurrent tendency for regionalism to divide people of similar class position tends to deflect challenges to the existing socio-economic order into demands for regional redistribution.

SPATIAL IDEOLOGY

While the spatial dimension of socio-economic inequality is important, it is not all-important. Space is a mediating and compounding factor in an economic system which systematically produces and reproduces economic inequality. As such, spatial inequality may be regarded as secondary to the unequal power relations within capital, labour and the state. Inequalities according to class, gender and ethnicity are manifest in spatial form. But to interpret those inequalities as primarily spatial in origin constitutes a form of spatial ideology. It distorts the causal role of spatial structure.

From a public policy perspective, it is also important to remember that redress of spatial inequalities can be sought through policies which are not explicitly spatial (e.g. tax reform, government expenditures on the social wage, prices and incomes policy, housing policy and interest rate policy). These policies are crucially important in the current political-economic context of growing social polarisation (as described in Stilwell 1993b). They may be just as effective as an antidote to urban inequalities as policies which are explicitly spatial (e.g. decentralisation policy, area improvement schemes for 'disadvantaged' localities, or busing of children to schools in suburbs of different socio-economic character). Striking a balance is an issue of judgement, both in respect of analysis and policy.

This issue of balance between spatial and non-spatial elements is necessarily a central theme throughout this study of Australian urban problems. It becomes even more so in the second half of this book when we turn to a more detailed consideration of how government policies have had differential spatial effects. One intervening step remains — to examine a particular constellation of changes to urban socio-economic structure in recent years. This is *gentrification*, a phenomenon which has been touched on already as one element influencing urban inequalities. Its significance in contemporary urban restructuring is such as to warrant more detailed consideration.

FURTHER READING

Badcock (1984): Part III provides an analysis of sources of inequality and redistribution within cities.

Stimson (1982): chapters 6–9 marshall information on dimensions of Australian inequalities.

Troy (1981): a collection of articles on urban inequalities ranging from housing and jobs, to transport, medical services and sewerage.

Horvath, Harrison and Dowling (1989): an atlas and commentary on the many dimensions of urban socio-economic inequality.

7

Gentrification

Urban form is never static. The land-uses and the socio-economic structures are continuously changing, usually incrementally but sometimes with quite dramatic surges. One obvious example of dramatic change in Australian cities, and many other cities around the world, is the process of residential change in the inner-city areas between the CBD and the more distant suburbs. Upper-income groups have partially displaced working-class and welfare-dependent residents there. Previously dilapidated housing has been renovated. Private renting has given way to owner-occupation as the dominant form of housing tenure. These interrelated processes have been labelled as *gentrification*, although there remains considerable confusion about the meaning and interpretation of this term. A flurry of books and articles in recent years has sought to describe the gentrification process, analyse its causes and assess its significance.

A parallel can be drawn with the phenomenon of *suburbanisation*. Attempts to analyse the causes, character and consequences of the growth of suburbia have been a recurring theme in urban studies (e.g. Thorns 1972, Davison 1993). Studies in political economy have sought to interpret its role in facilitating increased commodification, capital accumulation and social control (e.g. Walker 1981). The suburbanisation process continues apace, directly involving many more people than does gentrification. Its control and planning remains a central concern of urban policy, a matter to which we return in chapter 11. However, as often is the case in the social sciences, a focus on turning points, on qualitatively distinctive developments, can be a means of under-standing how the social system works and changes. Is the emergence of gentrification, as an apparently discordant trend in the established suburbanisation pattern, evidence of changes in social-spatial structure, in household preferences and in the economic functioning of the city? Is it a significant element in reshaping Australia?

This chapter explores these issues by:

- clarifying what gentrification involves;
- considering alternative explanations for it;
- commenting briefly on its consequences.

THE NATURE OF GENTRIFICATION

As commonly understood, gentrification involves the influx of relatively well-to-do, typically young, urban professionals into renovated houses in inner-city areas. Neil Smith (1987a) notes that 'to the popular press ... which generally extols the virtues of gentrifying urban 'pioneers', the link between the two icons — yuppies and gentrification — has been irresistable'. Actually, the connection is quite problematic: are yuppies the only gentrifiers? What is the spatial link: why the inner city? And what changes in economic and social structure are going on? The term gentrifica-tion literally suggests a role for the gentry, a word more tradition-ally used in the context of a landed aristocracy and of little apparent significance in the process of contemporary urban restructuring. In a book written when the process was just getting under way in Australian cities (Stilwell 1974) I characterised the changes taking place in the inner suburbs as part of a process of 'embourgeoisement', a more general sociological term connoting the spread of bourgeois values. More recently, the academic literature has been dominated by the association between gentrification and the 'new middle class' a term which has itself been the subject of ongoing contention among social scientists (e.g. Wright 1985). Some clarification is evidently needed.

Smith (1987a) formally defines gentrification as 'the process by which working class neighbourhoods are rehabilitated by middle class homebuyers, landlords and professional developers'.

This is useful in drawing our attention to gentrification being a *process* rather than a thing. An analysis of that process needs to encompass at least three interrelated elements:

- change in the physical condition of the housing stock;
- change in the social class structure;
- change in the form of housing tenure.

The change in the physical condition of the *housing stock* is the most visible manifestation. It is easy enough to conjure up a caricature of gentrified housing: Victoriana with modern bathrooms and kitchens; terraced houses with chipped-back sandstone walls; restored iron-lace balcony railings; flowering window-boxes poking through the security grilles. The essence is a neo-romantic combination of modernity with history, often with liberal doses of 'kitsch' whereby imitation takes precedence over authenticity (Jager 1986). However, it is difficult to define the boundaries. Do home improvements such as the installation of modern water systems in old houses previously lacking hot running water, or inside toilets in place of the back-yard 'thunder box', constitute gentrification? If so, then it is a long-standing and widespread phenomenon, characteristic of rural as well as urban areas. Even if we limit the concept to urban terraced housing we must ask whether, for example, the replacement of original wooden window-frames in Victorian terraces by modern sliding aluminium-framed windows (as is frequently done by older working-class residents or recent southern European migrants) constitutes gentrification? If not, then what forms of renovations are 'in' and what are 'out'? Is it all a question of style — of 'modernisation' versus 'raffish chic' (Knox 1987)?

It is impossible to resolve these issues separately from a consideration of the second dimension of gentrification — changes in the *class structure*. Can we define the physical changes which constitute gentrification as those which are undertaken by, or on behalf of, the incoming 'new middle class' occupants? If so, who are they, and can their class position be reasonably precisely defined? One simple answer would be to identify gentrification as houses previously occupied by low-income groups becoming occupied by upper income groups. However, defining the gentrifiers purely in terms of income is unsatisfactory. Most obviously, income is not an adequate defining characteristic of class, because it does not explicitly take into account production relationships — nor, for that matter, the distinctive patterns of consumption. Sure, there is a general association between a person's income and his/her relationship to the means of production — as owner, manager, employee or unemployed — and a broad association with levels of consumption expenditures. But is the issue of income less important than occupational status?

Pat Mullins (1982) suggests that what is distinctive about the gentrifiers is that they constitute 'educated labour', with employment characteristically in the professional and administrative category of occupations. Taking this definition, we can observe the change in the social composition of three inner-suburban areas in Sydney in the twenty-five years to 1991. The information is presented in Table 7.1. In terms of this indicator, Leichhardt is the most strikingly gentrifying area. At the start of the period, it was clearly the least preferred location for the houses of people in professional and administrative occupations, but it has since overtaken Randwick and nearly caught up with the more elite suburb of Woollahra. Ron Horvath and Benno Engels (1985) have used this type of analysis to provide a basis for empirical estimation of growth of yuppies in the inner city. It remains problematic in terms of the precision of the definition, the relationship between 'educated labour' and the particular set of occupational categories, and in terms of its relationship to more general theories of social class and stratification. Nevertheless, it does draw our attention to some aspects of the *social restructuring* as well as physical restructuring involved in the gentrification process.

Turning to the third aspect of gentrification — change in the form of *housing tenure* — the dominant trend is clear enough. The change is from private-sector rental to owner-occupation. This occurs typically through the sale of rental units to new owner-occupiers: Blair Badcock (1984) cites one survey which revealed nearly 40 per cent of sales of rental units in inner Adelaide resulting in such transfers. However, the gentrification process is not uniform in this respect. Some of the working-class people leaving the inner city owned their own houses, have cashed in on the capital appreciation and bought houses in the more distant suburbs or even further afield, sometimes timed to coincide with retirement from work. Some of the incoming gentrifiers rent their houses, a form of tenure which is understandably popular with many people in a young, mobile phase of their lives. Moreover, we have to distinguish the changes taking place in inner-city housing tenure from national trends. In Australia as a whole the proportion of the housing stock which was private rental halved between 1947 and 1991. As noted in chapter 2, levels of owner-occupation are still typically lower on average in Sydney's inner suburbs than in middle and outer suburbs, despite the changes in tenure of parts of the housing stock. If nothing else, this puts gentrification in perspective as a physical and social change which is more than marginal but less than overwhelming.

TABLE 7.1   THE CHANGING SOCIO-ECONOMIC STRUCTURE OF INNER SYDNEY

Professional and administrative occupational types as percentage of total workforce for selected local government areas

	1966	1971	1976	1981	1986	1991
Leichhardt	7.8	5.9	17.3	24.1	32.7	39.3
Randwick	17.2	18.3	18.9	19.8	22.8	26.2
Woollahra	37.9	34.3	36.0	37.0	44.5	45.5

Source: ABS Census.

EXPLAINING GENTRIFICATION

Having sought some clarification of gentrification and its main features, we can now turn to the still more difficult task of analysing its causes. Is it a consequence of changing consumer preferences for housing, both with respect to its character and location? Is it to do with preferences for related goods and services, such as an attraction to inner city pubs 'n' restaurants and an aversion to the alienating character of outer suburbia with its associated demand on travel time? And whose preferences are involved? Are there changes in the demographic or social structure which have advantaged particular groups in realising their urban 'life-style' ambitions? Or are the roots of gentrification to be found in the economy—in the changing structure of employment, the economic viability of house renovation and the role of financial institutions in urban redevelopment? Why the inner city? Why now?

Not surprisingly, the literature reveals competing viewpoints, associated with competing assumptions (consumer sovereignty versus institutional constraints), competing analytical focus (production versus consumption), competing methodologies (structure versus agency) and competing political perspectives (for and against the gentrifiers). How to sort this out? One way of doing so is to list various hypotheses which may contribute to a general understanding of the forces leading to gentrification.

The first explanation focuses on the *economic opportunities* for renovation of inner-city housing. The key concept is the 'rent gap', the difference between actual and potential ground rent levels. As noted in chapter 4, there is a close association between rent and land-use. The market value of a property depends upon the ground rent and the character and condition of the housing which stands on the land. A 'rent gap' arises where the character and condition of the existing housing is poor, thereby inhibiting the realisation of the potential ground rent. According to Neil Smith (1979), 'gentrification occurs when the gap is wide enough that developers can purchase shells cheaply, can pay the builders' cost and profit for rehabilitation, can pay interest on mortgage and construction loans, and can then sell the product for a sale price that leaves satisfactory returns to the developer. The entire ground-rent, or a large portion of it, is now capitalised; the neighbourhood has been 'recycled' and begins a new cycle of use.' Such reasoning could equally apply to large-scale urban renewal schemes as to piecemeal gentrification. It is a theory which has been subjected to much critical analysis (e.g. Badcock 1989, Bourassa 1992). What it usefully stresses is that gentrification will only be economically viable under certain circumstances. It does not explain when, where and how those circumstances will arise. That requires an analysis of urban decay and the rates of return on investment in real estate *vis à vis* industry, financial instruments, and so forth.

A second explanation begins with a rather more historically specific set of observations, focusing on the *changing economic structure* of the CBD in the transition from industrial city to corporate city. As Mullins (1982) puts it, 'where the inner city was once the location of working-class employment in factories, it is now the place of middle-class employment in skyscrapers and other office buildings. The growth of inner-city middle-class residents seems partly related to the development of the inner city as a place of middle-class employment.' To this one might add the observation that the demise of inner-city manufacturing activities has also made available various industrial properties and warehouses, some of which can be converted for gentrified housing (and other social uses attractive to gentrifiers.) But the main point is the changed composition of downtown employment. Mullins stresses that this can be only a partial explanation of gentrification. Indeed, it would not seem to apply so strongly to cities like Brisbane and Perth which, on his own reasoning, had never experienced a well-developed industrial phase before becoming corporate cities. Even in Sydney and Melbourne, where the transition is more evident, much of the new employment growth is of clerical employees and others who do not fit unambiguously into the 'middle class' category (unless the class division is crudely defined in terms of the 'white-collar' 'blue-collar' distinction). The explanation does have the merit of drawing attention to structural changes in the economic base of the city; but it leads us into another concern — why people employed in the CBD would want to live nearby anyway.

What of the growing problems of *urban transport*? As noted in chapter 3, the length of the average journey to work in major cities has increased. The socially prestigious and more environmentally attractive residential areas have tended to be well away from the CBD: Sydney's upper North Shore is a classic example. The relative accessibility of these areas diminishes as transport problems intensify. As cities become larger and more congested, the need for accessibility can be expected to rise. Those with the capacity to pay for accessibility to the inner city drive out (no pun intended) those who do not. The rising price of oil and the *energy crisis* buttress this tendency. This is not to say that the majority of gentrifiers are households moving to the inner city from the outer suburbs: American, British and Australian evidence suggests this is generally not the case (Badcock 1984). Nor is it to deny that the origins of the gentrification process pre-dated the steep climb in oil prices. Yes, the first signs of gentrification were already evident in the 1960s in Sydney's Paddington and Melbourne's Carlton. However, it did not become a generalised inner-city phenomenon until the 1970s, the decade in which OPEC drove up the price of oil, leading to substantial increases in transport costs. In effect, this explanation for gentrification sees it as a process of substituting extra housing expenditures for lower transport costs. However, note that the relative fall back in oil prices in the 1980s led to no reduction in the move towards gentrification — quite the contrary. Presumably one needs to see these issues in a long-term context. On this reasoning, widespread expectations of further rises in the cost of fuel, and therefore of transport, make it sensible to 'go inner-city' now (although, paradoxically, that is where environmental problems of congestion and pollution are currently most intense).

A fourth way in to the analysis of gentrification focuses on the changing *class structure*. In the words of Michael Beauregard (1986), 'the explanation for gentrification begins with the presence of gentrifiers, the necessary agents and beneficiaries of the gentrification process'. Some analysts have noted the direct role played by corporate capital and real estate agents in kicking the gentrification process along (e.g. Knox 1987). But for the most part the gentrifiers act individually, although having certain common socio-economic characteristics. Beauregard describes them as 'affluent, professional and ostensibly "afamilial" households'. Economically, they are a product of structural changes in the balance between manufacturing and service industries, technological changes and changes in the labour process which have led to a tremendous growth of professional, managerial, supervisory, technical, clerical and service workers at the expense of 'blue-collar' employment. To characterise the gentrifiers in terms of the distinction between 'middle class' and 'working class' is problematic: the more open-ended analytical category of 'contradictory class location' (Wright 1978) is an alternative. But what is more important in the current context is to explain the behaviour — particularly the locational behaviour — of this distinctive social stratum. Why the inner city? Or, to be more precise, why does a fraction of this stratum elect to live in the inner city?

One possibility is that inner-city living too is driven by the growing problems of *housing affordability*, as noted in chapter 2. As the more traditional affluent suburbs, like those on Sydney's upper North Shore, become so expensive that they move beyond the reach of young professionals, other options must be sought. From this point of view, renovating inner-city houses to acceptable bourgeois-aspirant standards may be a second-best solution, but it has an evident logic in the circumstances of a generalised crisis of housing affordability.

Another possibility arises because of the distinctive *consumption* patterns among the gentrifiers. This involves quite a different type of explanation in that it interprets gentrification, not as a response to changing conditions of production or relative prices of housing and transport, but in terms of changes in consumer preferences and life styles. In part the preferences concern the houses themselves, individually and collectively. In Mullins' (1982) words 'the inner city is perceived as a unique physical environment of old, gentrified, historically significant and attractive buildings, and it is this new "ambience" which is being consumed'. In part, the preferences also concern recreational and leisure facilities — theatres, cinemas, art galleries, museums, concert halls, and the intimate restaurants and pubs which are characteristic of the inner city areas. To quote Mullins again, 'whereas the suburbanisation process revolved around the mass consumption of goods, the contemporary residential development of the inner city appears to be resulting from the development of this site as the location for the consumption of unique leisure-oriented services'. Could this be seen as an expression of 'postmodern' life styles, emphasising diversity rather than standardised mass-consumption items? Could it be that the gentrifiers constitute 'the present day counterparts of Veblen's leisure class' (Ley 1980), fashioning a post-industrial city with a consumption landscape rather than a production landscape? If so, 'the world of productive industrial capitalism is superseded by the ideology of consumptive pluralism, and gentrification is one of the ways in which this historical transformation is inscribed in the modern landscape' (Smith 1987a).

Finally—and coming rather more down-to-earth—we should note that gentrification may also be linked to *demographic* trends. The growth of single-person households and more transient relationships among young people is one aspect. So too is the ascendency of DINK (double income, no kids) households. This is not to say that gentrifiers do not include families with children — obviously they do. But the inner-city housing stock offers more flexible living arrangements for a more socially mobile segment of the population. Picking up on this last theme from a more explicitly feminist perspective we may note Damaris Rose's (1984) claim that 'it is now increasingly accepted that women are playing an active and important role in bringing about gentrification'. As Ann Markusen (1980) puts it, 'gentrification is in large part a result of the breakdown of the patriarchal household. Households of gay people, singles and professional couples with central business district jobs increasingly find central locations attractive.' Gay and lesbian communities are readily observable in inner-city gentrified areas.

Which of these approaches to explaining gentrification is most useful? Each has its limitations, some of which have been noted in passing. However, each provides some partial illumination of this complex phenomenon. True, there may be some conceptual impediments to a synthesis of elements from competing paradigms—'consumer sovereignty' explanations which have their theoretical roots in neoclassical economies, class analysis which derives from Marxist and Weberian traditions, conceptions of post-industrialism and postmodernism, and so forth. Nevertheless, a holistic explanation must recognise the interacting and reinforcing (i.e. symbiotic) elements in the process.

For example, the explanation involving consumption patterns does not explain the reasons for the changed preferences nor why the inner city is the area which can be most readily transformed to satisfy them. One may postulate, for example, that the key to the process is the social-cultural revitalisation of the city itself—a sort of rebirth exemplified by street carnivals and ubiquitous harbourside redevelopments. The inner-city residences give access to these social goodies. However, as noted in the second explanation, the CBD's production focus is also changing; which raises the question of why changes in consumption patterns should be prioritised over production as explanatory factors? In any case, ignoring the transport aspects of the third explanation would leave open the question of why these production and consumption facilities in and around the CBD cannot adequately be accessed through commuting from the more distant suburbs.

The cause-effect relationships in gentrification are interactive. The growth of leisure consumption activities in the inner city is as much a consequence as a cause of the changing social structure. The changing social structure is, in turn, linked to production conditions, cost of housing and transport. Moreover, these are not simply structural imperatives; they interact with the attitudes and beliefs of the participants. From this point of view, gentrification may be interpreted as *a process of class constitution* (Williams 1986). It is a part of the means employed by the gentrifiers to distinguish themselves from the 'stuffed-shirt' bourgeoisie above them in the social hierarchy and the working class below. Thus, the changing conditions of production, consumption, transport and housing fuse with changes in social structure, demographic structure and prevailing ideologies, including beliefs about class. Gentrification is a more complex process than just fixing up old houses!

CONSEQUENCES OF GENTRIFICATION

So what? Why does gentrification matter anyway? The answers to such questions are necessarily linked to the discussion in chapter 6 of the consequences of urban spatial inequality. Indeed, to the extent that gentrification produces, in a prolonged transitional period, a breakdown in spatial segmentation, that earlier discussion can simply be turned on its head. Thus, because gentrification leads to upper-income professional groups living side-by-side with the traditional working-class residents of the inner-city areas, it apparently:

- breaks down the tendencies for social and economic problems to be concentrated in particular localities;
- generates greater social awareness of 'how the other half lives';
- helps overcome the impediments to social mobility, including educational quality and spatial discrimination in employment;
- injects greater dynamism into the electoral politics of inner-urban areas;
- undermines the tendency for class consciousness to be deflected into spatially-based interpretations of economic and social inequality.

This is a comfortable set of generalisations but it may be somewhat facile. Gentrification has two other effects which tend to compound the problems of an unequal society. Both concern the effects on the traditional inner-city working class. First there is the effect on those who stay in the inner city. Many do. Indeed, there is some evidence of a 'new servant class' in the inner city, employed in corporate support activities such as office cleaning or catering for the consumption requirements of the relatively affluent gentrifiers. If these low-income workers are in the private-rental sector of the housing market, the tendency is for them to be hit by rising rents as local property values escalate. Retail facilities and other local services also tend to start catering for the demands of the more affluent sections of the local population, which creates difficulties — including rising prices — for the local working class and older residents.

Second, there is the displacement effect. What happens to the working-class and welfare-dependent groups who are displaced from the inner city? Where do they go? And does the break-up of their communities further entrench their personal economic and social problems? One recalls Hugh Stretton's (1970) advocacy of spatial mix for housing types and socio-economic groups in the process of urban design, but the mixing associated with inner-city gentrification involves a different dynamic. There are big winners and big losers, and they do not divide unambiguously along class lines. Being an owner-occupier or a private housing tenant is one crucial dimension. So too, among owner-occupiers, is the time at which they bought their housing in the inner city—

before or after the escalation of prices associated with gentrification. Generational inequalities are a key dimension.

The losers in the process of gentrification in Australian cities
have not developed any coherent political organisation. This
contrasts, for example, with the role of 'Class Action' in London's
Dockland Redevelopment Area. The gentrifiers themselves have
been better organised here — e.g. through groups such as the
Paddington Society and the Glebe Society in Sydney and
through their growing representation on local government in all
the major cities. The 'Green Ban' movement in the 1970s did
show the potential for inner-urban restructuring to generate
major grass-roots political opposition, but that was reacting
more to large-scale redevelopment projects than to piecemeal
gentrification processes. We return to this issue in chapter 14 in
the context of a broader discussion of urban social movements.

FURTHER READING

Smith (1987a): an exploration of the causes of gentrification.

Smith and Williams (1986): a more comprehensive compendium of papers on the
   analysis of gentrification.

Kendig (1979): a description of the emerging gentrification trends in Australian
   inner cities.

Horvath & Engels (1985) and Mullins (1982): brief Australian case studies.

8

The State

What can be done to resolve urban problems? A commitment to social progress requires the identification of appropriate prescriptions. However, that is easier said than done. Were that not the case, one might have expected that well-intentioned persons, equipped with the requisite professional skills as town planners, traffic engineers and urban economists, would have provided the necessary solutions already. If the urban problems are rooted in the structure of existing economic, social and political institutions their resolution would require more fundamental structural changes. But what changes? And who is to bring them about? Is the state the avenue through which the solution can be found? Or is the state an obstacle to social progress, part of the problem rather than part of the solution?

Merely to pose the issues in this way is somewhat unusual in conventional urban economic studies, because the role of the state is seldom subjected to critical scrutiny. The typical approach is normative: urban problems are seen to arise because of 'market imperfections' (for example, externalities, imperfect information, lack of foresight or coordination in location decisions), so the government (as the central element in the state) should introduce remedial policies (for example, promotion of regional development, decentralisation or improved urban planning). This view underlies some of the discussion of public policies in earlier chapters of this book—employment policies, housing policies, transport policies, land allocation policies, and so on. The state is treated as *deus ex machina*, 'intervening' to implement policies on behalf of the community as a whole. This is pragmatic, perhaps admirably so, but it is innocent of the concerns of political scientists about the nature of the state itself, the limits on government policy and the competing interests influencing policy outcomes. A more coherent approach requires an analysis of the state as an integral part of the working of the socio-economic system, questioning rather than assuming a relationship between public policy and the national interest. In seeking to develop the foundation for that more systematic analysis of urban and regional policy this chapter proceeds in three steps:

- defining the state;
- identifying the various scales at which the state is involved in shaping urban and regional development;
- discussing alternative views of the state.

This involves a more generalised and abstract mode of reasoning than in the preceding chapters, but it is a necessary bridge to the more down-to-earth policy discussions which follow.

THE STATE

First it is necessary to clarify what constitutes the state. This is much debated in the academic literature, especially because the definition is not independent of the theory of the state which is adopted. Perhaps the simplest approach is to follow Ralph Miliband (1973) in defining the state as an interconnected set of institutions comprising the government, public service, judiciary, armed forces and police, political parties and parliamentary assemblies. These institutions are easy to list but more difficult to understand. Perceptions of the state range from a parasitic all-embracing monolith to a subtle and adaptable set of institutions for social betterment.

A systematic analysis of the state is a key focus of political economy. One useful starting point, following the reasoning set out by Alford & Friedland (1985), is to see the state as constituted through the intersection of democracy, capitalism and bureaucracy. Yes, the state is formally *democratic* to the extent that the selection of government from among the contesting political parties normally occurs through an electoral process. But other elements of the state are not normally subject to such democratic procedures. Yes, the state is *capitalist* to the extent that its activities are necessarily shaped and/or constrained by the prevailing economic system. Ensuring the conditions for capital accumulation and the legitimacy of capitalism is a recurrent concern, if only because failure to do so can be expected to cause economic or political crisis. But this may leave considerable discretion in the operation of economic and social policy. And yes, the state is *bureaucratic* because the implementation and management of those public policies is a task requiring a considerable state apparatus. Legions of public servants carry the burden. In the process some may develop interests and practices not necessarily in harmony with either the formal requirements of the democratically elected governments or the needs of capital. So the state is unlikely to function purely as the embodiment of the democratic ideal or as the ideal collective capitalist.

Setting out the issue in this way is helpful in showing the relationship between three deceptively simple questions about the state:

- what *should* be the public policies (to serve the interests of the people in a democratic political system)?
- are those policies *feasible* (in the sense of being possible in a capitalist economic system *or* helping to transform that system)?
- what are the *means* through which the policies can be imple- mented (through the state apparatus)?

The primary focus of each question is on the democratic, capitalistic and bureaucratic aspects of the state respectively. The trilogy is worthy of emphasis because so much disagree- ment about the state — as a vehicle for social progress, as an instrument of class domination or as a parasitic institution — is traceable back to a different emphasis on these three aspects. As we will see a little later in this chapter, the trilogy is also of significance in understanding the bases of competing theories of the state.

URBAN AND REGIONAL POLICY

Space is central to understanding the state. Indeed, it is its most obvious defining feature. National boundaries limit the state — hence the term 'nation-state'. As Michael Mann (1984) argues, each state's powers 'radiate authoritatively outwards from a centre but stop at defined territorial boundaries. The state is, indeed, a *place* — both a central place and a unified territorial reach.' In a world of increased integration, economically, socially and culturally, these discrete territorial limits remain a striking feature. Thus, to understand the broad patterns of regional and national development on a world scale inevitably focuses attention on the state. Our more limited concern here is to establish a framework for analysing the role of the state in relation to urban and regional development *within* the nation, with particular reference to Australia.

For this purpose we can concentrate primarily on the role of government. This is not to say that other parts of the state apparatus do not have an impact on the form of urban and regional development. For example, in Australia the judiciary has interpreted the Constitution in such a way as to restrict federal government initiatives which might involve location-specific expenditure and/or interfere with inter-State trade. The public service has also shaped regional and urban policies through the nature of its advice to government: Treasury public servants in particular have put a brake on innovative urban and regional policies (Lloyd and Troy 1981).

These are valuable reminders that the state and the government are not synonymous. Nevertheless, it is appropriate to have a primary focus on government as the central element in the formulation and implementation of urban and regional policy. That focus also draws attention to the importance of the federal structure in the Australian case and the division between *local governments, individual State governments* and the *federal government.** Each of these bodies has had an influence on the spatial dimension of economic development. The corresponding three-fold

---

* Note that here, as elsewhere in this book, State is used with a capital S to indicate the intermediate tier of government in the Australian federal structure, while state refers to the institutions of government and public administration as a whole.

distinction provides a useful basis for analysing the relationship between the three tiers of government and the three spatial scales of policy:

- inter-regional policy;
- intra-regional policy;
- intra-urban policy.

Inter-regional policy involves the largest sub-national territorial units. In the case of Australia this means the area bounded by the individual States of New South Wales, Victoria, Queensland, South Australia, Western Australia and Tasmania, together with the Australian Capital and Northern Territories. Given the historical importance of the State governments in shaping the form of urban and regional development, and given the continuing existence of the federal system, it seems appropriate to begin the analysis of the state at this scale. This is not to say that the States have particular significance as geographical entities or in terms of the conventional criteria for regional delineation. Rather, they are adopted as a practical recognition of the fundamental role of the federal system in the structure of the Australian space-economy.

Inter-regional policy (or regional policy for short) concerns the balance between these broad regions. In the Australian case, such policy has been primarily undertaken by the federal government. Indeed, only the federal government is really in a position to do it. Individual State governments compete with each other for investment projects, and their relative success has a significant bearing on overall regional balance. However, only the federal government can engage systematically in the overall planning of inter-State resource allocation and redistribution. The Australian government has done this explicitly through its fiscal policy, spending more in some States than it raises in taxes, and vice versa. The Commonwealth Grants Commission is a distinctive institution fashioned within the Australian state for this purpose. Other federal government policies, ranging from tariff policy to monetary policy, have implicit effects on inter-regional patterns of economic development. An analysis of these issues is the principal concern of chapter 9.

Intra-regional policy is the second level. It involves measures which affect the spatial distribution of resources within broadly defined regions. In the Australian context, if we continue to visualise the States as regions, this means policies which impinge on the shape of intra-State development. Within each of the individual States there is very considerable diversity but perhaps the most obvious aspect is the concentration of population and industry in the State capitals. In every State except Tasmania the capital city has more than ten times the population of the next largest town. The causes and consequences of the metropolitan primacy within each of the individual States have long been regarded as central to debates on Australian urban and regional development (e.g. Stilwell 1974, Burnley 1980). There has also been long-standing emphasis — in rhetoric if not in action — on policies of decentralisation. Both federal and State governments have been involved, although federal intervention has typically been minor, with the exception of the Whitlam government in the period 1972-5. This dimension of spatial policy is the subject of chapter 10.

Intra-urban policy (or urban policy for short) is the third dimension. This scale of policy impinges more directly on the internal structure and functioning of the cities. It is more complicated in that it often involves all three tiers of government: local, State and federal. Local governments regulate land use through the processing of development applications, although their capacity for more extensive planning is typically limited by meagre revenues (principally generated through local rates). State governments, because of their broader spatial coverage and their rather more extensive fiscal capacities, are able to engage in more comprehensive metropolitan planning as well as policies towards public housing, transport and the provision of public utilities, all of which have the potential to impact on the form of urban development — for better or worse. (Brisbane has a special status in this regard because, alone among the State capitals, it has a metropolitan government rather than more fragmentary local governments. This gives the third tier of government there some of the characteristics in the urban planning process that one associates with State governments elsewhere.) The

federal government's involvement in intra-urban policy is typically limited to providing grants which enable State and local
governments to carry out their functions. Here again though,
there was a significant exception in 1972–5 when the federal
government was active in various intra-urban policies, including
area improvement programmes, the provision of urban land for
new housing and inner-city housing rehabilitation schemes.

How such policies influence the metropolitan areas is a
complex matter. The spatial form of the major Australian cities is
very distinctive. Most obviously, the overall density of population
is very low by international standards, a feature which is linked
with the dominant emphasis (particularly since the second world
war) on home-ownership, rather than private rental or state-
provided housing (as noted in chapter 2). The housing policy of
federal and State governments is evidently a key factor influencing intra-urban development. Other distinctive aspects of the
metropolitan scene already noted include the changing form
of the CBD, the gentrification of the inner-city areas and the
suburbanisation of manufacturing. Metropolitan planning
purports to give some overall coordination and coherence to
these processes of urban development and redevelopment. How
successful it has been, or could be, continues to be a major
controversy. Chapters 11 and 12 consider some of the key issues.

These three levels of spatial disaggregation provide a framework for analysis of the state in urban and regional development.
Any one initiative affects all three scales. For example, if a
business corporation establishes a new factory in a Melbourne
suburb, this bears directly on the pattern of intra-urban development; but it also changes the balance of intra-regional development by further intensifying metropolitan primacy; and it
changes the balance of inter-regional development as between
Victoria and the other States. The selection of that particular
location by the corporation is a decision that takes place within
both a political and an economic environment. It presumably
reflects the firm's estimates of costs, revenues and other locational
characteristics, but it also reflects the incentives and constraints
determined by the different levels of government within the state
apparatus. An understanding of this sort of impulse in the urban

development process requires analysis of the purpose, character and impacts of the policy 'interventions' operating at the three different levels.

The preceding reasoning is summed up in Figure 8.1 as a three-by-three matrix of governmental bodies and the levels of spatial disaggregation at which their policies have operated. This indicates nine policy categories. In practice, some are much more important than others. The more important categories are indicated in Figure 8.1 by giving examples of relevant policies. Subsequent chapters consider these in more detail, also seeking to assess the Australian experience in the light of competing theories of the state.

FIGURE 8.1   A GENERAL CLASSIFICATION OF REGIONAL AND URBAN POLICIES

Spatial level of policy	Level of government		
	Federal	State	Local
Inter-regional	Taxation and expenditure policies: Commonwealth Grants Commission.		
Intra-regional	Development of Canberra; DURD initiatives for the development of growth centres	Decentralisation policies.	
Intra-urban	Other DURD initiatives e.g. area improvement programmes, inner-city housing schemes; Building Better Cities programme	Metropolitan planning; transport policy.	Processing development applications.

Source: Adapted from Stilwell (1983).

COMPETING VIEWS OF THE STATE

How can we interpret the activities of the state? Does it serve the national interest, albeit in difficult economic circumstances partly beyond its own making? Or, in responding to various sectional interests, does it recurrently violate the national interest? What of the Marxist view that the state primarily serves the interests of the dominant class? Or is the state more like an arena of struggle in which competing class and sectional interests confront each other? Then again, does it act in a managerial role, serving its own interests instead of the national interest or particular class interests? If we are to avoid a purely descriptive account of urban and regional policies, it is useful to set our discussion in the context of these competing views.

The first possibility is a *liberal pluralist* view which sees the state implementing public policies in response to the interests expressed by the people. A focus on electoral processes and pressure-group politics commonly leads to this interpretation of the state in the democratic process. There are many variations on this theme, but we can usefully distinguish two principal variants, one seeing the outcome as serving the national interest and the other seeing it as violating the national interest. In the former case, the state may be limited to correcting minor sources of market failure, or it may undertake large-scale government intervention to correct the various inefficiencies and injustices associated with a pure market system. J.K. Galbraith's (1974) notion of the state as a source of countervailing power to monopoly capital is a strong version of this view of the state. The liberal mainstream economists' conception of the state as an instrument for macro-economic management sits comfortably enough here too. Where a more explicit theory of the state is developed it focuses on how public policies come to reflect and reconcile competing interests — hence the emphasis, on the one hand, on electoral and pressure-group politics and, on the other, on the way in which economic and social policies contribute to serving the 'general interest' (for example, Keynesian economic policies directed towards the goal of full employment). The state's activities are regarded as generally benign, tempering the worst excesses of the free market economy with redistributive justice and social regulation. Regional and urban policy may be interpreted in this context as a response to a popular demand for modifying the spatial economic and social outcomes that would otherwise prevail in a market economy.

By contrast, the negative version of the liberal pluralist view suggests that the state's activities in practice, although responsive to political demands, tend to be harmful. This view dovetails neatly with 'new right' ideology. It is exemplified by the 'private interest theory of the state' which sees intervention by the state as a series of accommodations to sectional interests which violates the national interest. Tariff policy is often cited as a classic case — protectionism being interpreted as the consequence of the government 'caving in' to pressures from firms and unions in various industries, resulting in a macroeconomic outcome which impedes economic restructuring and efficiency (Anderson 1987, Pincus 1987). Similarly, regional policy is the outcome of accommodations to various regional interests. Responding to each and every parochial demand for special consideration leads to an outcome which is incoherent and wasteful.

A second general view of the state denies the usefulness of any concept of the national interest, arguing instead that the state systematically serves a particular class interest. This view is most evident in the traditional *Marxist* interpretation of the capitalist state as 'the executive for managing the common affairs of the whole bourgeoisie' (Marx & Engels 1848). From this perspective, the state can be expected systematically to serve the requirements of capital (although it may be noted that Marx's own empirical studies did not treat the state simply as an obedient tool of a monolithic ruling class). The interests of the class *as a whole* are of paramount importance here. This is because individual capitalists often do not perceive their common interests (or, if they do, they cannot coordinate their activities towards that end without 'external' assistance). Hence the need for the state. Since the interests of capital and labour are fundamentally antagonistic, the state can be expected to implement policies that work against the long-term interests of the working class, although interim concessions may be made to secure legitimacy and social reproduction.

Expressed rather baldly in this way, an underlying economic determinism is evident — the actions of the state follow more or less directly from the needs of the capitalist class. Analysis of the state therefore begins with an analysis of the requirements of capital. Urban and regional policy may be interpreted in this context as helping to open up new opportunities for capital accumulation or to provide the conditions for class-domination. There can be a tendency to tautology here. Either government policy directly meets the needs of capital accumulation or, if it involves progressive redistribution of income to labour and welfare recipients, it serves the needs of capital for legitimation and social reproduction. Moreover, the structuralist character of the reasoning tends towards a denial of the significance of different political parties in government. The 'logic of capital' rules OK.

A variation on this second approach — which one may, with some hesitation, label *revisionist* — emphasises the role of the state in relation to the broadened political conflict between capital and labour. The state is an arena of class struggle. It does not automatically serve the interests of only one class, and certainly not the interest of the community as a whole. The more orthodox Marxist view is rejected because it takes insufficient account of the extension of class and intra-class struggle from the economic to the political sphere. On the other hand, this revisionist view cannot be conflated with the liberal pluralist view because the latter denies the existence of fundamental antagonisms between classes which shape the role of the state. The liberal pluralist concept of a national interest against which the state's actions can be judged is held to be an absurdity, a point conceded even by one writer describing himself as 'a bourgeois critic of Marxism', arguing that 'in a class strati-fied society the very notion of a national interest is highly problematic' (Parkin 1972). Class struggle is central — a process which has extended and diversified to fill the expanded domain of the state. Thus, while the analysis of the state cannot proceed directly from the study of the 'logic of capital', the nature of the capital accumulation process shapes the conditions in which the class struggle takes place. Unlike the liberal pluralist view, this revisionist view of the state sees the political possibilities rooted in the economic conditions.

One particularly important aspect of this revisionist approach is the recognition of political possibilities arising from conflict between fractions of capital. For example, high rents from urban land benefit the owners of urban property at the expense of industrial capital; so there arises the recurrent possibility of an alignment between the working class and industrial capital, particularly the small business sector, in support of rent control. Intra-class conflicts, according to the more orthodox Marxist view, strengthen the need for the state to act on behalf of the capitalist class as a whole. However, according to this revisionist view, they also open up the possibility for members of the working class to exploit such conflicts in their own interests, thereby gaining more control over the state apparatus. Taking this chain of reasoning to the limit, there arises the possibility of the state being used for the transformation of a capitalist to a socialist system. Applied in the context of urban and regional policy, the state is regarded as having the capacity to use its policy instruments as part of a more comprehensive programme of radical reforms.

A third view may be characterised as *managerialist*, focusing on the organisations which constitute the state and the interests of the key players within the state apparatus. Again there are two variations on the theme, the first emphasising a 'gatekeeper' role for state and the second seeing the state as essentially a self-serving institution. The former variant stresses the function of the state in allocating public resources and guarding access to them from the diverse claimants within the community. To carry out this function requires the state employees to act as gatekeepers, in which capacity they have the potential to develop their own ways of working and allocative criteria. It is a view which has particular resonance in respect of urban and regional policy. State employees carry out the gatekeeper role by saying yes to some regions and no to others in the allocation of funding. The urban and regional plans which they formulate favour development in some localities and deny it in others. It is a process which, incidentally, generates recurrent opportunities for corruption. More generally it is a process which, although characterised by the application of planning techniques, embodies distinctive values shaped within the state apparatus itself. Hence the perception of Gurr and King (1987) 'that modern state and public officials have their own interests, institutional momentum, and the capacity to act with relative autonomy'. The state officials are not merely tools of capitalist class interests, certainly not disinterested functionaries in an arena of class struggle, nor even just mediators of diverse private interests. Their own identity and interests shape the functioning of the state.

Pushing this line of reasoning to its limits leads to the view of the state as a self-serving institution, as the private property of officials which they use for their personal advancement. There are elements of this view in early Marxist writings on the state as a parasitic institution. It is better developed in anarchist thought, where the oppressive consequences of the state are stressed as strongly as the exploitative consequences of capitalist economic organisation. Indeed the former aspect — the oppressive character of the state — is typically treated by anarchists as more fundamental and pervasive (Bookchin 1980). This view of the state also has a strange echo in the writings of conservatives such as Milton and Rose Friedman (1980) who contend that the expansion of the state has been, in effect, a mistake, the product of misguided reformism. However, the Friedmanite perspective involves an evaluation of the state from a normative standpoint favouring free-market capitalism. As such, it has more in common with what we earlier called the 'private interest theory of the state'.

The view of the state as a self-interested body is rather distinctive analytically in that it focuses our attention on the internal machinations of the 'state elite'. It goes without saying that its self-serving character requires a legitimising ideology, stressing various aspects of public interest. Regional and urban policy may even play a role in this respect. Charles Gore (1984), for example, claims that the logic of regional policy is in the *rhetoric* of intervention and redistribution, providing legitimacy for the state but not having any significant effect on regional problems.

More directly, urban policy may be used directly to improve the quality of the urban environment in the particular localities inhabited by the upper echelons of the State elite. To the extent that they share these localities (the more affluent suburbs) with the members of the capitalist class, there is a tendency for the outcome to converge on that predicted by a Marxist view of the state.

These various views of the state, interrelated as they are, are summarised in Figure 8.2. This is not intended as an exhaustive treatment of state theory, a topic which has filled numerous heavyweight tomes! Rather, it provides a framework for interpreting the Australian experience regarding urban and regional development, indicating competing hypotheses to be borne in mind while examining the various urban and regional policies.

FIGURE 8.2   ANALYSES OF THE STATE: PRINCIPAL CURRENTS

Analytical framework	Dominant view	Alternative view
Liberal-pluralist analysis	state serving the national interest	state responding incoherently to diverse private interests
Class analysis	state serving capitalist class interest	state as arena of class struggle
Managerial analysis	state as gatekeeper	state as self-serving institution

FURTHER READING

Head (1983): chapter 2 surveys competing views of the state, while other chapters deal with particular aspects of the Australian state, including urban and regional policy and federalism.

Alford & Friedland (1985): an examination of contrasting perspectives on the modern state.

Clark & Dear (1984): analysing the state apparatus as a system for ensuring the political legitimacy of capitalist society.

Johnston (1982, 1989): on the state and political geography.

9

Regional Policy

Regional economic development sets the broad context of urban problems and policies. This is particularly important in Australia because the federal structure shapes the capacity to address urban problems and policy issues. It provides simultaneously a basis for beggar-thy-neighbour conflicts and a mechanism for spatial redistribution. Policies for reshaping Australia must begin with an analysis of what can be achieved at this level.

Government policies to influence the pattern of regional economic development are more than common. They are effectively inescapable. For example, government expenditures necessarily have a regional economic impact, whether the spatial form of their allocation is consciously determined or not. As Ron Johnston (1982) notes, 'virtually all state expenditure is spatially specific, in that it is either allocated directly to a place (or to people living in a place) or it is spent on the purchase of goods and services produced somewhere'. In a federal system the regional allocation is particularly visible and usually highly political.

In Australia the economic policies of the federal government significantly affect the balance of regional development between the States. Ever since Federation there has been a general commitment to the pursuit of some degree of inter-regional equity. This involves countering the tendency for private sector investment to be concentrated in the more developed regions, reflecting the processes of circular and cumulative causation in regional economic performance. But how effective have government policies been in achieving the stated goals of more balanced regional development? And are regional policies compatible with the 'new right' push to roll back the state, replacing the Keynesian view of economic policy with so-called economic rationalism?

This chapter examines the general character of regional policy by:

- looking at the rationale of this type of policy;
- considering the available policy instruments;
- examining the Australian experience;
- reflecting on recent problems of restructuring and rivalry.

In so doing, we shift from the liberal-pluralist view of the state which usually underpins the advocacy of regional policy towards a more critical perspective on regional policy in practice.

WHY REGIONAL POLICY?

There are various reasons why regional economic inequality is a problem (Stilwell 1992: ch. 3). It violates the criterion of equitable access to comparable standards of living. It can undermine the efficiency of the economic system. It may generate political instability. In these circumstances it is not surprising that people commonly turn to governments for the implementation of remedial policies. Social equity is held to require policies to generate greater geographical evenness in *per capita* incomes and the distribution of life chances. Economic efficiency requires that policies be targeted at regions with unemployed resources in order to generate economic growth. Political integration requires that the central government attempt to reduce regional economic disparities which might otherwise lead to acute conflicts within the nation-state. These issues of equity, efficiency and integration comprise the triple foundations of the conventional wisdom about regional economic policy. It is hard to think of developed economies where it has not been accepted by governing bodies, and policies implemented more or less vigorously to influence the geography of economic activity.

A parallel may be drawn with *Keynesian policy*, an approach to macroeconomic management with which conventional regional economic policy has a close relationship. (To anticipate a later argument, this helps to explain why regional policy in practice has also been a casualty of the changed status of Keynesianism in public policy.) Put simply, regional economic policy may be regarded as the disaggregated equivalent of Keynesian macro-economic management — a means of generating full employment and/or avoiding inflation through state manipulation of the level of effective demand at the regional level. Indeed, regional policy can be regarded as a necessary adjunct to macroeconomic policies for stabilisation and economic growth, because of its role in evening out the spatial pattern of demand and supply in labour and housing markets and thereby alleviating a principal source of 'stagflation'. Politically, there is also a parallel in that regional policy complements Keynesian macro measures in providing reforms of capitalism. Underlying both strands of policy is a liberal-pluralist conception of the state as a vehicle for the pursuit of a general national interest within which competing regional interests are reconcilable.

From this point of view, the appeal of regional policy lies in its potential to enhance the achievement of national objectives, particularly economic ones. *Full employment* is achieved by steer-ing new investment to the labour-surplus regions, compensating for the failure of private enterprises to invest there, either because of imperfect information, inertia or risk-aversion. Fuller *utilis-ation of capital* (especially social capital such as transport, edu-cation or health facilities) may be achieved if policy bolsters up depopulating regions. *Inflation* is reduced by steering investment away from the 'hot-house' regions where excess demand in the labour and/or housing market generates rising prices. The nation's *balance of payments* situation is improved if the effect of regional policy is to steer economic activity to regions producing exports or import-substitutes. Finally, all of this may result in a higher rate of *economic growth* for the nation as a whole, to the extent that growth is constrained by the foregoing factors (i.e. under-utilised labour or capital, inflation and balance of payments problems).

Of course, it is not inevitable that regional policy *will* enhance national economic performance in these various ways. To the contrary, it is commonly argued that, since the effect of regional policy is to steer investable funds to localities where they would not otherwise go, the outcome may be reduced productivity. The private sector knows best: what is good for a firm like BHP is good for Australia! Well, no doubt regional economic policy may be poorly misjudged and have high opportunity costs. However, there are various reasons why private sector decisions about the location of investment may be problematic too. There is the problem of myopia in private sector decisions: 'building on the best' may have appeal from the viewpoint of short-run profits, but it is not usually the best way of opening up a broad array of investment opportunities in the long run. Large firms may seek to avoid this tendency through long-term planning for profits and growth but they still face the problems of imperfect information and lack of coordination. If private sector enterprises were aware of the possibilities for investment in other regions and were able to develop these opportunities simultaneously, then it might be in their collective interest to invest there. However, external economies will not be achieved unless they act in unison. This is a recurrent feature of capitalist enterprise: competition between individual firms may impede the achievement of collective (class) benefits. The coordination typically becomes a task for the state, albeit pursued with different degrees of vigour in practice according to whether there is a tradition of state involvement in industry policy. In Australia this has been notably lacking in any sustained commitment.

The *microeconomic* rationale for regional policy complements the macroeconomic reasoning. The underlying proposition is that there are pervasive reasons for 'market failure' in a space economy. Markets can provide an effective and decentralised system in many circumstances but there is no general guarantee that the resulting allocation of resources will be economically efficient where 'market imperfections' like monopoly, oligopoly and imperfect information exist. The situation becomes still more problematic when we take account of the externalities which impinge on the welfare of society as a whole. What is at issue is not just achieving external economies for the firms themselves through more coordinated decision making: there are also the more general effects of those firms' activities on, for example, environmental quality, the intensity of congestion or the incidence of poverty. No general mechanism exists to ensure that these effects are taken into account by the firms making investment decisions. Regional policy offers an apparent solution, the government redirecting the spatial allocation of investment in the attempt to maximise external economies and minimise external diseconomies.

This microeconomic rationale for regional policy, based on the limits of the price system and the recurrent problem of market failure, shades into a more explicit social or environmental rationale, based on the achievement of a more equitable or ecologically sustainable society. As with the preceding macroeconomic case for regional policy, it rests on a view of the state as capable of pursuing the national interest through its policy interventions within a capitalist economy. The underlying economic theory is that of the 'neoclassical synthesis'. Markets are held to generate efficient resource allocation subject to two general limitations — occasional microeconomic 'market failure' and recurrent problems of macroeconomic stabilisation. In dealing with the regional aspects, as with other dimensions of these problems, government 'intervention' is seen as being capable of providing the remedial fix. A rather benign view of the state underpins this position.

REGIONAL POLICY INSTRUMENTS

Four principal sets of policy instruments are available as components in a conventional programme of regional economic policy:

- regional expenditure policy;
- regionally differentiated price policies;
- controls on regional development;
- mobility policies.

The first involves the central government having a systematic regional variation in its own expenditure. The government may seek to achieve regional balance through running a budget surplus in some regions and a budget deficit in others. This would normally occur even without an explicit regional dimension in fiscal policy, so long as taxation rises and government expenditure on welfare payments falls with increases in regional income. In such a situation rich regions contribute disproportionately to total tax revenues, while poor regions draw disproportionately on government expenditures. An equity-oriented regional policy tends to increase the surpluses and deficits still more.

Government *infrastructure* expenditure is often said to be particularly potent. Indeed, the common justification for using infrastructure improvements as an instrument of regional policy is that, by altering the relative attractiveness of regions to new capital investment, they change the spatial distribution of industry in the long run. This may involve direct government expenditures channelled through public sector enterprises. It may involve the building of new towns to promote the development of laggard regions — a practical application of the 'growth pole' concept. The creation of entirely new capital cities such as Canberra and Brazilia are striking examples of this approach, although not entirely motivated by regional economic considerations.

Price policies are a second type of regional economic policy. These involve regionally discriminatory subsidies and taxes. They may apply either to inputs or outputs of the production process: either way the effect is to change the relative prices of goods and services between regions. The most obvious examples are regionally differentiated investment grants, payroll taxes, subsidies and low-interest loans. The desired effect is a reduction in costs of production in the less prosperous regions relative to those in the more prosperous regions, leading to a relative expansion of production in the former areas. Such policies have been widely used in many countries in pursuit of the objective of regional balance. However, their applicability in Australia is severely constrained by Constitutional limits on the capacity of the federal government to engage in policies which interfere with inter-State trade.

A third instrument for regional economic policy is *direct*

government controls of the pattern of regional development by private sector businesses. Controls can be considered as an extreme case of price policy: either permission for development is granted (implying zero tax) or it is refused (implying an infinite tax). In effect, the existence of controls alongside other regional policies (such as investment grants or employment subsidies) is an admission of the inadequacy of these latter policies. If they were successful, no controls would be needed. However, if location decisions are not based on short-run cost-minimisation calculations (as described in Stilwell 1992: ch. 4), then the choice of site may be quite unresponsive to regional input and output price differentials. (It may be more sensitive to the long-run strategic planning of transnational corporations, the climate, or even the availability of golf courses!) Hence, regulation on private sector locational choices may be called for in the interests of overall regional balance. Adding a locational test to the criteria applied in reviewing foreign investment proposals would be a case in point. There need be no sacrifice of economic efficiency in such regulations. Nevertheless, there is an understandable reluctance to apply controls on locational choices for fear of throttling the dynamics of the capitalist system. The recurrent fear is that the objective of regional balance may be associated with a process of 'levelling down'.

The fourth set of policy instruments aims at reducing *immobility* of labour and other factors of production. In the current political-economic context, such policies tie in with the more general concerns for workforce 'flexibility'. According to the figures in Table 1.1. there is still a long way to go. There are three main ways in which policy can act on regional immobility — by removal of 'market imperfections' causing immobility, by long-run policies to change the qualities least consistent with mobility, and by direct subsidies to migrant factors of production. All embody the characteristic reasoning of neoclassical economics. However, in practice the effects can be contradictory.

Consider, for example, what happens when a national wage fixation system is replaced by a more localised system such as the 'enterprise bargaining' which is in vogue in Australia. Yes, regional wage differentials are likely to more fully reflect differences in regional demand-supply conditions and regional unemployment differentials. This policy of greater 'labour market flexibility' thereby leads to greater wage inequalities. Whether this will promote equalisation of regional prosperity in the long run depends upon whether the consequential migratory flows have equilibrating or cumulatively disequilibrating effects (as discussed in Stilwell 1992: ch. 5). The latter outcome is always likely. Because demand and supply distributions for labour are spatially interdependent, labour mobility can fuel cumulative economic growth in the prosperous regions while causing further unemployment in the less prosperous regions. Moreover, labour migration can have social costs in terms of family unity or preservation of regional cultures.

This is a brief review of policy instruments whose advocacy is of long standing (e.g. Stilwell 1972). It is sufficient to illustrate that, while an array of instruments exists for the pursuit of greater regional balance, there are numerous limitations on their likely effectiveness. This is borne out by Australian experience.

AUSTRALIAN REGIONAL POLICIES

Regional policy has a long history in Australia, reflecting the origins of the nation in a set of separate colonies administered by 'the mother country'. The economic development of these separate colonies right up to Federation was a matter firmly guided by the state — not an Australian state but the British state and its colonial representatives. This involved everything from the earliest decisions about the location of convict settlements, through the practices of colonial administration and the development of transport infrastructure, to policy towards land tenure. It was not until Federation in 1901 that there was the possibility of regional policy by an Australian state. Therein lay a contradiction. On the one hand the newly adopted Constitution severely limited what the federal (Commonwealth) government could do in terms of location-specific interventions in the individual States. On the other hand, the federal government needed to implement regional policy as a precondition for national economic development, social equity and political cohesion. As Ronald May (1971) pointed out:

In Australia there were marked disparities in size, wealth and economic development between the colonies at Federation. In the process of national reorientation the small States suffered backwash effects from economic integration and their burden was increased by a national policy of developing manufacturing industry behind a protective tariff. In these circumstances, and having lost their major pre-Federation sources of revenue and facing a growing demand for national standards in taxation and the provision of social services, the governments of the smaller States began to find themselves in chronic financial difficulties.

These problems, and the policies to which they gave rise can be interpreted in terms of the distinction between horizontal and vertical imbalance in public finance. The quotation from May draws our attention mainly to the problem of *horizontal imbalance*, which has persisted in varying degrees throughout the century. This involves inequalities between the States. The State governments have had different fiscal capacities because of the different levels of economic development, with New South Wales and Victoria having a clear head-start over the others. The other States have had disabilities in tax-raising (e.g. because of lower *per capita* incomes) and/or disabilities in spending (e.g. because of higher costs of providing services to a more scattered population). The federal government addressed these problems through its own expenditure policies, giving special grants to the more disadvantaged States and, in 1933, establishing the Commonwealth Grants Commission as an institution for handling the inter-State distribution of funds. In more recent years though, the inequalities between the States have narrowed with the greater prosperity of Western Australia and Queensland, although Tasmania and South Australia remain laggards in terms of average income levels.

Attention has switched more to the issue of *vertical imbalance* in the system of federal-State finances. This involves inequality between the federal and State governments in their revenue-raising capacity relative to their expenditures. It came sharply into focus at the time of the second world war. The need for central coordination and financing of the war effort led to the Uniform Income Tax Agreement (1942) which, together with subsequent High Court decisions, put the bulk of tax-collecting powers in the hands of the federal government. Even since, the States have been reliant for the bulk of their funds on federal government grants, leading to a situation of vertical imbalance. It has been the focus of diverse twists and turns in federal-State financial relationships (Smith 1992). A system of Tax Reimbursement Grants was introduced when the States vacated their income taxing powers; later replaced by a system of Financial Assistance Grants, determined by a formula based on increases in population and a 'betterment' factor to improve the standard of public services. This system came to be a focus for the annual wrangling at the Premiers' Conference. It has been modified by various judgements of the Commonwealth Grants Commission about appropriate changes to the formula. Specific purpose grants increasingly replaced special grants, giving the federal government considerable control over the allocation of State funds to areas such as roads, housing, health, education, transport and urban development. Hence the charge that the States have tended to become spending agencies for the federal government, although the ideology and political priorities of State governments can lead to quite different types of public expenditure in practice.

There is a substantial tension here. On the one hand, there are recurrent proposals for a more decentralised system of federal-State financial relationships, generally described as 'new federalism'. This would involve the individual States being less reliant on tied grants, giving them direct access to a share of income tax revenues and the right to set tax rates above or below other States. On the other hand, there remains a strong centralist concern about the need for macroeconomic management and for uniformity of standards in various areas of economic and social policy.

The greater the vertical imbalance the greater is the capacity of the federal government to respond to horizontal imbalance. A measure of this potential is that the federal government collects about 80 per cent of the tax revenues but spends only about 50 per cent of the total outlays. The States collect only 20 per cent of the taxes but account for more than 40 per cent of total government spending. The combination of horizontal and vertical imbalance gives the federal government considerable scope (and justification) for the adoption of an explicit regional dimension in its expenditure policies. This emphasis on expenditure policies as the main instrument of regional policy in Australia is quite distinctive. The State governments are more highly dependent on the federal government for revenue transfers than is the case in other federal systems like Canada, Germany, Switzerland or the USA (Walsh 1992). By comparison, regionally differentiated price policies, development controls and policies encouraging mobility of factors of production have been less well developed in Australia, partly because of constitutional limits on the powers of the federal government. The failure to develop systematic industry policies, despite the commitment to do so in the 1983 Accord between the federal Labor government and the trade union movement, has also left regional policy without that potential link-up. In these circumstances the dominance of expenditure policy over other potential regional policy instruments is not surprising.

Anyway, even without an explicit commitment to spatial redistribution, fiscal policy always involves some *implicit* regional policy. A nationally uniform progressive income tax means that regions with an above average proportion of upper-income residents contribute a higher share of total revenues than those with more poor people. On the other hand, regions with more unemployed people or other welfare recipients normally receive a proportionately greater share of central government expenditures (other things being equal). The transfers are more in proportion to the expenditure needs of each region than to their financial contributions. So, some degree of interregional equity is generated automatically even in the absence of discretionary policies targeted at that goal (just as macroeconomic policy embraces both automatic and discretionary fiscal stabilisers). Both automatic and discretionary redistributions have operated in the Australian case over a long period. However, the reduction in the progressivity of the overall income tax scale which took place in the 1980s has tended to reduce the extent of inter-State redistribution through fiscal policy in recent years.

Implicit regional policy is a general feature of all government policies. *Tariff policy* provides one example. This policy is nationally uniform, involving the imposition of a levy on particular classes of imported goods. However, because tariffs vary between different types of goods, they have a differential impact on regional economies. In the Australian case, tariffs have applied particularly to manufactured products such as cars and textiles, clothing and footwear. The Australian States vary in their emphasis on the manufacturing industries which compete with these imports. Hence the policy effectively discriminates between them. To take the extreme cases, 13.8 per cent of Victoria's employment was strongly protected by tariffs at the time the federal Labor government came to power in the 1980s, compared with only 1.7 per cent of employment in the Northern Territory (Bureau of Industry Economics 1985). In these circumstances it was evident that a policy of tariff reduction would have its most adverse impacts on Victoria and, to a slightly lesser degree, on NSW and South Australia which have also relied strongly on manufacturing industry. No wonder that this came to be a source of pronounced political disarticulation (as discussed in Stilwell 1992: ch. 8). No wonder too that Victoria (with 11.9 per cent unemployment in June 1992) and South Australia (12.5 per cent), together with Tasmania (12.2 per cent) headed the league table of casualties as the recession deepened in the early 1990s. Tariff reductions were not the only factor involved in the regional economic inequalities, of course, but it is illustrative of how national economic policies can have differential regional effects.

Industry policy provides a second example. The steel industry plan which operated between 1983 and 1987 was simultaneously an industry policy and a regional policy, given the spatial concentration of the industry in Wollongong, Newcastle and Whyalla. Overall, its main impacts were in NSW. The car industry plan, on similar reasoning, has had disproportionate significance for South Australia and Victoria. The textiles, clothing and footwear industry plan affects all States since the industry is relatively dispersed, but has disproportionate significance for Victoria and Tasmania and, within them, for particular localities like Wangaratta and Launceston where local dependence on the industry has been strong. In general, there is a clear case for recognising this interdependence of industry policy and regional policy and using the combination as a means of tackling concentrations of regional unemployment and assisting regions with the processes of economic adjustment. Indeed, in current conditions of structural economic change, it is this combination of industry policy and regional policy which is potentially more powerful than the more conventional policy instruments considered earlier in this chapter.

Immigration policy provides a third example of implicit regional policy. Here the influence on *urban* growth patterns is very evident. Changes in the volume of immigration have a more major impact on the population growth of the metropolitan areas than on non-metropolitan areas. The focus on Sydney and Melbourne as the initial arrival and settlement points is particularly striking. Although the effect of immigration policy on the metropolitan/non-metropolitan population balance is greater than its effect on the distribution of economic activities between the States, the Sydney-Melbourne focus tends to make NSW and Victoria most immediately affected by changes in the annual intake. That is why concern with the pressures of urban development, including the housing crisis and growing urban congestion in those two major cities, has fuelled periodic calls for reductions in the annual immigration quota (Stilwell 1991).

These examples could be extended, although our knowledge of the spatial impacts of the different elements of government policy is generally poor. Take *monetary policy*, for example. Tight money and high interest rate polices, such as those adopted by the Australian government in the late 1980s, have very widespread economic and social costs. To the extent that high interest rates in that period exacerbated the crisis in the agricultural sector, the impact was disproportionately rural. However, high interest rates also hit particularly hard at the housing industry and at small business, impacting heavily on employment levels in the major urban areas, as noted in chapter 1. All of this illustrates the general observation of Lester Thurow (1989) that: 'macro-economic policies certainly have large impacts on regional economic development. Recessions differentially impact those regions where cyclical activities are located. High interest rate policies hurt these regions that specialise in capital intensive activities.'

Enough has been said to illustrate the importance and generality of implicit regional policies. One senior federal bureaucrat has even argued that, 'there would be little need for governments to have separate region-specific policies and programs if the resource implications of their existing programs ... took more account of the specific combinations of economic, environmental and social structure, circumstances, needs and potential that exist in Australia's local and regional economies' (Garlick 1991). That would not obviate the problem of general-ised recession caused by ill-judged macroeconomic policies, of course. What it would require is regional monitoring and budgeting by government departments as diverse as health, social security, employment, education, transport and communi-cation, primary industry, manufacturing industry, trade and commerce.

REGIONAL POLICY, RESTRUCTURING AND RIVALRY

Regional economic policy operates in a world of constant change. The relative fortunes of regions fluctuate for reasons beyond the control of the nation-state. The internationalisation of capital is a potent source of such dynamism, volatility and instability between and within regions. The resulting structural-spatial changes in turn impact back on public policy, particularly through implicit regional policies, generating new patterns of redistribution. State governments also respond with policies to deal with the new dimensions of competition.

This interconnection between changes in the prevailing economic conditions and changes in the character of regional policy is particularly evident in Australia. The policy changes in federal/State financial relations have taken place in the context of a wholesale restructuring of the Australian regional economy, initiated not by the state but by capital. The push for export-oriented resource developments and the growth of the financial services sector, to give just two examples, have had a substantial impact on the spatial structure of employment, as noted in chapter 1. Although the initiative in these restructurings has been in the hands of private capital — and transnational corporations in particular — Australian governments have also been closely involved. The 1970s saw the Liberal government under Malcolm Fraser making changes to economic and social policies which were designed to reduce the power of labour and to make Australia more attractive for foreign capital (Stilwell 1980). The Hawke government's Accord with the trade unions subsequently sought to generate economic growth by establishing a less volatile industrial relations climate with the cooperation of the labour movement (Stilwell 1986). In neither case was an explicit regional policy at the forefront of government concerns. However, there is an evident link between the form of structural economic change and the changing balance in the regional economy. For example, the focus on mineral resource development, particularly in Queensland and Western Australia, has linked these States more closely to other industrial countries, such as Japan, than to the relatively industrialised States in south-east Australia. Some foresaw these developments leading to a 'fragmentation of the nation state' (Stevenson 1977), although other analysts, with the benefit of a little more hindsight, have noted that the power of the mineral-based States in the federal system did not markedly increase as a result (Harman and Head 1982).

Perhaps the most general casualty of the last decade has been the commitment to resolving the imbalances in the process of structural change through economic policy. The liberal-Keynesian view of the appropriate role for the state has been radically challenged by the ascendancy of 'economic rationalism', emphasising the superiority of market forces over government intervention. Thus, the whole rationale of regional policy, as set out in early parts of this chapter, has been undercut. This is the point of stressing the connection between regional policy and Keynesianism, both at the level of ideology and in terms of available policy instruments. The two have tended to rise and fall together. This is not to say that regional policy disappeared with the ascendency of economic rationalism. As stressed earlier in this chapter, implicit regional policies are inescapable. Rather, the point is that the ascendant economic orthodoxies have tended to limit the role of the federal government in responding to structural economic change. The reluctance to implement an interventionist industry policy has simultaneously impeded the development of a systematic regional policy. This has thrown the burden of coping with an increasingly competitive environment onto the State governments.

How have the State governments responded to the growing competition for 'a slice of the action'? In an economic context of mobile capital, coupled with federal policies of fiscal austerity which have accentuated vertical imbalance, individual State governments have become ever more desperate to increase their regional share. Their responses fit readily into David Harvey's (1989b) taxonomy of the different aspects of regional competition. Drawing also on the analysis by Huxley and Berry (1990), these aspects can be identified as:

- Competition within the spatial division of *labour*. This involves the continuing quest to attract capital investment for local industry in an increasingly competitive inter-regional and international economic climate, and in circumstances of continued decline in overall manufacturing industry.
- Competition within the spatial division of *consumption*. What is at issue here is the competitive bidding process for consumption expenditures. Examples range from invest-ments in suburban shopping centre complexes to the quest to host major international events like EXPO (Queensland), the America's Cup (WA), the Racing Car Grand Prix (SA), the Olympic Games (NSW) ...
- Competition for *command* functions. This concerns inter-State rivalry to be the centre for financial institutions and regional headquarters of multinational corporations. It is a process in which Sydney seems to have led the way for NSW against the other States, albeit not without competition from Melbourne and, increasingly, from Brisbane.
- Competition for *redistribution*. Yes, the jostling for federal funds continues, both for revenue grants and direct govern-

ment expenditures (although not as strikingly regionally differentiated as in the USA, where the location of federal defence budget expenditures has been a major influence on the pattern of regional economic development).

STATE VERSUS THE REGIONS?

A curious mixture of competitive processes and policy commitments characterises contemporary regional policy. The question remains: does the Australian evidence on this aspect of public policy lend support to any of the general theories of the state set out in the preceding chapter?

The most obvious contender is the liberal-pluralist view of the state. There has been a general commitment to inter-regional equity through federal-State financial relationships and some evident measure of success. There has been a balancing of regional demands and some degree of coherence in the re-distributive policies. However, there are also elements of arbitrariness through the spatial effects of other policies where the regional objectives are not explicit.

A managerialist view of the state also has some apparant relevance. While regional policy has not been associated with the development of a major body of 'gatekeepers' or a particularly distinctive segment of the state elite at the federal level, bodies such as the Commonwealth Grants Commission have played an important role in shaping regional shares in government expenditures. More generally, it is evident that, because federal-State financial relationships are so central, regional policy is a product of the internal machinations within the state apparatus.

The Marxist view of the state also has some support to the extent that inter-State competition leads each State government, whatever the political complexion of the party in power, to be subservient to the needs of capital. Building power-stations to provide electricity below cost to potential investors in aluminium-smelting projects is an obvious case in point dating back to the 'resources boom'.

Finally, the Australian experience lends MOST support to the revisionist view of the state, in that the federal government's role in regional policy has reflected the competition between different fractions of capital and labour under changing economic conditions. The state has been an arena of struggle. The changing forms of policy have also reflected changes in the dominant ideologies about economic management — from Keynesianism to 'economic rationalism'. As such, regional policy is far from being a technocratic exercise in selecting the appropriate mix of policy instruments for the achievement of agreed national objectives. Rather, how the state deals with the consequences of the regional restructuring of capital — whether through accommodation, redirection or resistence — becomes the key political question.

FURTHER READING

Gore (1984): a critical reconsideration of the conceptual basis of regional analysis and associated regional policies.

Stilwell (1989): a description of regional economic policies in Britain, Italy and Australia and a commentary on the demise of the sort of 'Lib-Lab' reformist policies discussed in this chapter.

Head (1986): on fiscal federalism and different State economic strategies in Australia.

Alonso (1989): reflections on regional economic theory and policy in the light of contemporary regional restructuring.

10

Decentralisation Policy

What about the balance between city and country? How does public policy impinge on this important dimension of urban and regional development. Is rural-urban imbalance a problem anyway? To the extent that urban size is a key root of a wide array of urban problems, decentralisation policy offers an apparently obvious solution. However, if there is no clear basis on which it can be agreed that cities are too big, decentralisation policy loses its rationale. It is not surprising that this aspect of public policy has been the focus for continuous controversy. In Australia, with its pronounced degree of metropolitan primacy in each State, the issue of decentralisation has been particularly important. Arguably, it has been the key issue in public policy towards urban and regional development.

Historically, decentralisation policy in Australia seems to have had the properties of a miracle cure. Initially favoured as a means to encourage rural settlement, it also came to be regarded as a means of improving the nation's capacity for military defence. Then, in the 1960s, decentralisation was promoted as a means of alleviating the growing problems of traffic congestion in the major urban areas. By the early 1970s other urban environmental concerns, such as atmospheric pollution, buttressed these arguments. Gough Whitlam's government pursued decentralisation as one aspect of its commitment to a more egalitarian society. As the Minister for Urban and Regional Development put it, 'the faster a city grows around a single centre the greater will be the inequities in its population and the greater will be the segregation amongst its communities' (Uren 1973). Then the decentralisation issue came back into focus in the 1980s as a result of the intense problems of land and house price inflation in the major cities: non-metropolitan land and housing is certainly cheaper. Through into the 1990s, decentralisation retains a shadowy role in public policy pronouncements, not least in its advocacy by the Labor Party in NSW. It sometimes seems that decentralisation policy has achieved the status of a general panacea both for the problems of urban overgrowth and the problems of non-metropolitan neglect. Yet it is a policy which has not been vigorously pursued in practice. This paradox needs to be unravelled.

This chapter explores decentralisation from theoretical, historical and contemporary policy perspectives. The necessary steps are:

- appraising the theory of optimum city size;
- considering alternative arguments for decentralisation policy;
- examining the available policy instruments and strategies;
- evaluating the Australian experience;
- analysing the economic, cultural and political dimensions of decentralisation policy in practice;
- re-casting the issue — from dualism to mosaic.

AN OPTIMUM CITY SIZE?

Being for or against big cities is guaranteed to provoke lively debates. Critics point to the array of problems discussed in the first chapters of this book and link them directly with city size. Defenders of big cities contend that this methodology is spurious, that it confuses city size with more general characteristics of modern society. They argue, to the contrary, that urbanisation continues to be an ingredient in the march forward from 'the idiocy of rural life'.

These competing positions have had articulate proponents. G.K. Chesterton (1926) expressed the anti-urban view many years ago when he wrote of 'the growth of cities that drain and dry up the countryside, the growth of dense dependent population incapable of finding their own food ... the herding of humanity into nomadic masses whose very homes are homeless'. Federick Engels (1873) had earlier asserted the need to confront the urban problem as part of the socialist political project, claiming that 'civilisation has left us the legacy of huge cities and to get rid of them will cost us much in time and effort, but it will be necessary to get rid of them, and this will be done'. On the other hand, Robert Park (1967), inspiration for the development of the urban ecology research tradition wrote enthusiastically of cities as 'the most prodigious of human artefacts . . . the workshops of civilisation and ... the natural habitats of civilised man'.

From the more narrow perspective of economic analysis, two classic positions were laid down in the books by Max Neutze (1965) and Harry Richardson (1973). Neutze points to the tendencies which cause cities to expand beyond an optimum size, including the pervasiveness of negative externalities in cities, and the failure of a market system to ensure optimum spatial allocation of resources where there is inadequate information, lack of foresight or problems of coordination in location decisions. Richardson, on the other hand, claims that the case is not compelling, and that city size is better regarded as an 'intervening variable' rather than a root cause of economic and social problems. The latter position echoes the distinction between problems *in* cities and problems *of* cities (Stilwell 1993: ch. 2). It is also reflected in the conclusion of Hansen (1976) that, 'although survey results indicate that concern about human settlement patterns is widespread, almost nothing is known about the priorities people attach to spatial distribution issues in relation to other social and economic problems. Moreover, it may be more advisable to attack many problems directly rather than by trying to alter the size of places.'

In the light of these conflicting views a brief review of the arguments and evidence is appropriate. How, if at all, can a case for decentralisation policy, based on the assertion of an optimum city size, be justified?

One means of identifying an optimum city size concerns the average costs of providing *infrastructure* (schools, hospitals, sewerage, transport systems, electricity supply, etc.). There is some evidence that these costs tend to take the form of a U-shaped curve in relation to the size of the urban area. For small settlements the average costs *per capita* are high because initial costs are substantial and there are no economies of scale. The spreading of infrastructure costs over a larger population then leads to declining average cost. This is eventually offset when further urban growth makes the provision of infrastructure increasingly costly because of the high price of land and the complexity of reconstructing the facilities in the existing urban area to cope with the further expansion. In Sydney, for example, it has been estimated that the additional cost of providing serviced land for further outer western expansion had risen to more than $60,000 per unit by 1990 (Howe 1991). However, there is no general law which dictates that infrastructure cost provisions will conform to a conventional U-shape. Moreover, the argument is based on a rather narrow conception of the costs involved in further urban growth.

Broadening the conception of costs generates major conceptual and empirical problems. Ideally, we would want to identify and measure a wide range of costs and benefits associated with different city sizes — in effect, an overall *cost-benefit analysis* to identify the optimum city size. Neutze's (1965) classic study went part way towards this by estimating how much more traffic congestion costs were generated by adding an extra population to Sydney, by comparison with medium-size and small towns like Wollongong and Wagga Wagga. Other studies have tried to explore the connections between urban size and a range of other social costs, including the incidence of crime and indicators of psycho-social stress (Herbert & Smith 1979). On the benefits side, there is also the view that large cities may act as seedbeds for economic growth by providing a dynamic business milieu which is not typically found in smaller towns. Also, from a consumer's point of view, there are threshold levels below which towns typically do not offer various amenities, whether they be opera houses and cultural centres, sporting facilities or specialised retail services.

On all these matters, there is an enormous array of argument and evidence. However, the overall patterns are unclear. On items for which there is empirical evidence, the correlations with urban size are seldom strong. On other items it is difficult to frame the hypothesis in a readily quantifiable form. And the overall weighing of all the costs and benefits which would be necessary for a calculation of the optimum size is quite impossible. There are all the well-known problems of cost-benefit analysis (Self 1975) plus the difficulty of compiling the relevant costs and benefits for a range of city sizes. Moreover, as Charles Gore (1984) notes, 'a single measure of net benefits ... must be based on the researcher's own assumptions of, say, the relative costliness of pollution and crime. And if the distributional effects of city size are to be measured, the costs and benefits must be aggregated for different groups according to their goodness or badness.' There can be no generally agreed resolution of such fundamental conceptual difficulties and personal judgements.

An alternative approach seeks to escape from these problems by considering an optimum city size *distribution*. Rather than specifying a single optimum city size, this involves identifying a range of city sizes which any one national (or regional) economy should have. *If* an apposite array of city sizes can be defined, then presumably policy can be designed to fill in the gaps. In pursuit of this goal geographers have put much energy into the identification of empirical regularities in the city size distribution between nations. The rank-size rule stemming from the original contribution by Zipf (1941) is a case in point; but quite why any such regular pattern should have normative content remains unclear. Pragmatically, this chain of reasoning comes down to arguing the case for decentralisation policy in a country like Australia on the grounds that it has relatively few medium sized cities intermediate between the major State capitals and the numerous small country towns. The contention is that it would enhance locational choice (both for businesses and consumers) if the gap were filled. However, the case lacks conceptual clarity: it adds the problems of inferring what is an ideal distribution to all the empirical difficulties of measuring the costs and benefits of alternative city sizes.

An appropriate interim conclusion is that decentralisation policy lacks a clear foundation in theoretical and empirical analysis of optimum city size. The focus on size abstracts from other aspects of urban development which influence efficiency, equity and quality of life, for better or worse. These aspects include location, type of city, internal spatial form and class structure. However, while this interim conclusion knocks away one of the props from the general theoretical case for decentralisation policy, it does not destroy it. A basic concern does remain — that there *is* something about large cities which is appropriately a focus for public policy.

ALTERNATIVE ARGUMENTS FOR DECENTRALISATION

The city size issue may be approached quite differently. From a *distributional* perspective, for example, the question becomes 'optimality for whom?'. Is there a tendency — as implied by the quotation from Tom Uren cited earlier in this chapter — for large cities to disadvantage the lower income groups? And how, if at all, would decentralisation offset the processes generating and compounding economic inequalities? Who would be decentralised, and what would be the distribution of costs and benefits? What form of decentralisation would be most conducive to spatial equity? Exploring these issues can help to provide a more distributional, or class-based, rationale for decentralisation.

Likewise, an *environmentalist* approach to decentralisation can be developed. To the extent that large cities are associated with heavy energy usage and the generation of pollution, a partial solution to the environmental crisis may be sought through decentralisation policy. It would necessarily be partial for the various reasons identified in chapter 5. A spatial redistribution of environmentally degrading activities does not cause them to cease degrading the environment. However, together with the restructuring of cities on more ecological principles, this aspect of spatial restructuring can be expected to be an increasingly prominent concern as the environmental crisis intensifies. The quest for ecologically sustainable development must necessarily embrace the concern with appropriate spatial form.

Defence considerations have also loomed large in earlier discussions of decentralisation policy and the appropriateness of large cities. The vulnerability of large cities to military attack has been the main focus. The decimation of many British and European cities by bombing during the second world war gave particular impetus to this concern a half-century ago. It is also worth recalling that, in Australia, the entry of Japanese submarines into Sydney Harbour did actually lead to some rapid 'spontaneous decentralisation' at the time — away from the harbourside suburbs to the Blue Mountains! Governments have been understandably loath to stress strategic defense considerations in their more recent public pronouncements on regional policy. In any case, it is doubtful that they have quite the same force in an era of potential nuclear war in which global rather than regional destruction is a likely outcome.

Broader *political* and *ethical* considerations may also need to be taken into account. In an earlier book (Stilwell 1974), I argued that decentralisation policy is important as one dimension of a broader programme of decentralisation of political power. The general theme is not novel. In his definition of the optimum city size of 5040 persons, Plato's main consideration had been the size of a forum in which all (male) citizens would be able to efficiently contribute to the democratic process. Social anarchist Peter Kropotkin's case for decentralisation was based on a view of the perfectability of humankind once society was radically reorganised on the basis of cooperative communities, with self-management in place of hierachial and authoritarian social and economic institutions (Breitbart 1981). In China, Mao Tse-tung's espousal of decentralisation was linked to his view that the dualism of city and country, like that between mental and manual labour, industry and agriculture, must be transcended in creating a new society. Finally, if all that is not enough, there is the view that the development of autonomous local communities is part of a divine plan — hence 'God is for Decentralisation'! (Bhave 1974).

There is a panoply of issues here, ranging from the purely financial aspects of infrastructure provision through to environmental, strategic, political and even spiritual considerations in the decentralisation debate. It is hardly surprising that social scientists have been unable to weigh up the issues in an objective calculus. This gives scope for politicians to interpret the case for decentralisation policy with considerable elasticity.

POLICY INSTRUMENTS AND STRATEGIES

Certainly, there is no shortage of *policy instruments* which can be used in the pursuit of decentralisation. For the most part, they are the same regional policy instruments described in the immediately preceding chapter, but applied to deal with the balance between metropolitan areas and non-metropolitan areas, rather than the balance between States. For example:

- State governments may use their expenditure policies to allocate more funds *per capita* to non-metropolitan areas for infrastructure, services or capital works associated with new decentralised economic development;
- price policies may be introduced, such as spatially differentiated payroll taxes, subsidies and loans which are used as sticks and carrots to encourage businesses to locate in non-metropolitan areas;
- controls on building and land-use may be used as a means of prohibiting further investment in the metropolitan areas, in the hope that this will lead it to be relocated in non-metropolitan areas (rather than to be relocated overseas or to be abandoned altogether);
- policies may seek to facilitate mobility e.g. by giving allowances to defray the costs of moving house (although, given the major differentials between metropolitan and non-metropolitan housing prices, the material incentive for mobility is large already—as long as there is no intention of ever moving back to the big city!).

Two strategic concerns also need to be addressed in translating the principles of decentralisation into effective policy. The first involves the spatial definition of decentralisation. To take an example from NSW, we have to ask which of three *scales* of relocation is properly the subject for decentralisation policies— building up of secondary nuclei like Parramatta or Chatswood to offset the focus on Sydney's CBD; building satellite 'new towns' like the Macarthur growth centre at Campbelltown within commuting distance of the metropolitan area; or more distant developments State-wide in places like Bathurst-Orange, Dubbo, or Armidale. In the subsequent discussion the third dimension is given most attention, since the first, and to some extent the second, constitute issues of urban policy (or intra-metropolitan planning) which are the subject of the next chapter.

The other strategic concern involves the choice between *dispersed* decentralisation and policies focusing on *growth centres*. Building up a few decentralised urban growth centres has advantages over a more dispersed policy which moves people and employment out of the big cities, out anywhere. It requires a deliberate commitment in choosing between rival localities, and is correspondingly politically contentious. However, it facilitates the development of initial scale economies and maximises the propulsive growth effects. Ultimately, it also contains the contradictory potential to lay the foundation for new urban problems as these propulsive growth effects set in and new centre-periphery inequalities are generated. Meanwhile, leaders of local government and local businesses in other non-metropolitan regions may be resentful about being overlooked in the growth centre selection process. It is a difficult strategic choice.

DECENTRALISATION POLICY IN AUSTRALIA

The Australian experience illustrates the use of various policy instruments, the influences shaping decentralisation strategies, and some of the dilemmas and contradictions. Examining that experience also gives insight into the political and economic interests involved in decentralisation in practice and casts further light on general questions about the nature of the state, as discussed in chapter 8.

Australia is certainly a prime candidate for decentralisation in that the overwhelming feature of the distribution of economic activity within each State is the high degree of metropolitan primacy. This needs to be set in historical context, as a feature shaped by the early days of European settlement in the continent. The capital cities served as administrative centres, and as ports for the import of labour and for the export of primary produce, particularly wool. Service industries and such manufacturing activity as developed to supply local needs were also heavily concentrated there. Thus, the administrative, commercial and industrial functions tended to mutually reinforce metropolitan primacy. Unlike Europe, where a scattered population *preceded* the development of railways and other modern technology, the situation in Australia was not conducive to the development of village settlement, since large agricultural areas could be served by a modern transport system. Certainly, country towns did develop, but the radial focus of the transport networks, coupled with practical impediments such as variations in railways gauges between the colonies, focused the commercial activities on the capital cities. In these circumstances the development of metropolitan primacy within each colony was inexorable, though the same forces simultaneously ensured that metropolitan primacy would *not* be a feature of the continent as a whole.

In the twentieth century, consolidation of this uneven pattern of development has taken place. Industrial enterprises seeking large pools of labour, access to the markets and to ancillary services have shown a marked preference for metropolitan locations. The growth of the various State government bureaucracies has reinforced the process. These two forces led to a growing metropolitan dominance which was particularly marked during the first 25 years after the second world war. The share of total NSW State population in Sydney rose from 55 to 59 per cent between 1947 and 1971: it had only been 36 per cent in 1901. Corresponding figures for post-war growth in the other States were 63 to 68 per cent in Victoria, 36 to 45 per cent in Queensland, 55 to 62 per cent in Western Australia, 59 to 69 per cent in South Australia and 30 to 33 per cent in Tasmania.

A growing concern with decentralisation was a predictable consequence of this metropolitan dominance. Steering growth away from the major urban areas had long been seen as part of the general objective of 'populating the interior'. After the second world war, these concerns intensified, and there was a marked increase of interest in the decentralisation issue. This was encouraged by the federal Labor government in the 1944–49 period through the activities of the Department of Post-War

Reconstruction (Coombs 1981). In New South Wales and Victoria the commitment to decentralisation was on-going. Various forms of financial assistance were given to local authorities for the provision of community and industrial services, and to decentralising firms so as to reduce their costs of production and distribution (Searle 1981). Numerous individual State government reports reconfirmed the commitment to decentralisation. A specially convened group of federal and State government officials endorsed it, albeit tentatively, as an objective of national policy (Committee of Commonwealth/State Officials on Decentralisation 1972). The Labor government backed it with federal funds in the period 1972–75, concentrating mainly on particular growth centres such as Albury-Wodonga and Bathurst-Orange, the former being a particularly important experiment in cooperative federalism because it straddled the boundary between two States (NSW and Victoria).

However, after the demise of the Whitlam government, federal government promotion of decentralisation policy was abandoned. Neither the Fraser nor the Hawke governments had any enthusiasm for involvement in this type of policy. Rather, they evidently made the judgement that decentralisation policy should 'stay in the too hard basket'. This is understandable. Changing the distribution of population and economic activity is a long business, requiring big up-front government expenditure on infrastructure and the cooperation of capitalist investors. Non-metropolitan population growth had been burgeoning anyway in the 1980s and early 90s, especially in coastal areas associated with tourism and retirement. Even the federal government's revival of interest in urban policies in 1991–2, associated with Deputy Prime Minister Brian Howe's push for the 'Building Better Cities' programme, effectively side-stepped the decentralisation issue in favour of urban consolidation (a theme to which we return in chapter 12).

State government policies towards decentralisation have also been varied. Only in NSW and Victoria has the decentralisation commitment been substantial. In other States 'decentralisation' has often been interpreted as changing the balance between south-east mainland Australia and Western Australia, South

Australia, Queensland and Tasmania, effectively redefining it as an issue of *inter-State rivalry*. Even in NSW and Victoria the commitment to decentralisation has not been without contradictions. The location of the NSW government's own Department of Decentralisation in the heart of Sydney's CBD was for many years a striking case in point! Nevertheless, various services, grants and loans have been made available to decentralising firms on a case-by-case basis. Regionally differentiated payroll tax was also introduced in the 1970s in NSW and in Victoria: in NSW, for example, companies in the Sydney metropolitan area had to pay the full tax, but companies in the band around Sydney stretching from Port Stephens through Maitland, Lake Macquarie, Gosford-Wyong, Blue Mountains, and Bowral to Kiama were able to claim 50 per cent rebate, while firms further afield in the State could claim 100 per cent rebate. These State policies were substantially restructured in the 1980s: the NSW Liberal government effectively marginalised decentralisation relative to the broader concerns with promoting big investment projects through its Office of State Development, while the Labor government of Victoria abandoned its commitment to decentralisation policy in the mid 1980s, preferring to rely on industry policy as the vehicle for economic restructuring.

Evaluating the overall effectiveness of this history of decentralisation policies is difficult. As with the effects of any government policy, it is hard to know what would have happened if different policies had been pursued. To isolate the effects of a particular policy is extraordinarily difficult. Furthermore, given that all public policies have an implicit spatial dimension, it is difficult to disentangle the effects of those few policies whose spatial dimension is explicit. The uneven participation of various governments, federal and State, further confuses the issue.

Nevertheless, it seems that the overall effects of decentralisation policies have been marginal. To take the case of NSW, particular firms have been steered to non-metropolitan locations, one university was established in a country town (Armidale) — long before the up-grading of existing colleges of advanced education to university status — and some government employment has been relocated (e.g. the Central Mapping Authority at

Bathurst and the Department of Agriculture at Orange). However, in terms of offsetting the metropolitan dominance of population and economic activity, the impacts of policy have been modest. This is not to say that no major urban developments have occurred outside the major metropolitan areas. Taking the nation as a whole, four types of non-metropolitan development are strikingly evident — the establishment and growth of Canberra as a national capital; towns such as Broken Hill and Mt Isa based on resource extraction; towns like Gladstone based on mineral processing; and areas such as the Gold Coast, the Sunshine Coast and the north coast of NSW based on the tourist industry and retirement resettlement. The growth of decentralised growth centres like Albury-Wodonga and Bathurst-Orange are modest achievements by comparison.

The usual explanations of decentralisation policy's ineffectiveness are the reluctance of people to leave the metropolitan areas and the additional cost to business associated with non-metropolitan locations. However, neither explanation is persuasive. Survey of people's attitudes to moving to non-metropolitan areas reveal predominantly positive responses; while analyses of the costs of industrial location typically indicate a greater spatial elasticity than the current imbalance between metropolitan and non-metropolitan economic development would suggest (Stilwell and Johnson 1991). Pertinent in this context is Stuart Holland's (1976) argument about the limitations of liberal regional policies in a world of transnational capital. Firms *do* decentralise from the metropolitan areas. However, by 'striding the globe in seven-league boots', they often step over non-metropolitan regions and resettle in the most-developed regions of less-developed nations.

What can we conclude from these reflections on the experience of decentralisation? Most obviously, that it is very difficult to reverse the tendency to metropolitan primacy through piecemeal policies. The dominance of the big cities is the legacy of complex historical, geographical and political factors. It has come to be a cumulative phenomenon because individual capitalist enterprises have sought to capture the economic advantages of a metropolitan location and their locational interdependence reinforces centre-periphery inequalities. The growth of State bureaucracies in the metropolitan centres has consolidated the process. Meanwhile, the nominal commitment to decentralisation policy has been uneven and largely ineffective as a counter to the cumulative agglomeration pressures. The policy has not been vigorously pursued in practice. Indeed, its vigorous pursuit in any one individual State tends to run counter to the objective of maximising regional economic growth, since the more locational constraints are imposed the more likely is capital to take flight elsewhere. With the increased mobility of capital on an international scale, non-metropolitan regions tend to be by-passed by structural economic change. These interacting aspects of *federalism* and *capitalism* help to explain why the state as a whole does not play a leading role in shaping regional development towards a more decentralised outcome.

ECONOMIC, CULTURAL AND POLITICAL DIMENSIONS

How can this experience of decentralisation in Australia be interpreted in terms of the competing views of the state discussed in chapter 8? The nominal commitment to decentralisation policy by at least some federal and State governments gives some support to the liberal-pluralist view of the state in that it embodies a concern with general community welfare (e.g. spatial equity and the negative externalities associated with urban living). However, the failure to deliver substantial reforms suggests important limits on the processes of 'popular sovereignty'. A managerialist view of the state also has some credibility, to the extent that State bureaucracies have acted as gatekeepers in apportioning funds between decentralising firms seeking subsidies, although the overall funding and bureaucratic involvement has been relatively small.

In general, the Marxist view of the state as serving the needs of capital, while seeking legitimacy through its apparent concern with community welfare, appears most consistent with the evidence. When the needs of capital are consistent with non-metropolitan development, as in the case of resource-based towns, some decentralisation has taken place. Particular aspects of decentralisation policy have also aided the process of capital accumulation (e.g. capital subsidies) while others have facilitated the reproduction of labour power (e.g. labour subsidies). Yet, as Glen Searle (1981) notes, 'the prevailing ideology of competitive capitalism' sets limits on state action, in this case limiting the extent of subsidy so as to prevent the spatial pattern of capital becoming too 'inefficient'. There is little evidence that the highly skewed distribution of population and industry between metropolitan and non-metropolitan ares has generated a crisis of capital accumulation: as such there has been little call for the state to play a more actively interventionist role as 'crisis manager' in this aspect of regional policy.

However, an adequate explanation of the role of the state in decentralisation policy needs to go beyond economic reasoning and take account of cultural and electoral influences. The *cultural tradition of anti-urbanism* is a case in point. This is a distinctively British tradition which has its roots in the disdain of an aristocratic 'upper class', whose socio-economic position is based on rural landownership, for the 'middle class' of urban capitalists with its nouveau-riche life-styles. It also embodies a reaction against the squalor and degradation historically associated with the joint processes of industrialisation and urbanisation. This anti-urban cultural tradition is discernible in English literature (Williams 1975) and in the 'garden city' movement initiated by Ebenezer Howard (as described in the following chapter). It is reflected also in the continued quest by the upwardly mobile to establish their 'country house', however modest in practice and however mock the Tudor, as a symbol of disdain for the commercial vulgarity of the city.

The transfer of this cultural tradition to Australia is incomplete, resulting in an Antipodean compromise of sprawling low-density suburbs which are neither fully urban nor rural. The physical harshness of much of the non-metropolitan areas in Australia is the obvious explanation for the compromise: the concept of 'countryside', which in England conjures up conceptions of a much more mellow and hospitable terrain, has much less applicability 'down-under'! Yet the unsatisfactory character of the Australian suburban compromise generates a recurrent interest in the possibility of establishing a wider range of settlement options. To be 'in tune' with these social concerns requires the state to keep decentralisation policy on the agenda.

The *electoral* basis of decentralisation is more down-to-earth. The advocacy of decentralisation by political parties vying for office appears as a win-win situation. It appeals to country electorates on the basis that more funds will be steered in their direction for infrastructure improvements and the promotion of economic growth. It appeals to urban electorates on the basis that decentralisation will syphon off the growth pressures that recurrently threaten the amenity of urban living. This seems neat, although it doesn't always pan out that way in practice.

None of the major Australian political parties is consistent in its support. The most obvious backer, the National Party (formerly Country Party), has its electoral base in country areas many of which are depopulating, so it faces a long-run decline unless it can maintain an electoral 'gerrymander' or increase the proportion of people living in country areas. But there is simultaneous fear that an active decentralisation policy would bring in electors who do not support the Nationals, so their political heartland would be lost anyway. The fear of an influx of ALP-voting workers in decentralised growth centres is a case in point, although it is one which has dissipated in recent years with the general demise of employment in manufacturing industry, whether metropolitan or non-metropolitan. The Liberal Party meanwhile has a recurrent, albeit not consistent, ideological aversion to the sort of government intervention involved in decentralisation policy. For its part, the ALP has tended to focus political attention on marginal urban electorates, frequently in the outer-metropolitan areas which are expanding as a result of the continued urban growth. It has been the most vigorous exponent of decentralisation policy, but its vigour has been tempered by the pragmatic concern with servicing the needs of the expanding urban areas.

For all political parties, there is the problem noted by Searle (1981) that 'the selection of one (non-metropolitan) area as the location for a growth centre could alienate voters elsewhere'. Also, it is pertinent to recall the reflection by France and Hughes (1972) on the political process involved: 'It has been said that a policy of decentralisation will take fifteen years to take hold. In Australia that means a span of five federal elections and five state elections. What electorate would have such staying power?' Yes, more than fifteen years later, a 'we told you so' would be in order!

These considerations help to explain why decentralisation policy has had a recurrent presence in public policy debates, but is seldom translated into consistent and vigorous policy. In Max Neutze's (1965) prescient phrase, decentralisation has been 'everybody's policy but nobody's programme'. Indeed, it seems to have taken a step backwards in recent years in that it is no longer everybody's policy. The concern with the 'urban crisis' has not abated. The need for revitalisation of rural areas also remains strong. However, conventional decentralisation policy, despite its economic and cultural basis, seems out of tune with the processes of contemporary spatial-structural change.

FROM DUALISM TO MOSAIC?

The simple dichotomy between metropolitan and non-metropolitan regions used throughout this chapter has become increasingly difficult to sustain. There is growing evidence of a re-focusing of population growth towards areas like the Gold Coast, the Sunshine Coast and the north coast of NSW. These areas do not fit neatly into either the 'city' or 'country' categories.

As in some other countries, some spontaneous elements of 'counter-urbanisation' are visible (Champion 1989). These are more to do with individual re-location, often involving complex commuting patterns, than the product of public policies for de-centralisation. The metropolitan/non-metropolitan dichotomy is being breached by structural economic changes and new communications technologies (Stilwell 1992: ch. 12).

The focus on the metropolitan/non-metropolitan dualism also obscures significant intra-regional variations. These quite properly need to be taken into account in assessing any region's suitability for economic development. Rob Carter (1983) has suggested the following typology, reflecting the variety of regional categories and their relationships to economic re-structuring in recent years:

- restructuring agricultural regions, based on the processing of agricultural products e.g. the Riverina (NSW), Goulburn Valley (NSW);
- remote resource development regions e.g. the Pilbara (Western Australia);
- urban-based resource development regions e.g. Gladstone (Queensland), Portland, Latrobe Valley (Victoria), Hunter Valley (NSW);
- restructuring basic manufacturing regions e.g. Wollongong, Geelong, Newcastle, Whyalla;
- environmentally sensitive regions e.g. south-west Tasmania, NSW rain forests, much of the Northern Territory;
- warm-climate coastal regions attractive for tourism and retirement e.g. Gosford-Wyong (NSW), Gold Coast, Sunshine Coast (Queensland);
- underdeveloped regions: remote, sparsely populated areas.

How to achieve balanced development in the face of this diversity of regional needs and potentials? A more 'tailored' approach to decentralisation and regional development policy is implied, replacing the conventional metropolitan/non-metropolitan dualism with a more complex mosaic. This situates the decentralisation issue in a broader framework of regional economic policies. Equally, it links it to a reconsideration of policies towards intra-urban development, an issue to which we turn in the following chapter.

FURTHER READING

Neutze (1965) and Richardson (1973): classic studies for and against decentralisation policy – a tale of two city sizes!

Searle (1981): an attempt to interpret the Australian policy experience in terms of theories of the state.

Carter (1983): a review of appropriate policies in contemporary conditions of regional economic restructuring.

Murphy & Burnley (1990): on demographic and economic factors influencing infrastructure planning and regional policy.

11

Urban Policy

Urban policy is the most contentious aspect of the state's participation in shaping the spatial form of development. It is in the cities that the economic, social and environmental problems are most visible, although not necessarily more severe, and where the conflicts associated with the provision of public services and the regulation of private interests are most pronounced. By comparison, the two broader spatial dimensions of policy — regional policy and decentralisation policy — seem rather removed from the day-to-day concerns of most people. The two preceding chapters have argued their strategic importance in reshaping Australia. However, it is urban policy that is the focus for recurrent demands on the state as planner, regulator and provider. In a predominantly urban society like Australia, the success or otherwise of the state in responding to these often-conflicting demands has a major bearing on the overall quality of life and the political process.

This chapter seeks to analyse urban policy by using a similar methodology to that adopted in the preceding two chapters. This involves:

- examining the rationale of urban policy;
- identifying the nature of urban planning, with particular reference to Sydney as a case-study;
- examining the relationship between the three tiers of government involved in urban policy;
- considering the implications for the analysis of the state.

In effect, this involves the exploration of two competing hypothesis. One is that urban policy can make important contributions to solving economic and social problems. This is reflected, for example, in the observation by Spearritt and DeMarco (1988), that 'imaginative planning can make Sydney a better city for all its citizens' (although they note that the record to date has been very uneven). The other view, more critical, was captured in Leonie Sandercock's (1975) conception of urban planning as a 'case study of ruling-class operations and capitalism at work'. It is expressed more wittily in the words of cartoonist Bruce Petty (1976): 'The importance of town planning has long been appreciated and careful research, co-operation and ingenuity among land-owners, sub-dividers, finance institutions, shire councillors and MPs, has resulted in some incredible profiteering. The towns are hopeless.'

WHY URBAN POLICY?

The rationale for urban policy derives from the general liberal concern with reform and social progress. It assumes that the government — whether central, state or local — is the necessary instrument for the realisation of that goal. Modern cities are beset with a range of problems. Governments are responsive through the democratic process to the will of people. *Ergo*, governments can be expected to redress urban problems through public policies. It is not a view that is universally shared. Edwin Banfield's (1974) classic conservative critique of urban planning argued that 'we cannot solve our serious (urban) problems by rational economic management. Indeed by trying we are almost certain to make matters worse.' A similar view was echoed locally by the chief economist in the NSW Department of Planning when he said 'the best thing planners could do for the inner city would be to leave it alone' (John Patterson, quoted in Kilmartin & Thorns 1978). The contemporary influence of 'economic rationalism' has reinforced these *laissez-faire* perspectives.

On the political left there is an echo of the scepticism about urban policy, albeit deriving from different reasoning. Chris Paris (1982), for example, argues that 'development plans often do little more than accept the location of big industries and commercial concerns: the plans are drawn around them.' Chris Pickvance (1982) asserts that 'physical planning has little influence on urban development when compared with market forces'. More bluntly, there is the Marxian view that urban planning is one of the mechanisms whereby the state serves the interest of the owners of capital and urban landowners. The social reformers also have their reservations. Sandercock's (1975) assertion that urban planning 'has failed to improve the welfare of our city dwellers' rests on an acceptance of the claim that it is about progressive redistribution: the problem is that it hasn't been effective in practice. Even Jane Jacobs, a long-standing liberal contributor to proposals for urban improvement, warned at an early stage of the tendency for urban planning to negate the very elements of urban living that account for its vitality and dynamism (Jacobs 1961).

However, the range of urban problems (discussed in chapters 1–6) understandably raises recurrent demands for reformist measures. It has long been thus. And there has been no shortage of visionary thinkers and practitioners seeking to show the way forward to a better planned urban future. Ebenezer Howard, Frank Lloyd Wright and Le Corbusier are three striking examples. They were not the first nor the last urban visionaries. Long before them came 'utopian socialists' such as Charles Fourier and Robert Owen who envisaged the possibility of new communities creating a more rational and cooperative society. More recent visionaries have included, for example, Paolo Soleri whose experiments in building extraordinarily compact settlements in America have embraced radical environmental principles. But Howard, Wright and Le Corbusier are particularly interesting because of the pervasive influence of their ideas on urban design. In their own ways, each was responding to the inadequacies and problems of cities in the late nineteenth and early twentieth centuries. In Robert Fishman's (1977) words, they 'hated the cities of their time with an overwhelming passion. The metropolis was the counter-image of their ideal cities, the hell that inspired their heavens.' The salvation of civilisation was to be found in their particular urban visions. It is pertinent to review the nature of those ideals and their influence on contemporary urban policy.

Howard's vision was of 'garden cities', planned urban environments with shops and cottages at the centre of a geometric patterned settlement with farmland surrounding. As set out in his famous study *Garden Cities of Tomorrow* (1902), this was a vision of social order. It was a plan for a better life for ordinary working people otherwise condemned to the squalid and degraded conditions of the major industrial cities. It was to be a very influential view, laying the foundation for a 'new town' movement whose influence was particularly evident in Great Britain. New towns on garden city principles were developed around London — such as Welwyn Garden City — and later around other major conurbations. As the research by Rob Freestone (1989) documents, the ideas were also influential in Australia. The garden suburbs of Daceyville in Sydney and Garden Village in Melbourne were developed on the basis of Howard's ideas, while some influences of the British new town movement are evident in the subsequent development of Elizabeth as a new town in South Australia (Peel 1992).

Frank Lloyd Wright's vision was very different but also influential. Walter Burley Griffin, designer of Canberra, had been one of his students. For Wright, urban planning was to have a distinctive political mission. His ideal 'Broadacre City' was conceived as the expression of an American individualism, as described in *The Living City* (1958). He set out a conception of an integrated urban-rural form where every citizen would have sufficient land to provide for their economic and social independence. This was to be the ultimate suburb where the automobile was king and modern technology would facilitate the necessary integration of economic and social activities. In Fishman's (1977) succinct phrase, 'Edison and Ford would resurrect Jefferson'. Cynics might contend that this spatial pattern, albeit not the political goal, has since been the almost universally dominant tendency — not through conscious design but through the incoherent sprawl of urbanisation in a car-oriented society. The result, evident in Australia as well as American cities, is a 'fast-buck' version of Broadacre City, falling woefully short of Wright's democratic ideals.

Le Corbusier's ideal city emphasised a more strikingly urban rather than suburban form. As set out in *La Ville Radieuse* (1935), the city was to comprise cruciform skyscrapers set out in open parkland. It embodied a vision of perfect Cartesian order, quite at odds with the messy, disorderly aspects of existing cities which were at once the source of their problems and their vitality. It was to become the model for public housing and urban renewal projects in many countries, including Australia, centred on high-rise towers in a parkland setting. Indeed, the proliferation of high-rise residential and commercial development in inner-city areas has established Le Corbusier's conception as an urban norm, albeit usually without the beneficial environmental effects which were a principal purpose of the original conception. The parkland setting and countryside access are casualties of the adaptation. A high-rise central business district, surrounded by sprawling suburbia and a few satellite new towns is not the 'synthesis' any of the three visionaries would have welcomed!

While far from exhausting the various conceptions of urban planning, the ideas of these three visionaries are interesting for their focus on how urban form could be remodelled to serve human needs. They show the reformist character of town planning. Of course, in any process of reform, it is important to have clear notions of the objectives sought and the means to implement them. What has dogged the town planning movement in practice is the difficulty of integrating socio-economic objectives with physical land-use controls. This was evident right from the start in Australia with the emergence of the town planning movement as a serious force in the first two decades of the twentieth century. The movement's aim of 'urban improvement' then was particularly concerned with the poor sanitary conditions and with 'slum' clearance. The basic conception was social progress through physical planning. This is what Sandercock (1975) labelled a 'facility-centered theory of social change'. In her words, the reformers believed:

... that if the poor were provided with a set of properly
designed facilities, ranging from a house and garden, which
the poor were expected to pay for, to better work places and
parks and play-grounds, they would not only give up their
slum abodes but would also give up the pathologies associated with poverty. This theory of social change, based on assumptions of environmental or physical determinism, was
the conventional wisdom of the early town planning movement and was supported by many businessmen, property
owners and their economic and political associates (banks,
councils and the like). These groups were interested in ensuring that the slums did not 'infect' the central business
area. They were concerned primarily with buildings and
facilities and they made common cause with the early
reformers.

More succinctly, 'the first step to taking the slum out of the man is
to take the man out of the slum' (letter, *Sydney Morning Herald*,
3.7.47, cited in Spearritt 1978).

Contemporary town planning theory and practice is more
sophisticated but still subject to recurrent criticism. Not usually
embracing the big pictures sketched by the urban 'visionaries',
the planners adopt a more pragmatic approach to steering urban
development. They nonetheless claim to be contributing to the
development of more efficient, equitable and environmentally
attractive cities. It is not an unreasonable claim. The pressures
for urban growth and restructuring are strong and relentless:
some management of this process — whether piecemeal and pragmatic or motivated by grander goals — appears inescapable. But
how effective are the planners in helping to build better cities? Is
urban planning a 'neutral, technical and progressive force for
gradual social improvement in an essentially harmonious
world' (Berry 1986); or are the class interests and institutional
impediments such as to create a quite different agenda?

URBAN PLANNING

As Blair Badcock (1984) notes, 'urban policy is an umbrella term
that tends to subsume the resource allocation that is undertaken

within a number of sectors of the economy including transportation, housing, construction and industrial development'. As
such, it involves most aspects of public policy. Urban *planning* is a
sub-set of those broader concerns, involving the formulation
of strategic plans for urban development and the systematic
application of controls on the urban development process. For a
city facing pressures of population growth, the usual priority for
planners is to identify the appropriate areas for the accommodation of that growth, whether on the metropolitan periphery
or within existing built-up areas. To accompany that residential development, necessary additions to urban infrastructure
(for the provision of water, electricity, transport, sewerage and
social services) are identified and policies implemented for its
financing. Zones for residential use, industrial uses, transport
corridors, recreational and green belt areas are specified and
development applications are processed according to their
consistency with these broad urban plans.

That is the theory anyway. The practice is rather more
complicated for at least three reasons. First, there are a *range of
institutions* involved. In the Australian case both State and local
governments and an array of public instrumentalities and
corporations are involved in the provision of transport, electricity, gas, water, and other urban services. Coordination is a
recurrent problem, diminished only a little by the replacement of
local governments by a single metropolitan government, as in
Brisbane.

Second, there is the problem that while the planning is
public — or, to be more precise, in the hands of the state —
the sources of initiative in urban development are largely private.
The *interest groups* include industrialists and commercial capitalist businesses, private land-owners, developers, residential construction companies, financial institutions and real estate
agencies. Therein lies a recurrent tension. To the extent that the
restrictions involved in urban planning may impede private
profit, it is not surprising that the pressures to vary or even
abandon planning guidelines are recurrent.

Third, there is the related problem of *finance*. The public
provision of infrastructure for urban development requires

capturing part of the economic surplus generated in the development process—whether through taxes and rates or special
development levies. This is inhibited by competition between
different local and State governments to attract developments
to their localities. Beggar-thy-neighbour tendencies recur and
development standards come to be compromised in the process
of spatial competition.

To give more specificity to this discussion it is appropriate to
consider particular cases. Brian McLoughlin's (1992) study of
Melbourne is an examplar. Sydney also makes a good case study
of urban planning. First, it evidently needs it! The lack of any
coherent initial plan (comparable, for example, to Colonel
Light's design for urban development in Adelaide) has left it
with a legacy of narrow streets in the CBD and limited options
for the further development of transport corridors. The relentless
population growth has led to more peripheral sprawl and
growing pressure on the very environmental resources which are
the basis for its distinctive appeal. The pollution of Sydney's
harbour and beaches and the major environmental threat to the
Nepean-Hawkesbury river basin to the west are all-too-obvious
cases in point. Sydney is also a good case-study because there
have been a series of comprehensive urban plans. These bring
into focus the choice between *urban consolidation* and further
peripheral expansion, two models for dealing with the continuing
pressures of growth.

More thorough studies of planning in Sydney are to be
found elsewhere (e.g. Spearritt & De Marco 1988), but a brief
evaluation can give concrete form to some of the broader
generalisations in this chapter. We can identify three key plans, at
twenty year intervals, since the second world war:

- the County of Cumberland Planning Scheme (1948);
- the Sydney Region Outline Plan (1968);
- the Metropolitan Strategy (1988).

The first of these plans was the product of a bold experiment
which has been interpreted, perhaps a little grandly, as embodying 'the practical socialism of post-war reconstruction' (Wilmoth
1989). Local governments came together to establish a vision for

more rational land use within a clearly bounded urban area. The planners projected a population growth for Sydney of a little over half a million people in the next quarter-century, and determined that this should be focused on urban districts comprising 'communities or groups of communities, largely self-sufficient in shopping, entertainment, education, culture and amenities, with local industrial areas'. This district system would 'correct the defects of sprawl, nonentity, lack of independence and inadequacy of utility and amenities' (Cumberland County Council 1948). Most importantly, sprawl would be limited by the imposition of a green belt, creating 'a girdle of rural open space encircling the urban districts'. In practice, the rate of population growth turned out to be over twice that anticipated by the planners, largely because of the vigorous programme of national immigration implemented by the federal government. Sydney, as a major port, got a disproportionate share of the arrivals. The green-belt was invaded. Commercial interests, seeking profits in residential and commercial building, dominated over the visionaries. Local government cooperation was not sustained. 'Sydney's Great Experiment' collapsed as 'owner-builders, developers, speculative builders and the Housing Commission vied with each other to cover the landscape with freestanding houses' (Spearitt & DeMarco 1988).

Ostensibly, the Sydney Region Outline Plan was better placed to control these processes. It was the product of a *State* government department, the State Planning Authority, with greater power to control urban development than local governments had under the Cumberland County Council plan. However, the grand vision had faded. Here was a plan to accommodate the pressures for further urban growth through further peripheral expansion, albeit channelled to some extent into distinctive corridors. Sydney would expand south to Campbelltown and west to Penrith and beyond, with major options on further expansion in a north-western corridor and in the Gosford and Wyong areas well to the north of the existing metropolitan area. It was claimed that these would not be 'dormitory suburbs', based on the expectation of corresponding growth of employment opportunities (over which the planners have no control). The basic task was seen as the accommodation of 2.75 million people, of whom it was hoped that 0.5 million would go to the Gosford-Wyong area and a further 0.5 million would be decentralised elsewhere in the State. Few concrete steps were taken to achieve the decentralisation which was assumed. Indeed, the report simultaneously emphasised the desirability of continued metropolitan primacy. It beat the drum for 'Australia's premier city' while warning against its overgrowth, leading Hugh Stretton (1970) to comment that 'perhaps planners and politicians wrote alternative sentences'. Other critics have argued that, in practice, the plan involved accommodating to 'promiscuous suburbanisation' and to 'the vehicle that made such spectacular suburbanisation possible — the private motor car' (Spearritt and DeMarco 1988).

A revision of the Outline Plan took place in 1980, reconsidering some aspects of the rate of population growth in the metropolitan area. However, its basic principles remained intact until the publication in the bicentennial year of the Metropolitan Strategy for *Sydney Into Its Third Century* (1988). A more modest growth of about 1 million persons in the Sydney region in a 25-year period was now anticipated. The planners reasoned that this would generate a demand for nearly 600,000 new dwellings, taking account of changing patterns of household size and composition. Over half of these dwellings would be steered to new urban areas on the metropolitan fringe, with particular focus on new housing areas in the north-west sector, south-west past Liverpool to Bringelly, south to Macarthur and north to the Central Coast beyond Wyong. Urban consolidation would play a major role in accommodating the rest, increasing the density of dwellings and population in the existing metropolitan area. Was this to signal the end of 'urban sprawl'?

The 1988 Metropolitan Strategy report considered two principal alternative strategies for accommodating growth — a 'concentrated alternative' and a 'dispersed alternative'. The former embodied urban consolidation and the promotion of strong commercial centres. The latter, more a continuation of current trends, involved low residential densities and less emphasis on the promotion of commercial centres. The contrast is one of degree. As the report acknowledged, even a strong urban consolidation push would not eliminate all the pressures for peripheral expansion. The preference for the concentrated alternative was mainly because of the costs of urban land and additional infrastructure. However, the report simultaneously earmarked areas for Sydney's continued peripheral expansion. By carefully identifying the constraints imposed by national parks and other recreational uses, steep terrain, soil hazards, floodplains, prime agricultural areas and so forth, it whittled down the areas under consideration for potential urban use. Particular localities with capacity for major additional residential development were said to include Macarthur and Bringelly in the SW Sector, Scheyville, Rouse Hill, Marsden Park and London-derry in the NW Sector, Warnervale-Wadalba near Wyong in the north, plus some smaller pockets in outlying areas such as West Gosford and Helensburg. Of course, this identification of new urban development areas is essential for systematic planning of land releases and rezoning of land uses. However, there remains the perennial problem, noted in chapter 4, that the plan, like its predecessors, has simultaneously provided a punters' guide for land speculators. Despite the brave words about urban consolida-tion, peripheral urban expansion remains the main game, with all the attendant problems of transport, social isolation and environmental decay.

The planning process remains dominated by the traditional concern of accommodating additional urban population growth. This relegates other considerations, especially employment, unemployment and structural economic change to a secondary status. They are not wholly ignored in the Sydney Metropolitan Strategy report, for example, but the issues of major youth unemployment in outer suburbs, of the demise of manufacturing jobs, of the increased mobility of capital and of technological restructuring, all have a rather shadowy existence behind the soothing generalisations. Predictions of employment growth quickly proved inappropriate in the context of economic recession in the 1990s.

The integration of physical, economic and social planning is a massive task, especially in circumstances where the government does not have control over the rate and direction of economic growth. Sandercock (1975) summed up the problems of urban planning in Australian cities by noting that 'the political power of business and property interests ... has forced planning authorities into the role of responding to private developments rather than initiating and controlling urban growth and change'. It is a tendency which is commonplace in capitalist societies, reflecting a continuing tension between the individualist basis of economic decisions and a collective interest in the outcomes. Certainly, urban planning is presented by its proponents as having a reforming role — a means of achieving more equitable, efficient and environmentally attractive cities. However, it is applied in a particular political-economic context which obviates the achievement of that goal.

The relationship between capital and state is perhaps at its most transparent at this 'micro' level of spatial development processes. It is an arena which is notorious for corruption, as noted in chapter 4. More generally, the normal workings of the urban system operate in a class-biased manner. In part this arises simply because much urban development is undertaken in the pursuit of profits; while the community as a whole bears the external diseconomies associated with unplanned development. Of course, it is this that urban policy is ostensibly designed to redress. However, the institutions of the state have tended to share the same pro-growth ideology and have generally accommodated to the forces generated by the capitalist system. It is a conclusion with strong echoes of the Marxist theory of the state described in chapter 8. But what of the democratic and bureaucratic aspects of the state which coexist with the capitalist aspects, as argued concurrently in that chapter? To understand their influence requires a rather more thorough examination of the different levels of government involved in urban policy.

THREE TIERS; THREE TEARS?

The role of *local government* is limited by its territorial fragmentation, its financial resources and its restricted range of functions — commonly categorised as 'roads, rubbish and rating'. With the exception of Brisbane, no local government in Australia is of sufficient magnitude to cope with metropolitan planning. Moreover, in comparison with local government in the United Kingdom, Canada or the United States, local government in Australia handles a tiny and declining share of total government expenditures. Though originally entrusted with a wide range of functions, ranging from community health and welfare to town and country planning, its role has shrunk to the management of libraries, parks, swimming pools, secondary roads, garbage disposal, and so on — and these functions have been increasingly sub-contracted. There are exceptions where local government has a key strategic role in the urban development process — as in the case of the councils of the Cities of Sydney and Melbourne — and local business interests have been particularly active there to ensure that policies are sympathetic to their requirements.

There have been various attempts to revitalise local government, long seen as the Cinderella of the state apparatus, including proposals for financial arrangements whereby the federal government makes transfer payments directly to groups of local councils. Local governments remain short of funds, particularly in areas characterised by low-income residents, which intensifies their general tendency to be subservient to business interests, competing with each other for commercial and residential developments which add to rate revenues. This is not to say that local government is irrelevant: it is the seed-bed of diverse political activities (Halligan and Paris 1984) and its financing has important distributive and ideological effects (Mowbray 1982). For those on the political left, there has been a growing interest in the possibilities for intervention at the level of 'the local state' (Fincher 1989a). However, as an avenue through which a more coherent urban policy can be pursued, it is invariably frustrating. Certainly, the detailed form of urban development is modified by the structure and implementation of local development controls, but local government typically has neither the scope nor the resources to take the initiative in transforming the overall form of cities.

The role of *State governments* is more important. These have long had a major role in shaping urban development. Obviously, the urban planning statements discussed earlier in this chapter are key elements in this process. However, urban policies are implicit in nearly all State government policies (in much the same way that regional policies are implicit in all federal government activities, as argued in chapter 9). The structure of the public transport system provides an example. The form of the metropolitan areas was shaped historically by radial expansion associated with the development of the railway system (and trams in some cases), changing subsequently to a more scattered development as public expenditures were channelled into more flexible forms of road transport. Housing provides another example, not only in respect of the location of public housing, but also in relation to the legislation regulating private housing, such as minimum lot sizes. The release of publicly owned land for housing is a matter over which there is direct State control. Policies towards the spatial distribution of expenditures on education, health and community services have also had a significant impact on the form of urban development (Stimson 1982). The State governments are the direct providers of most of these items of collective consumption, albeit heavily dependent for their financing on grants from the federal government.

To the extent that urban planning and the provision of these items of collective consumption has led to a distinctively suburban form of urban development in Australia, it has been conducive to the maintenance of a high level of demand for goods and services (at least one television set, washing machine, car, and so on per household) and to the dominance of individualistic ideologies which underpin social and political stability. This is the classic dualism — the state ensuring the conditions for capital accumulation while legitimising the existing economic and social order. Not that capital and the state have been unified in orchestrating this outcome. On the contrary, there have been important conflicts between fractions of capital in the process of urban development. Moreover, capital and the state have met opposition to many features of the urban development process — urban protest groups have been an important countervailing force (a phenomenon to which we return in chapter 14). So, while the activities of State governments in the urban development process have been generally consistent with the needs of capital for accumulation and legitimisation, they have also been an arena of class conflict.

Finally, what of the *federal government*? Historically, its direct role in the urban development process has been minimal, with the exception of a couple of periods when a more interventionist approach was in vogue. After the second world war there was a strong surge of concern for improved urban and regional planning. As one of the leading public administrators for the Labor government recalls in his autobiography, there was avid reading and discussion of the works of Frank Lloyd Wright and other urban planners, even the anarchist Peter Kropotkin, as well as the establishment of administrative structures to promote regional development in each State (Coombs 1981). These were years of hope. In Manning Clark's (1991) words, they were 'heady times ... [when] the great dreams of humanity were about to come true'. The reality was more sobering, in urban planning as in other fields of economic and social policy. The reforming federal government was swept from office by the conservatives and direct federal involvement in urban planning was eschewed for the next 23 years.

It was not until the election of the Labor Party in 1972 that there was a further surge of enthusiasm and innovation. Gough Whitlam and Tom Uren were the political exponents of this revival while Hugh Stretton, Max Neutze and Pat Troy were the leading intellectual forces behind it. In place of the earlier 'facility centred view of social change' was an explicit emphasis on urban policy as the means for environmental improvement linked to equity objectives and the redistribution of urban resources and services (Lloyd and Troy 1981). The principal vehicle for this, the Department of Urban and Regional Development (or DURD, to use the usual acronym) initiated a wide range of policies dealing with urban development. These included area-improvement programmes (designed to assist local governments to improve facilities in relatively deprived suburbs), provision of expenditure to deal with backlogs in the provision of sewerage, the establishment of Land Commissions (seeking to stabilise the price of urban land) and direct purchase of housing in areas such as Glebe in Sydney (in order to maintain low-income housing in inner-city areas). NSW Premier Wran was later to reflect, drawing attention to the sewerage programme in particular: 'It was said of Caesar Augustus that he found a Rome of brick and left it of marble. It can be said of Gough Whitlam that he found Sydney, Melbourne and Brisbane unsewered and left them fully flushed' (Whitlam 1985).

Various assessments of DURD have been made (e.g. T. Logan 1979, M. Logan 1978, Lloyd and Troy 1981, Sandercock and Berry 1983). Some see it as a challenging attempt to attack the problems of social inequality via urban policy. Others have argued that its policies effectively redefined inequality in terms of spatial issues, and thereby redirected attention away from the roots of inequality in the capitalist mode of production (Catley and McFarlane 1974). No doubt the main beneficiaries of some policies included property developers, speculators and urban planning consultants. However, with the benefit of hindsight it is hard to sustain the argument that DURD was merely serving capitalist interests by providing the conditions for further capital accumulation in the cities. Equally, it would seem rather simplistic to regard DURD as an instrument of popular sovereignty in pursuit of general urban improvement, since it exposed fundamental class antagonisms and bureaucratic checks on progressive reform. The evidence would seem most consistent with the view of the state as an arena of class struggle (while itself generating changes in the nature of the class structure through the development of the bureaucracy). Yes, DURD was a classic experiment in social democratic reformism, generating momentum for progressive changes but simultaneously bringing into focus the economic, political, ideological and administrative impediments to progressive outcomes.

Certainly, the changes in policy after the Liberal Party was returned to office, following the constitutional crisis which its leaders precipitated in 1975, indicated a major shift in the balance of forces. DURD was disbanded and, although a successor called the Department of Environment, Housing and Community Development existed for a couple of years, direct intervention in urban affairs was truncated. The federal government pursued a general economic strategy which intensified the problems of urban areas. Promoting a 'resources boom' was a key element, as noted in chapter 1, leading to expenditure on the cities being siphoned off into the major resource-based projects (Australian Institute of Urban Studies 1980). In the 1980s, as it became clear that the 'resources boom' would not materialise, this tendency for the redirection of capital expenditure became less acute but the commitment to federal intervention in urban policy was gone.

The ALP federal government elected in 1983, under the leadership of Bob Hawke, did not seek to establish another actively interventionist department like DURD to shape the pattern of urban development. Ex-DURD Minister Tom Uren sought for a while to pursue similar objectives through the Department of Local Government but the government avoided significant direct involvement in the cities as it concentrated on the process of macro-economic management. There were glimmerings of an urban policy revival by the end of the decade. Treasurer Keating called for a renewed involvement of the federal government in this aspect of policy, a call which he restated in his personal campaign for the Prime Minister's position in 1991. Deputy Prime Minister Howe was a more steady and committed campaigner and managed to get a financial allocation for a 'Building Better Cities' programme in the 1991-2 budget. This was a significant initiative, providing federal funds (totalling a projected $816 million over five years) to back proposals coming up from the States for urban consolidation, improved transport and urban environmental quality.

There is a recurrent problem of incoherence, which is exemplified by 'Building Better Cities'. Social justice objectives are stressed, together with reducing the costs of peripheral metropolitan expansion and providing more diverse housing to cater for the changing population structure. But an interventionist approach to urban policy is basically incompatible with 'economic rationalism' and the ideology of a 'level playing field' which have been the hallmark of the Hawke and Keating government's economic policies. The deepening recession in 1991-2 prompted some State premiers to call for infrastructure and public works expenditures as an instrument of Keynesian 'pump-priming', with some response from Prime Minister Keating in 1992. However, urban policy has remained marginal to an increasingly problematic economic 'big picture'.

STATE VERSUS THE CITIES?

What are we to conclude about this experience of urban planning? As Jon Gower Davies (1982) points out, 'it is because of its antagonism to capitalism that planning has often been associated with socialism'. The reality is evidently otherwise. Urban planning, as illustrated in the Australian case, has typically had market-augmenting rather than market-replacing effects. No doubt, the efforts of the planners have been well-intentioned, often concerned with equity as well as efficiency objectives, even aspiring on occasions to the 'practical socialism' ascribed to the post-war planners. However, the process has been fraught with contradictions, including the use of urban plans as blueprints for land speculators and urban consolidation policies that have the potential to trigger processes of land price inflation and regressive wealth redistribution.

How this experience fits with the competing theories of the state in chapter 8 is a matter of conjecture. Each element in the 'democracy-capitalism-bureaucracy' trilogy is clearly in evidence. *Citizens' concerns* about urban problems generate recurrent demands for better planning. *Capitalist interests* constrain what is possible. *Bureaucratic structures*, including the recurrent problems of coordination between the different tiers of government and public instrumentalities, limit what is achieved. The whole sits most uneasily with a liberal-pluralist view of the state, despite the attempts to couch planning statements in terms of a generalised public interest. The Marxian view has more plausibility in that the urban planning process holds out the recurrent promise of social reform but remains ultimately subordinate to the interests of capital. Yet the continual contestation over the appropriate form of urban planning indicates scope for competing class interests, different housing tenure groups, public and private transport users, environmental action groups and others to address the state as an 'arena of struggle'. The managerialist view of the state also has credibility to the extent

that planners are able to act as 'gatekeepers' in restricting the release and uses of urban land. The problems of cooperation between the different tiers of government can also be
interpreted in this context, suggesting a more negative view of
the managerial process. Developing this perspective, Martin
Painter (1979) argues that effective coordination of government
policies at the urban level is impossible.

So, as with the earlier analyses of regional policy and
decentralisation policy, it seems that elements of each of the
competing theories of the state are compatible with the experience of urban policy in practice. This may appear as a wimpish
conclusion but it is of some methodological significance. It
means that the empirical evidence is not a basis on which
competing hypotheses (about the state) can readily be accepted
or rejected. Rather, the role of the competing theories is to steer
our attention towards particular modes of inquiry, raising particular questions in the context of empirical studies. Yes, the state
is an arena of struggle in which competing classes and class
fractions seek to shape regional and urban policies. Meanwhile,
official ideologies recurrently stress a broader public interest
while bureaucratic structures impart distinctive biases to the
policy outcomes. Underlying it all, the structural characteristics
of capitalism set limits to what is economically feasible.

What is hard to deny is that the impact of urban planning, for
better or worse, has been less spectacular than the claims made
on its behalf. The Australian experience is broadly consistent
with Pickvance's view, quoted near the start of this chapter, that
the influence of planning is secondary to that of market forces.
The general thrust of urban policy, the periodic attempts by
federal Labor governments notwithstanding, has not been
sufficient to cope adequately with urban externalities, let alone
chart new directions towards more efficient, equitable and
ecologically sustainable cities.

FURTHER READING

Sandercock (1975): a standard reference on the history, limits and contradictions of urban planning, with particular reference to Sydney, Melbourne and Adelaide.

Fishman (1977): for more detail on Howard, Wright and Le Courbusier.

Lloyd & Troy (1981): a detailed assessment of the Whitlam government's initiatives in urban and regional policy.

Spearritt & DeMarco (1988): a popular treatment of the development of urban planning in Sydney, commissioned to accompany the State government's Metropolitan Strategy plan.

12

Urban Consolidation

The issue of urban consolidation warrants further consideration. As noted in the preceding chapter, it is a distinctive feature of the latest phase of official planning for Sydney. It has come to be an increasingly prominent goal for planners in the other major cities as an antidote to urban sprawl. It has been given a more national focus as a key element in the federal government's 1992 commitment to the Building Better Cities programme. Is it merely 'flavour of the month' or something which promises to have a more long-term impact on the planning process and urban futures?

What is at issue is urban policy which aims to increase the density of residential land uses within the existing urban area, rather than growth through further fringe metropolitan expansion. 'Compactness without congestion and spaciousness without sprawl' (Bunker 1986) is a neat phrase to capture the essence of urban consolidation in its most positive light. 'The end of the quarter acre block' is a phrase more likely to generate concern about the fracturing of conventional Australian expectations. Either way, urban consolidation can be expected to involve some combination of more multiple-unit dwellings and other medium-density housing, smaller residential lot-sizes and sub-division of existing lots, dual-occupancy of dwellings, the construction of 'granny flats' in the grounds of existing houses, houses being built up to the site line, narrower streets and a generally more economical use of land for transport purposes.

This chapter explores the urban consolidation issue in three steps:

- Why bother? Key aspects of the case for consolidation.
- Contradictions: problems of implementing a consistent policy.
- Prospects for more compact urban forms.

WHY BOTHER?

Five strands in the increasingly influential case for urban consolidation may be identified. First, there is the observation that the *infrastructure costs* of further fringe development have risen sharply. Estimates of the cost of providing schools, hospitals, police, water, sewerage and drainage, main roads, community health and other necessary facilities have risen as high as $47,000 for each new house on the outskirts of the mainland capital cities, and over $60,000 in the case of Sydney (Howe 1991). This cost is initially borne by the public authorities who are already complaining of fiscal crisis. If it is not passed on in direct charges to the new residents, there is an effective subsidy which encourages more outer-urban development (yes, sprawl, to use the more emotive term). On the other hand, if the full cost is imposed on the new residents, according to the user-pays principle, many will be encouraged to look instead at housing within the existing built-up areas.

Second, better use can be made of *existing urban infrastructure*. In the situation where population trends, including the gentrification process, have led to a 'doughnut effect', existing urban infrastructure tends to be underutilised. This has been evident in some degree of surplus capacity in inner-city school facilities, for example. However, it is a point to refrain from over-generalising. Much of the existing infrastructure in the major cities needs upgrading and renewal even to cope with existing demands. As Pat Troy (1989) wryly observes, 'the main "economic" benefit may be the illusory one of being able to count work [on infrastructure improvements] in the inner suburbs as maintenance of the system whereas work in fringe areas is new capital work'.

Third, there are *environmental constraints* on further fringe development. Valuable agricultural land is being lost. Particular ecologically sensitive areas, such as the Hawkesbury-Nepean river basin and the Blue Mountains to Sydney's west are under threat from the environmental impacts of further urban spread. What is at issue here is not just the spatial form of development, but also the degree to which it is planned in ecologically sensitive ways. Urban policies can have quite unintended environmental impacts. A classic example is the sewerage programme of the Whitlam government to which reference was made in the preceding chapter: sewering Sydney's west added substantially to the effluents pouring out into the ocean to the east, the effects of which on Sydney's beaches came to be of acute social and political concern in the 1980s (Beder 1989). Now the toxicity in the Hawkesbury-Nepean is reaching danger levels as a result of the further westward expansion of the metropolitan area.

Fourth, *demographic changes* mean smaller dwellings are needed. The ageing of the population has led to a growing proportion of single and two-person households. Changes in the pattern of household formation, numbers of children and the incidence of divorce also require more flexibility in the array of housing choices. The three- or four-bedroom detached cottage with its own relatively spacious garden may have been the standard basis for the nuclear family pursuing the 'great Australian dream', but it does not serve the diverse needs of the contemporary urban population. Sub-division and 'granny flat' construction may be a more effective way of catering for the demands of many elderly pesons, while a greater array of smaller town-houses and multi-unit dwellings could more effectively be tailored to meet the demands of other population groups. These forms of dwellings are usually also cheaper to construct per person housed.

Fifth, *transport needs* may be economised. As noted in chapter 3, the low density sprawling urban form is very expensive in terms of its transportation requirements, and very difficult to serve with public transport rather than private cars. Both the private costs and the collective depletion of scarce energy resources set limits on this form of urban development. Ironically, the suburbanisation of employment in conjunction with further outer-area residential development can compound the problem further, because the growing volume of criss-cross movements is still more difficult to service by conventional modes of public transport. Urban consolidation, focusing on settlement clusters or urban villages, provides a potential solution to this problem. As Beed and Moriarty (1988b) note, very large increases in density would be needed to have significant effects.

These five considerations seem to provide a fairly persuasive case for urban consolidation. This is not to gainsay the difficulties involved in any reconstruction of the existing physical urban fabric. It is not to ignore the legitimate interests of people who may oppose change which is seen to impact unfavourably on the amenity of their existing area of residence. It is not to underestimate the capacity of local governments, particularly in more wealthy low-density suburbs, to block urban consolidation proposals coming from State and federal governments. Nor is it to imagine that such policies could readily transform existing Australian cities into the more compact forms characteristic of European cities. Rather, it is simply to point out social, economic and environmental advantages of urban consolidation from a liberal perspective on what constitutes 'the good city'.

CONTRADICTIONS

It is equally important to question the existence of a collective interest in urban consolidation. There are four fundamental concerns. The first is that urban consolidation can increase the *cost of land*. Changes in planning regulations which permit more intensive land uses can be expected to raise the price of land within the existing urban area. This benefits existing landowners at the expense of new purchasers. It widens the wealth gap between those who already own land and those who do not. As such, the distributional impacts are predictably regressive. To counter that, the sort of land-use policies discussed towards the end of chapter 4 could be instituted, but they would involve a greater degree of public intervention in the ownership of land and/or control of land markets than most existing land-owners (and many aspiring land-owners) would find acceptable.

The second problem is that fundamental *attitudinal changes* would be required for a successful policy of urban consolidation. The social expectations of people are strongly conditioned by their own experiences. The quest for the quarter acre block as the fulfillment of the 'great Australian dream' will not easily be diverted into more high-density living. Of course, not everyone shares the same ideal and a shift towards urban consolidation promises to cater more effectively for diverse preferences. Moreover, the more conventional option will continue to exist; and those who are prepared to pay for it, including full user-pays costing of infrastructure provision, would not be denied it. Be that as it may, the political pressure to continue with policies that make the conventional-sized residential lot available to most people at an affordable price remains substantial.

Third, there is a contrary perspective on the *environmental* benefits of urban consolidation. Troy (1993) puts this forcefully as follows:

> Increasing housing density decreases our capacity to cope with wastes, reduces our capacity to cope with the rainfall and runoff and reduces opportunities for recycling. Increasing density makes it harder for urban residents to produce much of their own food and fruit and increases air pollution because it reduces chances of growth of trees to purify and cool and reduces growth of wood for fuel, and reduces habitat for birds and other native fauna.

These concerns have to be set against the environmental problems of further urban sprawl.

Fourth, a paradox in urban consolidation policy arises because higher residential densities are easier to achieve on the *urban fringe*. Constructing housing at, say, ten rather than six units to the acre is more readily done in new outer-suburban estates than in existing urban areas with all the constraints imposed by the current form of housing, transport facilities, and so on. Building 'urban villages' well served by modern, efficient public transport facilities tends in the first instance to be an outer-metropolitan phenomenon. There may be the expectation of a demonstration effect regarding the advantages of more compact living; but meanwhile the metropolitan area continues its peripheral and satellite expansion.

PROSPECTS

Because of the contradictory features of urban consolidation and the interests opposed to it, it is not surprising that the policy commitment in practice is rather shaky. It is equally important to put consolidation in some quantitative perspective. According to Ray Bunker's (1986) estimate, less than 3 per cent of the additional housing demand in Sydney could be expected to be diverted into more consolidated forms by the end of the century. The scope for urban consolidation in other cities is not markedly greater. In these circumstances, and in the absence of a vigorous commitment to decentralisation policy (for the reasons explored in chapter 10), it seems that accommodating peripheral urban expansion will continue to dominate the urban planning process. Indeed, it is rather tempting to draw a parallel between decentralisation and urban consolidation in terms of the 'everybody's policy but nobody's programme' theme. The failure of either policy to substantially change the dominant form of metropolitan expansion means that the corresponding urban problems—economic, social and environmental—grow apace.

But the concern with urban consolidation is unlikely to be dissipated. It has been around for a long time, underpinning the long-standing concerns with urban containment (e.g. the 1948 Cumberland Council Plan for Sydney). It is embodied in the current plans for all the major cities, as illustrated in Figure 12.1. Its renewed backing reflects significant changes in economic, demographic and environmental conditions.

Economically, the persistent fiscal crisis of the state makes the quest for cost-savings relentless. The costs of urban infrastructure provision are an obvious target. Federal government estimates indicate a projected total cost to State and local government of $6 billion over five years to provide services and facilities for an estimated 700,000 dwellings on the fringe of the major cities (Howe & Staples 1991). Anything that can be done to reduce this economic burden, either by making more intensive

FIGURE 12.1   ESTIMATED NUMBER OF NEW HOUSEHOLDS AND
              THEIR LOCATIONS FOR FIVE AUSTRALIAN CAPITAL
              CITIES, 1900–2030

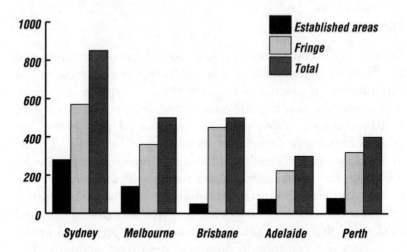

Note: 'Fringe' refers to areas of new subdivision at the edges of the city.
Sources: Perth: A planning strategy for metropolitan Perth.
          Sydney: Sydney into the Third Century, *Department of Planning*, 1988.
          Melbourne: The urban development program for metropolitan Mel-
                     bourne.
          Brisbane: A city strategy, Brisbane City Council, February 1991.
          Adelaide: Long term development plan for Adelaide, September 1987,
                     Department of Planning and Environment.
Source: Howe (1991).

use of existing infrastructure or by shifting the burden to new
house-buyers through user-cost pricing, has obvious appeal to
governments. It may be objected that the cost-cutting appeal
of urban consolidation is somewhat spurious in a period of
protracted unemployment, since such infrastructure provision is
an ideal focus for job-creation. As such, it leads to more income
flows and tax revenues for government. However, this Keynesian
economic reasoning has tended to be subordinated to a more
short-term accounting approach to dealing with the fiscal crisis.

The influence of 'economic rationalism' can be seen more
generally in the deregulationist aspect of urban consolidation.
Permitting more sub-divisions of urban land and a greater

variety of structures to be built can be interpreted in this context. As Carolyn Stone (1985) puts it, 'any attack on the lack of variety in housing is therefore bound up with adjustments to the regulation of residential development'. However, seeing urban consolidation as 'part of the deregulation thrust of the early 1980s' (Bunker 1986) sits awkwardly alongside an interventionist interpretation. From this latter perspective consolidation is seen as a more vigorous attempt, including stronger control by State government planners over local governments, to change the outcome of market processes. A cynic might note that the critical stance taken by the Industry Commission in its 1992 report on urban consolidation supports this 'interventionist' interpretation, since the Commission invariably supports the deregulationist option on any issue! On this reasoning, the problem with consolidation is that it is too interventionist, distorting urban development options away from the 'consumer sovereignty' ideal.

The *demographic* considerations are more clear-cut. As federal Housing Minister Brian Howe (1991) has noted, 80 per cent of current dwellings are single detached houses, but the projected changes in household structure make such a housing stock less suitable. By the year 2006 it is estimated that 75 per cent of all households will not include children: almost half of income units will consist of single persons or childless couples over 35. The numbers of old people are also expected to increase by over 50 per cent in the next twenty years. Figure 12.2. presents an official projection of the changing age profile. In these circumstances, it is evident that changes in the array of housing options will be needed. This does not necessarily require urban consolidation but it does suggest the need for a wider array of housing types which are affordable, less demanding to maintain and which integrate better with the provision of public transport.

If urban consolidation is to be more vigorously pursued, one of the most contentious questions is 'where?'. Inner city areas and the surrounding suburbs, particularly in Sydney and Melbourne, already have relatively high housing densities, although falls in population have been associated with the gentrification processes described in chapter 7. To focus the push for consolidation in those areas provokes a predictable outcry about the

FIGURE 12.2   POPULATION STRUCTURE BY AGE, AUSTRALIA, 1990
              and 2031

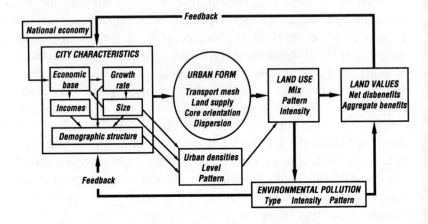

Source: ABS Australian Demographic Statistics (3101.0), ABS Projected Population
of Australia. 1989–2031 Series D, including migration since base year.

problems of congestion and deficient recreational space. A case
in point is the conflict in the early 1990s in the Sydney harbourside suburb of Balmain, following proposals to use vacated
industrial land for medium and high-density housing. Proposals
for urban consolidation in areas more distant from the CBD,
like Sydney's upper north shore, provoke similarly vociferous
opposition, rooted in the concern to preserve the class character
of the localities. Of course, other possibilities exist. The area
bounded by Epping in the north, Parramatta in the West,
Bankstown in the south and Balmain in the east is an obvious
focus: it currently houses about 100,000 people, yet it is roughly
the same size as some European cities with a population in excess
of a million. Targeting areas like this in the middle-outer zones of
the major cities would mean consolidating 'middle Australia'.

The *environmental* rationale for urban consolidation also
remains an open question. The arguments are clear enough—
conservation of scarce land resources, switching to less energy-
intensive housing types and transport systems and reducing
the emissions of greenhouse gases. What remains unpredictable
is whether the necessary urban restructurings will be forced

on us all, for example, by the need to adhere to international agreements reducing the use of hydrocarbons. Or will it be the case that adjustments will come in a more *ad hoc* manner, as intensifying problems of congestion and pollution, for example, provoke individuals to seek residential locations well served by existing public transport facilities? In general it can be expected that the growing need for concern with 'ecologically sustainable development' will put the planning of compact integrated urban settlements ever higher on the public policy agenda.

Whether urban consolidation is an appropriate policy also depends crucially on its consequences for *distributional equity*. This underpins many of the reservations expressed by academic critics (e.g. Bunker 1986, Stone 1985, Troy 1989). There is understandable concern that urban consolidation could intensify the tendency to spatial socio-economic segregation identified in chapter 6. Impacts on land and housing prices are one obvious channel through which such effects operate. However, the use of public housing as an instrument of consolidation could play an important role in countering regressive tendencies. It could help to create a greater mix of socio-economic groups in the inner areas which are otherwise becoming enclaves for gentrifiers. It could also help to provide a wider array of housing types in the middle suburbs. Careful planning would be needed to deal with the recurrent potential for formation of new ghetto areas. In other words, such a policy would only be effective in countering the trends to social-spatial polarisation if it concurrently involved the broadening of the public housing sector role as discussed in chapter 2.

Ray Bunker (1986) has said that 'heroic measures' are needed to deal with the problems of contemporary Australian cities. Whether urban consolidation has more than a marginal role in that scenario remains an open question. Our brief review indicates that while urban consolidation addresses key problems in the cities, it generates new contradictions. By itself, it offers no cure for the complex array of urban problems considered in earlier chapters of this book. Indeed, it would be unreasonable to expect any single form of spatial reshaping to provide such a generalised quick-fix. However, as part of a broader programme of reforms, it could contribute to creating more efficient, equitable and ecologically sustainable cities. Such a package would need to embrace:

- policies for higher housing densities in existing suburban areas;
- revitalisation of downtown areas for more residential purposes to complement their specialisations in commercial and entertainment facilities;
- development of compact urban village settlements rather than more sprawling suburbs on the metropolitan fringes;
- policies to upgrade public transport and re-orient travel demand away from its domination by the car;
- job-generation policies focussed on nodal points in that public transport/housing system;
- policies to control speculation and stabilise land prices;
- greater emphasis on the provision of public housing;
- general economic policies for a more equitable redistribution of income and wealth.

Such a policy programme would situate urban consolidation in a more equity-oriented and energy-conserving context. It would integrate the spatial elements in reshaping Australian cities with more radical socio-economic reforms. These would be 'heroic measures' indeed.

FURTHER READING

Bunker (1986): a review of the arguments, experience and potential for urban consolidation.

Stone (1985): on the problems and prospects of urban consolidation.

Glazebrook (1992): proposals for transport policies to facilitate consolidation, more efficient movement and land use in Sydney.

McLoughlin (1991): on the limited contribution of policies to increase urban densities.

13

New Cities, Fast Trains

What about major regional redevelopment projects? Are these indicative of qualitatively different forces shaping urban development in an era of monopoly capitalism? Certainly, the nature of urban and regional development has been changed by the internationalisation of capital (as discussed in chapter 1). The most commonly cited aspect is the development of 'world cities' such as London, Tokyo and New York, whose key institutions orchestrate the internationalisation process. Second-order cities like Sydney, Melbourne, Brisbane and Perth also serve as regional centres for multinational capital. The development of 'new industrial spaces' has been posited as another feature of the increasingly complex territorial division of labour which the internationalisation of capital both permits and requires (Knox & Agnew 1989, Stilwell 1992a: ch. 12). Now we are seeing the emergence of international agreements for capital-state participation in big new town developments and transport infrastructure projects. The proposals for a Multifunction Polis (MFP) and a Very Fast Train (VFT) in Australia are cases in point. At the time of writing the former is still on-going, though rapidly losing momentum, while the latter has been abandoned, albeit not without its flow-on implications for transport and regional policy. This chapter examines these two case studies as a means of identifying some of the new forces at work in urban and regional development, the associated opportunities and hazards.

MFP: CONCEPT

The MFP proposal is for a new town to be built at Gillman, on the northern outskirts of Adelaide, based on 'high-tech' industry together with the most modern facilities for consumption and recreation. What makes it distinctive is partly the ambitious nature of the integrated project, and partly the direct participation of the Japanese state and Japanese capital in its planning and financing.

The proposal had its origins in comments made by the Japanese Minister for International Trade and Industry (MITI) in January 1987 at a meeting attended by his Australian counterpart, the Minister for Industry, Trade and Commerce. It seems to have been suggested as part of a broad commitment to closer cooperation between these two increasingly economically interdependent nations. It was pushed along by a planning group established by MITI which submitted an outline plan to the Australian government in September 1987. MITI drummed up the necessary corporate support from 86 companies, including giant corporations such as Mitsubishi, Kobe Steel and Kawasaki, as well as construction and financial enterprises. On the Australian side 62 major companies, including the largest banks and financial institutions as well as manufacturing firms, expressed a similar commitment. In August 1988 a joint steering committee made up of seven representatives of each side took over responsibility for pushing the project ahead, while the Australian government commissioned private consultants to undertake the main feasibility study which was completed in December 1989 (Arthur Anderson Consulting/Kinhill 1989).

What the proponents of the MFP originally envisaged is a new city of up to 100,000 people, comprising both Australians and 'international workers' and their families coming to the MFP to live for anything from a few days to several years. The project's steering committee stated its intention that the 'vast majority' of residents and workers will be Australian, but parts of the consultants' report refers to up to 80 per cent being international. As for its *financing*, the development of the MFP was originally estimated to cost $A 13 billion, of which about 20 per cent might be financed by Australian governments (federal and State) and 80 per cent would be privately financed, with that latter component being split about equally between funds raised by Australian business (including overseas borrowings) and by international interests (Bureau of Industry Economics 1990). In practice, these public/private boundaries in the financing of the project are inevitably fuzzy, as for example where the private 'world university' to be established in the MFP draws on the facilities and resources of existing public tertiary educational institutions. However, right from the start the public promotion of the project stressed that it would be primarily financed by private enterprise rather than being a fiscal burden on the Australian state.

The economic activities on which the MFP is to be based have always been uncertain. The original proponents of the project recurrently stressed 'high-tech' industries which would give a stimulus to the flagging Australian economy, while the planning documents have also emphasised the scope for various service sector developments, including health services, education services, and telecommunications/media services, oriented towards export sales to an international community. As one report from MITI puts it, 'the MFP would be a fusion of high-tech industries destined to comprise core industries in the 21st century and high-touch oriented industries which support creative human people accompanied by their families' (MITI 1987). The term 'high-touch' is not yet so well established as 'high-tech', but it is clearly designed to encompass sport, leisure and recreational activities, as well as the production of health, education, media and other services. International business and professional conventions are particularly relevant in this context, expressing what Gary Gappert (1989) has called 'the new symbiotic relationship between the 'business' of information exchange and the 'play' of resort tourism'. Equally, the focus on 'high-tech' and 'high-touch' activities leaves little role for 'high-tension' activities — class struggle has no place in 'serendipity city'!

Of course, as Margo Huxley (1990) reminds us, Australia already has a number of 'multi-function polises' — literally, cities in which the various functions of work, residence, reproduction, recreation, health and education are carried out in an integrated manner. Qualifiers would include Sydney, Melbourne, Perth, Brisbane, Adelaide and Hobart! In that sense, the terminology is misleading. What distinguishes the proposed MFP from existing metropolitan areas is partly its *size*—the capacity to carry out these varied functions on a scale well below the million-plus populations of existing metropolitan areas. Also, it is partly its *modernity* (some would say post-modernity), involving the integration of these functions through the use of the most advanced technology. As such, the MFP has been promoted as a prototype of twenty-first century living.

MFP: LOCATION

What about the site for the MFP? In the lead-up to the selection of Gillman, the question of how the MFP would impact on regional development had to be considered. Would it be better to have the MFP as a spatially distinct entity (on a 'greenfield' site) or for it to be grafted on to one of the existing metropolitan areas ('brownfield' site)? And, in the latter case, would that mean the elements of the MFP being integrated into the existing city or kept reasonably distinct in one suburb or satellite town (as favoured by the Japanese interests)? From the perspective of regional development, the 'greenfield' option has appeal, but Australian fears of the MFP becoming an enclave led to proposals for the more integrated type of approach. In practice, these alternatives were considered jointly with the question of which State would host the MFP. Australia's federal political structure generates recurrent rivalry, as noted in chapters 9 and 10. Not suprisingly, the issue of location became the subject of an inter-State competition. The principal contenders were Queensland (which proposed a distinct site near the Gold Coast), New South Wales (which had the MFP split between three separate sites within the Sydney metropolitan area), Victoria (which linked the MFP to its inner-city Melbourne docklands redevelopment) and South Australia (which proposed a satellite town at Gillman).

And the winner is ... South Australia. Actually, it wasn't the original winner. The Queensland proposal was selected by the national committee charged with reviewing the options. However, the Queensland State government was unwilling to meet the required conditions, declining to formally commit itself to compulsory acquisition of privately owned land in the area. So the South Australian proposal which faced no similar impediments, involving land already largely under public ownership, was given the go-ahead in July 1990. Nevertheless, its selection, even as second best, was in many respects a quite surprising outcome. Among the contending States, South Australia is the most distant from Japan; it has the least experience of Japanese investment, and the smallest gross regional product. It would be unfair to call it the Cinderella State, its political leadership having developed a reputation for its 'developmentalist' ethos, but it is from the main centres of Australian economic development.

MFP: RATIONALE AND INTERESTS

The official assertions that the MFP would provide a 'biosphere offering renaissance living', and claims that it would be 'Vital, Responsive and Intelligent' (Anderson/Kinhill 1989) obviously invite some wonder, if not sheer cynicism. Nonetheless, it is possible to discern a three-pronged rationale for the project from an Australian perspective, quite apart from its appeal to the South Australian government as an instrument for increasing that State's share of national investment.

First, there is the need for a boost to the Australian economy, dogged by a persistent current account deficit and a high level of overseas debt. These problems are often misinterpreted as primarily due to merchandise trade imbalances and/or government borrowing overseas. In fact, the balance of payments deficit is largely due to the interest payments on overseas borrowings and most of these were undertaken by private corporations rather than government in the 1980s (Jones 1989, Dieter 1991). Nevertheless, one can readily observe a political climate, accentuated by the recession of the early 1990s, in which finding an economic fix is a top priority. More generally, it remains the case that the Australian economy continues to feature a strong dependence on the production and export of primary products, such as coal, wool and wheat, and that this makes the economy vulnerable to changes in international market conditions and the terms of trade between primary products and manufactured goods. To the extent that the MFP has been seen to offer some correction to this economic imbalance, through stimulating a more diversified economy, it has evident appeal.

Second, there is the issue of *technological stagnation*. The average age of plant and equipment used by Australian industry has remained high by international standards. This adds to the difficulties of international competition in a world of rapid technological change. Innovations occurring in Australia have often been taken overseas for their development and application to industrial production. There has been no major development of high-tech industry, although there have been important contributions to the advance of knowledge in various scientific fields including in vitro fertilisation and solar energy. There is no equivalent to Silicon valley or even Britain's M4 corridor, nor any evident parallel to the model of 'flexible specialisation' characteristic of the 'third Italy'. Sure, these latter forms of development are not unproblematic (as noted in Stilwell 1992: ch. 12), but their relative absence in Australia enhances the apparent appeal of any project such as the MFP which promises to pave the way for the growth of sunrise industries and other forms of economic modernisation. The expectation of 'technology transfer' from Japanese companies is a specific aspect of this appeal.

Third, there is the potential role of the MFP in promoting *regional development*. As noted in chapter 10, a concern with decentralisation policy and regional development has been of long standing in Australia, albeit more frequently evident in political rhetoric than in practical policies. Of course, the capacity of the MFP to make some contribution here rests critically on the choice of location, whether it be 'greenfield', fringe-metropolitan or inner-metropolitan. In practice, the selection of the Gillman site is clearly in the middle category and, as such, has little to do with decentralisation. It is more compatible with the recurrent tendency for the State govern-ments to interpret regional development as capturing big investment projects for their own State, irrespective of the location of the project within that State.

To identify these three elements as components in a rationale for the MFP is to presuppose that there is some 'national interest' which the project can serve. It is equally pertinent to note the particular interests of Australian-based capital, such as the 62 companies who made the initial commitment to the project. The interests of local capital lie partly in the construction process which offers major opportunities for profit, partly in capturing the gains in land values, and partly in the hoped-for benefits arising from economic partnership with Japanese corporations. There may also be the anticipation of a 'demonstration effect' arising from having a mini-economy in which the role of trade unions is minimised, fitting in with the 'new right' vision of industrial relations. Finally, when all is said and done, there is the expectation that because of the special character of the project, the state would underwrite it, effectively ensuring the conditions for profitable capital accumulation *or* socialising the losses.

What of the Japanese interests? They are a little less obvious, given that the investment is to be in Australia, with the secondary and multiplier effects, including the presumed benefits of technology transfer, being concentrated 'down under'. After all, the Japanese have built some twenty 'technopoles' in their own country. Why Australia? Gavan McCormack (1989) suggests that it is explicable in terms of the interrelated effects of 'economic rationalism, economic imperialism and utopianism'. The first aspect involves Japan's growing trade with Australia, and the need for international economic friends in a world recurrently threatened by moves towards the development of international trading blocs. Imperialism enters to the extent that the bilateral relationship involves 'incorporation, control, exploitation of the resources, people or territory of one country by foreign states and corporations' (McCormack 1990a). This makes sense from the perspective of Japanese capital because of its need to secure access to Australia's supply of raw materials and energy sources. Equally important, corporate construction businesses, so central to the functioning of the Japanese political system as well as its economy, have exhibited a strong expansionist drive, already manifest in various tunnelling, hotel, casino and resort development projects in Australia (Tanaka 1990; Rimmer 1988b). Thus, Japanese economic interests, in the context of the increasingly integrated economies of the Asia-Pacific region, have a particular concern with Australia.

Although facing growing economic problems, Japan is a surplus capital economy and has been looking for ways to use it in the region to further secure access to land, materials and labour. This process involves close cooperation between Japanese capital and the Japanese state, which are fused in a much more intimate fashion than in other capitalist nations. In particular, MITI, under whose auspices the MFP proposal was conceived (in its Leisure division), has an interest in maintaining its central role in the steering of the Japanese economy. In other words, the MFP is designed partly to resolve problems of Japanese economic institutions, and to further the Pacific Rim strategy whereby Japanese-based capital maintains and entrenches its premier position in the international division of labour.

The element of *utopianism* is also important. There is nothing specifically Japanese about the quest for a perfect city in which all human endeavours are given full opportunity to flourish. As noted in chapter 11, it has been a recurrent theme of urban 'visionaries' in countries like Britain, the United States and Australia. However, the quest for conditions of harmony is particularly central to *shinto*, the foundation of Japanese spirituality. It sits uneasily with the pressing intensity of urban problems characteristic of modern Japanese cities. Australia's huge and relatively unspoiled continent seems to offer more potential for realising an urban utopia. It is notable in this context that a forerunner of the MFP proposal was the abortive 'Silver Columbia' project, involving the development of retirement villages for Japanese people in Australia and elsewhere in the Asia-Pacific Region (Huxley and Berry 1990). Likewise, the attractiveness of Australia for holidays by Japanese tourists has become well-established. Golf course fees are modest, gambling facilities are accessible, the beaches are attractive and the lifestyle is relaxed. To conflate utopianism with access to golf courses and casinos may seem overly cynical, but it is illustrative of the various levels at which a project like the MFP may be rationalised.

The development of the MFP proposal evidently involved some dovetailing of the interests of capital and state in Australia and Japan. This reflects the almost opposite circumstances of the two countries — the one technologically advanced, with surplus capital and a high overall population-land ratio, and the other needing additional investment and technology to enhance its economic position and to foster regional development, with a low population-land ratio. It appears as a marriage of convenience between unequal partners, propelled by the concerns with over-development and under-development respectively. It remains unclear whether the marriage has good prospects.

MFP: PUBLIC CONCERNS

The MFP project was extremely controversial from the beginning. It became a substantial issue in the 1989 general election when the leader of the Liberal Party declared himself opposed to the establishment of the 'enclave' he said the MFP would become. Some of the objections had a racist character, as has also been the case with some of the more general opposition to Japanese investment in Australia. Of course, Japan was Australia's immediate adversary in the second world war and, despite the successful development of Australia as a multi-racial society, anti-Japanese sentiments remain significant among segments of the population. Local graffiti in Adelaide quickly featured 'No Jap City Here' once the Gillman location was selected. Indeed, fear of fuelling racist sentiments soon caused some opponents of the MFP to mute their criticisms. Nevertheless, legitimate grounds for concern have been recurrently voiced, including economic problems, adverse environmental impacts, and political problems arising from the processes of decision-making.

A principal *economic* concern is that the MFP has the potential to blow out the size of the Australian foreign debt. This is indicated by the section in the Joint Feasibility Study based on research done by the National Institute of Economic and

Industry Research (Arthur Anderson Consulting/Kinhill 1989). A variety of assumptions are used to estimate the impact of the MFP on the economy. The most striking results concern the balance of payments. The projected net trade impact after 10 years (for a MFP with a 100,000 population of which 20 per cent is foreign) is to increase Australia's annual current account deficit by $0.5 billion. It is argued that this adverse impact could be reduced if a higher proportion of the population were to be from overseas and there was a higher proportion of the funding coming from foreign equity. Hence the conclusion that the 'optimal' characteristics of the project would be for 'an MFP primarily based on foreign capital, with the investment outcomes reinvested in the Australian economy, and a workforce of 60–80 per cent highly skilled international workers who take up residence in Australia'. The subsequent study by the Australian government ruled out this outcome by setting a limit of 25 per cent on the foreign-sourced population. However, it confirmed that the effect of the MFP would be to increase foreign debt — one of the very problems it is supposed to resolve — for up to fifteen years before its boost to output and exports was fully developed (Bureau of Industry Economics 1990).

Even in the long run there is doubt whether there would be a positive effect on the external trade balance. Of course, there can be no guarantee that profits generated in the MFP would be reinvested locally; if they are not, the outflows of interest and dividend payments add to the balance of payments problem. Also, to the extent that the 'international workers' maintain a preference for the consumption of goods and services from their own countries of origin (because of familiar products and brand-names), it is a prescription for deterioration in the balance of trade. This would only be offset in the long term by dynamic effects of the MFP on the structure of the Australian economy. These would depend in turn on the type of industries developed, the consequential labour market impacts, and the extent of technology transfer.

As previously noted, education, healthcare, telecommunication and media production/broadcasting have been identified as a starting point for an implementation strategy for a MFP.

However, the balance between 'high-tech' (e.g. computer-based industries) and 'high-touch' (e.g. convention centres, leisure and recreation pursuits) remains ambiguous. The resolution of this matter is extremely important because, together with the issue of the proportions of the population who will be local and 'international', it has a major bearing on the type of employment opportunities provided. The official scenario is one of quality jobs for a 'clever Australia'. An alternative scenario is one in which the local workers are concentrated in a secondary labour market, as golf-caddies, cleaners, and maintenance workers serving an elite group of internationals either at work or play.

Proponents of the MFP claim that this latter outcome, although unfortunate, may be a necessary social price to be paid for the transfer of technology and the modernisation of industry. Certainly, the Australian economy has evidenced technological backwardness and outdated capital stock in many areas, and this needs addressing in any programme of economic restructuring. As the Australian government's own economic analysis noted, the gains to industry 'depend crucially on the degree of technology transfer and the diffusion that the MFP gives rise to (Bureau of Industry Economics 1990). However, there are strong reasons for scepticism about the technology-transfer argument. Japanese industrialists are understandably concerned to maintain a degree of technological control or monopoly as an ingredient in their success. Equally, to the extent that the MFP remains distinct spatially and socially, it is also likely that it would be limited in its economic integration.

The *environmental* concerns are more specifically related to the particular site selected. Gillman is about 15 kilometres from the Adelaide CBD. Part of the site has been used as a garbage dump, including toxic wastes and heavy metals. Various hazardous industrial activities have been located nearby, including a factory producing chlorine and ammonia, another producing sulphuric acid and sulphur dioxide, petrol storage tanks and a major power station. It is very low lying, much of it only 20–30 cm above sea level, and therefore vulnerable to the potential impact of the greenhouse effect on water levels. The area is ill-suited for major construction, being based on a combination of low bearing-strength sediments and underlying stiff clays which offer considerable resistance to pile-driving, excavation and dredging operations. There have been proposals to turn the bordering wetlands into a national park: its mangrove forests are a sensitive nursery ground for the fishing industry. Overall, the combination of natural wetlands and degraded land uses is highly problematic. The area has been variously described as vital for maintaining ecological balance in an area bordered by offensive industries and as an 'ecological disaster' area (Smith 1990). One journalist has described it, with some poetic licence, as combining 'the pollution of the Ganges, the pestilence of Mexico City and the stinking swamps of the Louisiana bayous' (Hills 1992). To say the least, its transformation presents a challenge!

Finally, there has been strong concern about the *political* processes associated with the development of the proposed MFP. The secrecy surrounding the early stages in the project's development was a major focus for disquiet and criticism. The early involvement of corporate interests was not matched by a similar concern with public information and participation. The minutes of one meeting of the MFP Joint Secretariat Committee stated the view that 'it is necessary to control the consciousness of public and related organisations very carefully' (Sugimoto 1990). A 'leaked' federal Cabinet minute fuelled these concerns about manipulation of public opinion. Despite efforts by the South Australian government to redress this legacy, the proposal for the local government of the MFP to be appointed by the State government, rather than elected, inevitably rekindled these concerns. Overall, critics of the project have characterised it as the product of an 'enclave of technocrats' with an 'absence of democratic participatory processes' (Sugimoto 1990).

VFT: A MEGA-PROJECT DERAILED?

Many similar economic, environmental and political concerns arose when a Very Fast Train was proposed to connect Sydney, Canberra and Melbourne. This is worthy of study as another project with major implications for urban and regional development. The VFT proposal was formally abandoned in 1991 but not before it had stirred up some lively discussion on transport infrastructure policies. It was revived in 1993 during the federal election campaign when spending on infrastructure projects was an issue, although it simmered down again afterwards. It is of ongoing significance in the context of understanding how transport and urban regional development can interact.

The scheme originated in 1984 with an idea by the Director of the CSIRO for a super-fast train linking the major cities of south-eastern Australia. It was quickly taken up by a consortium of private corporate capitalist interests, notably TNT, BHP, Elders and the Japanese construction firm Kumagai-Gumi. Like the MFP, Japanese capital, technology and management was important to the venture. As such, both projects are expressions of the closer East Asia-Pacific regional integration described by Abe David and Ted Wheelwright (1989). The VFT was originally estimated to cost $4.5 billion for the construction of the new track and associated facilities. What was envisaged is something equivalent to the Japanese bullet-train (*shinkansen*). Estimated passenger travel time from Sydney to Melbourne was as low as 3.5 hours, on which basis it was anticipated that there would be a major diversion of air, road and existing rail traffic to the new facility. How much diversion and how much new travel would be generated is obviously crucial in the assessment of economic viability. There have also been important environmental concerns, particularly with the route originally chosen (James 1990). As with the MFP, an overall evaluation of the project also needs to take into account the social and political implications of how the economic decisions are made.

First, it is clear that, although privately financed, the VFT would not have been free of the problems of public finance. The cost of construction was expected to be generated by the consortium of private enterprises, presumably mainly through equity and/or loan financing. In other words, the public would ultimately provide the funds, not through contributions to tax revenues or the purchase of government bonds as is the usual case for public sector infrastructure, but through the purchase of shares and debentures and through savings in banks. Even the use of accumulated past profits by corporations in the consortium means that these funds would not have been available for other investment purposes. Financing the VFT would thereby have added an extra strain on the supply of investable funds in the Australian economy. As such it would have tended to add to the international inflow of capital, either directly or indirectly, with adverse consequences for the balance of payments and overseas debt. Against this, proponents of the scheme contended that 'the VFT offers to provide a major boost to investment in the traded-goods sector, [and] therefore, is fully in accord with the Government's own prescription of the requirements to escape from the external debt trap' (VFT Consortium 1989).

Whether or not that secondary boost to the economy would have occured is necessarily a matter of conjecture. What is more certain is that the immediate effect would have been to put upward pressure on interest rates as the competition for available investment funds increased. These high interest rates could then be expected to curtail other domestic investment projects, thereby intensifying the nation's long-run economic difficulties. This is not to argue against major infrastructure investments. Indeed, the economic development of Australia has depended upon governments taking a leading role in this respect and, in conditions of recession, it is a particularly appropriate policy response to the unemployment problem. Rather, the point is that the macroeconomic outcome is an unpredictable effect of two competing tendencies: the stimulus of the initial investment and the secondary effects resulting from changes in the availability of investment funds and the rate of interest.

Private financing also presupposes that a profit will be generated. That likelihood would have been enhanced by three conditions:

- substantial diversion of existing traffic from existing inter-urban rail, road and air movements; *plus* additional demand for passenger travel;
- generation of revenue from associated sources, such as property development and accretions in land values along the route;
- the possibility of an eventual subsidy from the government in the event of revenues being insufficient to cover the operating

and maintenance costs plus the interest costs on the capital employed.

The first condition would seem to depend in turn on the extent of three factors:

- the development of areas around intermediate rail stations as commuting belts;
- the development of new business areas to be served by the VFT;
- the development of additional domestic and/or international sources of passenger demand.

In other words, the volume of traffic necessary for the profitability of the project would have depended on major changes in the distribution of population, regional economic development and international economic relationships.

The regional aspects are particularly interesting. If the VFT were conducive to decentralisation of population and industry, it could be said to serve the goals discussed in chapter 10 more effectively than the piecemeal policies of State governments have done in the past. But would that have likely been the case? The annihilation of space by transport technology doesn't necessarily promote decentralisation. Bringing Sydney and Melbourne closer together in time, if that is what would have been effectively achieved, may promote their economic restructuring and closer economic integration, but the likelihood of economic development occurring at intervening localities is less certain. Of course, much would depend on the number of intervening railway stations. Areas around intervening stations on a VFT line could flourish as commuter centres and possibly as sites for service, commercial or industrial developments. But the more stops the less speed and, hence, the less overall effectiveness of the scheme as an inter-metropolitan link. No doubt, a combination of rapid through-trains and slower stopping-trains could have been programmed to achieve some compromise. However, it must also be borne in mind that the VFT proposal was principally for the carriage of passengers, which limited its potential for stimulating decentralised industrial developments where rail-freight carriage (other than expensive high-speed freight) is a relevant consideration.

The effect of the VFT would have been to link regional policy, at least in south-east Australia, to the success or otherwise of a particular private enterprise infrastructure development. That would have made any newly developed regional centres particularly vulnerable to the continued existence and efficiency of the VFT. That is why the spectre of eventual public subsidy necessarily hung over the project — and eventually signalled its demise — despite protestations about the essentially private character of the enterprise. As with the first railways in Australia constructed by private enterprise, the state could have been expected to take over when national interests are at stake. 'Privatise the profits and socialise the losses' is a familiar theme in relationships between the private and public sectors of the capitalist economy. Indeed, this aspect surfaced very early in the VFT proposal because of the claim by the VFT consortium for specially lenient initial tax arrangements from the federal government — an effective subsidy for the project — as a condition for its commencement.

The project also raised questions about whether the VFT consortium would benefit from the increased land values associated with the development. One might say that the mode of transport was never the sole issue in the VFT proposal. The financial trump-card of the consortium was its plan to capture the increases in land values expected in the vicinity of intermediate stations on the VFT line. (This has a precedent with the ill-fated Bond University on Queensland's Gold Coast.) If implemented it would have given the consortium a vested interest in generating inflation in land values. That could have been expected to intensify the general problem of inflation, particularly in housing costs, which would offset the claimed advantages of the project in lowering costs of housing and infrastructure in the metropolitan areas.

It is difficult to put values on these various items in an economic evaluation of how the VFT project would have fared. The evaluation in monetary terms of the environmental and noise impacts is also highly contentious. From the information available, it seems that there were always substantial grounds to doubt its overall economic viability, especially by comparison with the upgrading of the existing Sydney-Canberra-Melbourne rail connection. The latter approach has been estimated at less than a third of the cost of the VFT. It would have less acute environmental impacts and would improve freight transport as well as passenger transport services, with potentially important implications for the development and decentralisation of industry (Ferris 1990). However, a systematic evaluation of these alternatives seemed to have little place in the process of policy formulation. In the end, the deregulation of the airlines and consequent falls in airfares, together with the federal government's unwillingness to accept the proposals from the consortium for capturing land values and getting tax concessions, brought the proposal to an end. From the viewpoint of political process, it had been a revealing trip.

The decision-making process itself had seemed to be semi-privatised. There was no process of public tendering, as was also the case in other projects involving the Japanese construction firm Kumagai-Gumi, such as Sydney's Harbour Tunnel. Little attention was paid to providing the conditions necessary for effective public debate about alternatives. The VFT project stood and fell on its private commercial viability and the capacity to secure special deals with the state apparatus. These are the hallmarks of a corporatist system in which the public interest is subsumed into a calculus of corporate profitability.

PROSPECTS

The scale of mega-projects like the MFP and the VFT is comparable historically to the Snowy Mountains scheme or the early stages of building Canberra as the national capital. However, the role of government seems to be primarily as co-ordinator and facilitator, effectively restricted to creating the conditions necessary for private sector development.

At the time of writing the South Australian State government is still committed to the MFP. Some of the local criticisms of it have become rather more muted, as the practicalities of constructing it in South Australia have begun to be addressed

(McCormack 1990b). However, other opposition remains, particularly from environmentalists and left-wing political groups, while the local trade unions have identified particular necessary conditions for their cooperation (South Australia: United Trades & Labour Council 1991). Even the academics have got organised, forming a group called Academics Against the Multi-Function Polis! The business interests remain committed, although the strength of that long-term commitment was dissipated by the deepening economic recession in Australia in the early 1990s. As for the Japanese interests, one may detect some significant erosion of their support for the MFP project since the idea was first floated. This is not surprising. The original gesture of international cooperation had become a catalyst for anti-Japanese sentiments in Australia, a focus for a messy inter-State competition, and the target for many other economic, social and environmental concerns. The Australian people as a whole are evidently not grateful for the offer, and the Australian processes of public controversy and dissent sit uncomfortably with the tighter corporatist processes which are the Japanese norm.

The contradictory features of regional development are also evident in the study of these projects. Building an MFP away from the eastern seaboard may be justified in terms of regional balance. However, it is evident that the selection of the South Australian site was a serious setback in practice. Adelaide lacks the proximity to Japan that the Queensland site would have had and it lacks the abundant leisure resort facilities with which so many Japanese have already become familiar on Queensland's Gold Coast. Also, the South Australian site is not connected to the dominant Sydney-Melbourne axis (which the VFT would have served). Many commentators originally envisaged a symbiotic relationship between the two schemes, with the MFP being located on the VFT route, thereby enhancing the access and economic potential of the new town while generating more demand for the rapid transportation services (Stilwell 1990). That ceased to be the case with the selection of the Gillman site for the MFP and the abandonment of the VFT proposal, at least for the time being.

It can be anticipated that new urban developments and

regional infrastructure projects directly linked with international capital will become more common. This is evident in various other mega-projects for urban development and redevelopment (as analysed by Huxley and Berry 1990). The MFP and VFT schemes are illustrative of both the possibilities and hazards. They have raised key issues about where the Australian economy and society is, or should be, heading. Improved transport infrastructure, more efficient and equitable cities, more decentralised forms of regional development, and how to achieve them — these are properly the stuff of widespread concern. The big question is the political one about how these issues are posed and resolved.

Meanwhile, the games are coming! The decision, announced in September 1993, to stage the Olympics in Sydney in the year 2000 switches attention to another mega-project with major implications for urban and regional development. As with the MFP and VFT, a series of questions about economic, social and environmental impacts necessarily arise. How reasonable are the assumptions underlying projected costs and revenues? What of the relationship between public sector expenditures and private sector interests? What will be the use made of the Olympic facilities beyond the big event? What of the links to transport and other infrastructure developments? Can potentially inflationary impacts, particularly in the housing market, be controlled? In these and other respects there is much to be learned from the experience with other mega-project proposals. Then let the games begin ...

FURTHER READING

James (1990): a collection of critical articles on the MFP and VFT projects.

McCormack (1989): a consideration of the initial MFP proposal by a leading scholar of Australian-Japanese relations.

Paris (1992): further details on the VFT proposal.

Huxley and Berry (1990): a review of other 'mega-projects' in Australian cities.

14

Urban Conflict and Protest

The intensity of urban problems and the inadequacy of reforms implemented by the state have been matched by a proliferation of urban protests. Internationally these protests have taken various forms. At one extreme there are potentially revolutionary confrontations such as that which occured on the streets of Paris in May 1968 and the waves of urban violence which occurred in various British cities in 1981 and 1985 and in Los Angeles in 1992. At the other extreme there are the activities of numerous parochial residents' groups concerned to protect their domestic property values. In between are a range of urban protests which have posed significant challenges to the economic interests of capital and the legitimacy of the state. In Australia the range of organised protests includes:

- the 'Green Bans' movement involving builders' labourers joining with local residents to obstruct urban building projects;
- organised squatting in vacant housing, such as that in the inner Sydney suburb of Glebe;
- groups protesting about the impact on their neighbourhoods of urban freeway developments;
- campaigns against urban airport developments e.g. Residents Opposed to Runway Three in Sydney;
- environmental protection groups such as Stop The Ocean Pollution;
- various pressure groups for more and better public housing, public transport, health and child-care facilities.

What, if anything, is the common element in these diverse forms of urban protest? And what is their significance? Are they reactionary, reformist or revolutionary? In what sense can they be described as 'urban social movements'? This chapter addresses these general issues and then examines two case studies — the Green Bans and the Glebe squatters. The former is a famous political movement of international repute while the latter is characteristic of more localised action. In both cases our concern is to explore the dynamics and limits of urban protest. The following theoretical discussion is necessary to set the context for the case studies.

THE SIGNIFICANCE OF URBAN PROTEST

Systemic social conflicts inevitably arise in large cities such as Australia's metropolitan areas. The problems analysed in this book, especially in the first six chapters, are pervasive. The origins of the resulting conflicts are partly in the process of *production*, including capital-labour conflicts, irregular capital accumulation, periodic economic crises and uneven development. Their origins are partly in the system of *distribution*, involving inequalities structured according to class, gender and race, mediated by space and place. Their origins are also partly in the sphere of *exchange*, arising from externalities, monopoly pricing and problems with the provision of public goods.

To a considerable degree, these various conflicts are contained, individualised and domesticated. Grumbling is their most general manifestation! Alcoholism and drug abuse, domestic violence, psychological disorder and even suicide may also be involved in the personal responses. However, from time to time people get together into organised groups to address the urban problems from which they collectively suffer.

What is the significance of these protest groups? As with other social movements which cut across class boundaries, it is tempting to see them as secondary to the more conventional organisations of the left and the labour movement which more directly challenge the interests of capital (Miliband 1991). A traditional Marxian view sees the workplace as the primary focus of class struggle, classes being defined in terms of ownership and non-ownership of the means of production. Such struggle, involving wages and working conditions but also raising demands for industrial democracy and worker control, is the motor force for fundamental economic change. It is through this process that social progress occurs, sometimes evolutionary and sometimes revolutionary. Urban protest groups are not at the centre of this action. They do not directly challenge the ownership of the means of production. Their principal focus is often not privately-owned businesses at all but state-owned enterprises providing public services like housing, transport, child care, health or education. Nor do they directly impact on the rate of exploitation and the distribution of income between capital and labour. The capitalist class has little to fear.

To this summary rejection of the political significance of urban protest groups can be added some observations of their structure and activities in practice. The leaders are typically articulate professionals who in their working lives would usually see themselves having a stake in the maintenance of the existing socioeconomic order. While alliances with trade unions are not unknown, the political style of urban protest groups usually owes more to a 'middle class' tradition. The characteristic focus on submissions, petitions, public meetings and alternative plans for urban design is in contrast with the more working-class tradition of direct action. Urban protest groups may even have the effect of undermining the cohesion of classes. This is because the interest groups involved in urban conflicts often divide along lines other than those of class; e.g. owner-occupiers and renters, private motorists and public transport users. The organisational focus is characteristically local — not evidently compatible with the call for workers of the world to unite! Thus, the social divisions and alliances involved in urban protest groups set them aside from 'the main game' of capital/labour conflict which gives capitalism its dynamism, its principal contradictions and its potential for radical change. Urban protest groups are, at best, reformist. At worst, they are parochial and reactionary, fully deserving of the NIMBY (not-in-my-back-yard) epithet.

Against this dismissal of urban protest groups as incidental to the dynamic forces operating in capitalist society can be set various counter arguments. First is the obvious point, a theme running throughout this book, that *location is important*. Residential location (and its relationship to the location of workplaces, commercial, cultural and recreational facilities) has major consequences, economically, socially and politically. People involved in paid work outside the household normally spend 35–40 hours working and most of the rest of the 168 hours each week in household-focused activities and transport movements for which the residence is the base point. The conditions of housing, transport, local social services and environmental amenity are crucial to standards of living. They also have a major bearing on ideology, including attitudes to community, state and political process. In other words, both production and consumption — mediated by place and space — are important influences on the living conditions of ordinary people and their responses to those conditions. Location, production relationships and consumption patterns interact in complex ways in shaping class structure and political action.

Second, the provision of 'collective consumption' goods has become a key element in the modern capitalist city. This concept of *collective consumption*, closely associated with the analysis of Manuel Castells (1977, 1978), is central to urban political economy. The provision of collective consumption goods by the state is essential for the functioning of monopoly capitalism. On this reasoning, conflict over the provision of items like public housing, public transport and other social services addresses an element of the economic system no less fundamental than conflict over wages and working conditions. The adequacy of the provision of collective consumption goods in different locations has a major bearing on the material well-being of population subgroups in the city. So, urban protest groups addressing deficiencies in these collective consumption goods and their distribution are not marginal but central to the functioning of contemporary capitalism. They challenge the system at a key point of contradiction.

Third, urban struggles may threaten *social reproduction*. Capitalism is not just an economic system for the production of goods and services and for the distribution of rewards: like any system it must also have features which ensure its reproduction. This chain of reasoning in political economy has been particularly stressed by feminists, drawing attention to the crucial role of women in the process of reproduction, socially as well as biologically. However, it also derives partly from the writings of Antonio Gramsci on the importance of ideology in the reproduction of the social order. From this point of view urban protest groups may be very important. To the extent that they challenge the legitimacy of the existing institutions, they are destabilising and more potentially radical than groupings in the labour movement whose primary concern is with re-distribution of income shares. They have the potential to challenge the hegemony of capital within the existing social order.

Fourth, urban protests typically involve *confrontation with the state*. Does this make them less or more radical than trade unions who confront employers? Both employers and the state are key elements of the capitalist system — indeed the state is typically the largest employer in cities. More generally, the state has become central in ensuring the stability and reproduction of the system in its monopoly capitalist phase, albeit at the expense of generating new contradictions. So urban protests may be regarded as a reflection of the changed form of class struggle in this particular period of capitalist development. In an increasing number of aspects of economic and social life, labour does not confront capital directly, but is mediated by the state. In this sense urban protest groups are to the fore in what Cynthia Cockburn (1978) has called 'the new terrain of class struggle'.

The outcome is an increasingly *politicised* urban economy and society. The provision of goods and services becomes essentially political when the state is the provider. Demands for improved provision may translate into support for particular political parties (and, increasingly, for independent candidates). More strikingly, when urban protest groups engage in direct action, they challenge the legitimacy of the capitalist state. Here are non-governmental organisations purporting to act on behalf of the people, raising questions about the adequacy of existing structures of political power. The recurrent demand is for 'power to the people', although co-optation and dissipation of energies are ever-present tendencies.

These propositions can be summarised in terms of five defining features of urban protest groups:

- their urban place/space focus;
- their concern with collective consumption;
- their challenge to social reproduction;
- their confrontation with the state;
- their politicised character.

These are features that are applied later in assessing the two Australian case studies.

URBAN SOCIAL MOVEMENTS

The discussion so far has largely avoided the term 'urban social movements.' This is because, following the influential use of this term by Castells, a more restricted meaning is usually implied. Some clarification is appropriate. The typology of Kilmartin & Thorns (1978), drawing on the early work of Castells and reproduced as Figure 13.1 is a useful starting point. Three types of organisation—urban social movement, protest and community—are identified according to their characteristic levels of consciousness, political line and effects. They broadly correspond to the three political positions—revolutionary, reformist and conservative. On this reasoning, the term urban social movement is applicable only to groups that adopt 'contestatory strategies aimed at the structural transformation of the urban system or towards a substantial modification of power relations in the class struggle, that is to say, in the last resort, the power of the state' (Castells 1977).

This view interprets urban social movements as representing secondary contradictions in advanced capitalism. They are a characteristic response to the intervention by the state in the provision (or lack of provision) of the items of collective consumption required for capital accumulation and social reproduction. Although urban social movements may have varied social compositions and practices, they are regarded as being capable of generating qualitative transformation only if they link up with the more advanced sectors of the working class. Hey presto, the Marxist focus on the primacy of *production* relations is re-established. It is the structural changes in the economy which bring urban social movements into existence. It is the alliance with working-class organisations which is the requirement for practical success.

FIGURE 13.1   CLASSIFICATION OF URBAN PROTEST GROUPS

Levels of consciousness	Political line of the organisation	Effects	Type of organisation
Revolution	Contestatory	Structural transformation of the urban system	Urban social movement
Conflict	Reformist	Reform	Protest
Communion	Redress of actual or anticipated grievance	Community advancement/ defence	Community

Source: adapted from Kilmartin & Thorns (1978).

Castells has subsequently modified this analysis in significant ways. Indeed, both the methodological shifts and political implications are quite striking. Greater autonomy is accorded to urban social movements in his later writing which moves away from the formal structuralist analysis influenced by Althusser's Marxism. Castells identifies social conflicts which are not derived from the structure of the capitalist economy. He further argues that the political effectiveness of urban social movements may be enhanced by broad alliances with political parties. An evident parallel is with the strategy for socialist politics involving a popular front, gradually infiltrating the state rather than continuously confronting it (Castells 1978). This is altogether a less restrictive conception of the origins and character of urban social movements. It is a more pragmatic view of the ingredients for their success through making use of the existing political structure of the bourgeois state.

Yet more recent analysis involves a total break with the emphasis on the primacy of class struggle (Castells 1983). This emphasises the diversity and specificity of urban social movements in various countries. Yes, there are conflicts over the provision of collective consumption, but also conflicts between local communities and the broader structures of mass society, and conflicts generated by local groups attempting to wrest control over provision of services from the centralised bureaucratic state. Politically, there is a rupture too: now, according to Castells, the success of urban social movements requires organisational and ideological distinctness from all political parties, even including parties based in the working class. Gone is the essential nexus with working-class organisations and even the pragmatic alliances with political parties. In their place is a stress on the importance of autonomy, a belief that anything more than an arms-length relation to political parties is likely to be fatal (Lowe 1986).

These elastic but influential views on the nature of urban social movements may be regarded as complementing our earlier discussion. The five characteristics of urban protest groups which give them their radical potential are also in evidence here. There is no fundamental disagreement on that score. What remains contentious are the conditions necessary for the realisation of that potential. We can seek to throw some further light on this through the examination of the two Australian case studies, one involving an alliance of activists with trade unions; the other a single group in confrontation with the interests of capital and the power of the state.

THE GREEN BANS

The Green Bans are typically cited as the principal example of an urban social movement 'down under'. The movement brought resident action groups and trade unions together in effective opposition to urban developers and the NSW State government in Sydney in the early 1970s. It had a major impact on the urban development process at the time, and it has had a lasting effect on the way many people perceive possibilities for progressive political action.

What were the key elements in the emergence of this phenomenon? A constellation of factors came together in a potent mixture, of which the three central elements were:

- rampant urban redevelopment with little regard for environmental quality;
- the increasing importance of resident action groups;
- the involvement of trade unions in helping to put a brake on the urban redevelopment process.

The first point is important in setting the scene. The period of the late 1960s and early 1970s was one of rapid *economic restructuring*, within which the movement of capital into speculative CBD office development was one important aspect. Other aspects (described more fully in chapter 1) included the crisis in manufacturing profitability, its consequences for the concentration of capital and for spatial relocation, and major changes in technology and the structure of the workforce. The Liberal State government in NSW was intimately involved in seeking to create the conditions for continued capital accumulation, particularly through coordinating major urban redevelopment projects and transport infrastructure schemes. The scale of physical, economic and social change in Sydney was enormous. As Maurie Daly (1982) notes, 'banks, finance houses, and related business services such as accounting were at the centre of a boom in office construction which began in the mid-1960s and accelerated during the mineral boom'. There was a massive inflow of capital associated with this reorientation of Sydney as a significant financial centre. Urban redevelopment schemes proliferated. As Andrew Jakubowicz (1984) puts it, 'the initiatives by the state and capital shattered the peace of suburbia'. In the inner-city areas the conflicting interests became particularly pronounced. The expansion of the CBD was physically impeded by the legacy of an earlier set of production and consumption structures in the inner-city suburbs — small manufacturing businesses, warehouses, working-class residential areas and the associated local pubs and other community facilities. Something had to give.

The second ingredient in the looming confrontation was the increased importance of *resident action groups*. The political structures of the inner-city areas had traditionally been dominated by the ALP, whose local branches had taken on the characteristics of 'family businesses'. The emergence of the process of gentrification was threatening to these cosy arrangements. The new residents, typically white-collar and professional workers, formed separate societies in areas like Paddington and Glebe. Within the ALP they constituted a distinct faction which struggled to wrest control of branches from what was sometimes called 'the old Irish Mafia' (Jakubowicz 1984). Resident action groups proliferated, partially coordinated for a while by the Coalition of Resident Action Groups (CRAG). There was no general presumption that governments—local, State or federal—could be relied on to provide the necessary safeguards for urban environmental quality and residential amenity. Rather, as Richard Roddewig (1978) notes, 'most of the major threats to neighbourhood environment which spurred the rise of resident action groups ... were state-sponsored projects'. A mood of social activism was evident.

The third ingredient was *trade unions* prepared to use their industrial muscle in pursuit of broad urban environmental objectives. The particular trade union which pioneered the Green Ban tactic and remained at the forefront of the action throughout was the NSW branch of the Builders' Labourers' Federation. Its leaders, Jack Mundey, Joe Owens and Bob Pringle, had proved their effectiveness in more conventional union struggles over wages, working conditions and security of employment. The leadership persuaded the union's members that broader social goals could be pursued through extending the traditional union tactic of black bans to projects adversely affecting urban quality of life. Jack Mundey was—and still is—particularly persuasive in arguing that workers' welfare depends not only on the wages which their labour earns but also on the social usefulness of the products of their labour and, more broadly, on the character of the urban environment in which they live and work. This diversification of trade union objectives and tactics was certainly innovative. It was not welcomed by the Establishment. *The Sydney Morning Herald* (14.8.72) was moved to editorialise that 'there is something highly comical in the spectacle of builders' labourers, whose ideas on industrial relations do not rise above strikes, violence, intimidation and the destruction of private property, setting themselves up as the arbiters of taste and protectors of our national heritage'. Such effrontery ...

The first of the Green Bans was at Kelly's Bush in the affluent harbourside residential suburb of Hunters Hill. The local residents, once decribed by Mundey himself as 'upper middle-class morning-tea matrons', called on the BLF in 1971 to help prevent destruction of local bushland for new housing developments. The union agreed; so BLF members refused to work on the site and the housing was not built. More requests for the union's backing followed. A standard strategy was devised for dealing with such appeals: the union would request a meeting with the residents, invite the developers and also consultants more sympathetic to the residents' concerns, listen to the debate, take a vote and act on it.

In quick succession a series of other Green Bans were established:

- at Eastlakes, a working-class area where the development of high-rise flats in a new estate impinged on the limited recreational space;
- at The Rocks, a traditional working-class area bordering the CBD and the wharves, where a major redevelopment of high-rise offices, hotels and expensive town houses was planned;
- in Glebe, where proposed expressways would require the demolition of inner-city housing then mainly occupied (pre-gentrification) by working-class residents;
- at Waterloo, where further high-rise public housing developments were proposed, displacing existing working-class tenants and owner-occupiers;
- in Woolloomooloo, where a State government plan involved massive high rise office and commercial development and an urban freeway, demolishing housing occupied by the working class, welfare recipients and squatters;
- at Victoria Street in Kings Cross, where working-class tenants and other occupants of Victorian terraces, many of which had been converted to boarding houses, were to be displaced by the construction of high-rise apartments.

Other Green Bans were placed on the demolition of two theatres, the loss of parkland in the Botanical Gardens and at Centennial Park and on a number of historic buildings scheduled for demolition to make way for urban redevelopment. At the peak of the movement, over 40 Green Bans had been declared, halting an estimated $4 billion worth of construction projects (Roddewig 1978). Other unions, such as the Federated Engine Drivers and Firemen's Association (FEDFA) and the Building Workers Industrial Union (BWIU) also supported the bans.

Classifying the types of project involved is not easy because many bans involved more than one issue. The dominant aims were preserving existing buildings, stopping inner-city redevelopment, maintaining housing standards, obstructing demolition for expressways and retaining parkland (Camina 1975). A few bans were applied for other reasons, e.g. a ban on building work at the University of Sydney until the authorities withdrew their refusal to allow a course in feminist thought; a ban on work at Macquarie University for discrimination by a residential college against a homosexual student; and a general ban on doctors' new dwellings in a campaign against higher doctor's fees. The targets of the bans were thereby diversified.

The responses by capital and the state to the Green Bans were rapid, powerful and relentless, particularly where urban redevelopment was thwarted. The Rocks and Victoria Street were the classic cases. Forcible evictions of residents occurred. Gangs of armed thugs were hired by developers to 'encourage' residents to leave. Activists obstructing 'scab' labourers were arrested. Fires were lit in vacant buildings. Individual terraced houses were demolished even where this affected the safety of adjoining houses. One local newspaper proprietor, active in voicing opposition to the developers, disappeared and was never found, presumed murdered. Public support for residents and the Green Bans was substantial, despite a generally unsympathetic media which highlighted the violence (as usual) rather than the issues of urban amenity, moral responsibilities and citizens' rights. As Jack Mundey put it, the Builders' Labourers showed 'that intelligent action around an issue does tap a real feeling among people, even though it may be dormant. A type of action which punches through mass apathy and captures people's imagination, as it were, brings in mass support and attracts all sorts of people' (Manning and Hardman 1975).

The eventual demise of the Green Bans was the product of various factors. Moves were instituted by big business interests, in conjunction with the State government, to deregister the NSW branch of the BLF. These interest groups backed the federal branch of the union in its bid to take over the membership of the NSW branch. The federal branch was led by 'big Norm' Gallagher, a long-time opponent of Mundey and his colleagues, whose opposition was rooted in a factional political split — Mundey was prominent in the non-aligned Communist Party of Australia (CPA) while Gallagher was prominent in the pro-Chinese Communist Party of Australia (Marxist-Leninist). For the capitalist interests to have backed Gallagher as the agent for dismantling the NSW union and the bans was the height of pragmatism, to say the least. However, in the deteriorating economic conditions of the mid 1970s, building workers could no longer be assured of continuous employment. Most joined Gallagher's branch of the union to secure what jobs were available. Some other unions, such as the FEDFA and the BWIU, maintained bans for a while, but the momentum was lost. By 1975 the Green Ban movement was effectively finished.

In what sense were the social forces involved in the Green Bans an *urban social movement*? They certainly conform to the five criteria identified earlier in this chapter as characterising urban protest groups. The focus was on *urban place/space*, indeed overwhelmingly on the city of Sydney and its inner suburbs. The need to defend and extend the provision of items of *collective consumption* — particularly public housing, transport and recreational spaces — was a recurring theme. There was a challenge to *reproduction* of the existing economic and social order, particularly to the legitimacy of existing structures of power. The *state* was central, both as an urban demolisher/developer in its own right, and as an enforcer of the interests of private capital. The Green Bans were also manifestly *political*, both in the narrow sense of challenging the authority of the NSW Liberal government and in the broader sense of triggering changes in expectations of the political process, including demands for more environmental protection. This may have fallen short of the irreversible 'values revolution' for which Jack Mundey has recurrently called, but the experience contributed to a growing public awareness of the importance of urban environmental issues.

Most strikingly, the Green Bans involved innovation in the formation of *cross-class alliances*, bringing together militant blue-collar workers with the 'middle-class' mums of Kelly's Bush, students, professionals, welfare recipients and other disaffected groups. Fusing trade unions, the traditional organisations of the working class, with such groupings comprised a bridging of production and consumption concerns and was a forerunner of broader environmental political activism. On Castells' early formulations of what comprises an urban social movement, this linkage with the working class was a crucial element. So too were the wide-ranging demands, transcending the limiting concerns of piecemeal reform. Of course, the ultimate failure of the Green Ban movement to carry through a full 'structural transformation' could be held to disqualify it as an urban social movement, according to a strict interpretation of Castells' early formulation — but on that basis, the world has yet to see one! On the other hand, the close connection of the residents with trade unions and, increasingly, with the sympathetic federal ALP government would, on Castells' later formulation, be regarded as a limiting factor. It certainly did not seem so at the time ...

Retrospective appraisals of the impact and significance of the Green Bans vary considerably. Ironically, the Green Bans may have been useful to capital in the medium term, putting a brake on over-zealous urban expansion schemes which would otherwise have generated a crisis of over-production, most obviously in over-supply of CBD office space. The retention of the original character of areas like The Rocks has also proved to be a valuable commercial asset for a city increasingly geared to the promotion of tourism, an asset which would have been lost if the short-sighted redevelopments had gone ahead. It has also been argued that maintaining the original inner-city housing stock has proved to be a boon for the middle-class gentrifiers, who are now among the main beneficiaries (Badcock 1984). However, other commentators have stressed the more radical consequences of the Green Bans, politically and ideologically. The creation of an 'imagery of resistance' (Jakubowicz 1984) is a case in point. Community concern with urban environmental amenity, and a belief in the efficacy of direct action in defending it, is an enduring radical legacy.

THE GLEBE SQUATTERS

The second case study has less notoriety but is interesting both as contemporary urban social history and for showing the limitations of urban social protest. It concerns squatters in the inner-Sydney suburb of Glebe in 1984–5. The episode has a connection to the Green Bans movement in that it took place in an area of housing which would have been partly destroyed if the NSW State government's plans for new expressway developments had not been thwarted by a Green Ban in the 1970s. However, the more immediate trigger for the protest was the intensfying housing crisis of the 1980s.

The particular housing in question comprised some 700 homes on 19 hectares of land in Glebe. The houses had been bought from the Anglican Church by the federal ALP government in 1973. The Whitlam government, as we know, was keen to place a high priority on urban affairs. Retaining housing for low-income groups in the inner city, extending public ownership and community control, maintaining urban environmental quality and opposing further decimation of the inner city by inner urban expressways — these were goals which fitted neatly into the broader philosophy of the federal government's policy objectives. The Minister for DURD claimed that the public ownership and management of the Glebe Estate would retain the opportunity for low-income individuals and families to live in close proximity to the city centre as part of a wider community; to improve environmental conditions and social conditions of residents of the Estate and surrounding area; to avoid the sudden displacing of the existing population and to avoid any disruption to existing community networks and to preserve the townscape and sympathetically rehabilitate it (Uren, 1974).

Renovation of the run-down housing stock began quickly after the transfer of ownership to the federal government. However, the dramatic change of government in 1975 provided a set-back to the development of the Glebe Estate — and to many other social reforms too. Because the incoming Liberal government did not share the ALP's interventionist philosophy or commitment to urban and regional planning, it cut the funds for the Glebe project. Rehabilitation of the housing dwindled. Many houses were allowed to remain empty, becoming increasingly dilapidated. The Fraser government, recognising the political odium it would incur by abandoning the project, did not seek to sell the housing to the private sector, as its political philosophy would have otherwise suggested. Instead, it began negotiations with the NSW State government regarding a possible land-swap, whereby the ownership of the Glebe Estate would be transferred to the State government in exchange for other land and/or payment. The victory of the ALP at the federal election of 1983 helped to remove political obstacles to the negotiations but progress was very slow. The State government was apprehensive about taking on the Glebe Estate at a time when it claimed to be de-ghettoising public housing, and it was reorganising its overall housing policy.

It was during the period of negotiation between the federal and State governments that the squatters moved in, bringing to a head some ten years of indecision about the future of the Glebe Estate. The initial 'invasion' in October 1984 was organised by the Squatters' Union, involving about 100 squatters in 40 houses. More joined in and the number of occupied houses rose to about 100–120 at the peak in February 1985, with about 200–300 squatters in residence in previously vacant houses. The social composition of the squatters was varied. In the early days, there were nuclear families and at least one extended immigrant family, though the character of the squatters came to be dominated increasingly by young single people, including students at the nearby University of Sydney. For the most part their principal objective was simple — free housing. For some there was also an appeal in the social and political aspects of the squatting, involving the formation of an 'alternative' community, a challenge to the authorities and a dramatisation of the housing crisis for low-income groups.

The relationship between squatters and local residents was problematic. Many locals were apprehensive or hostile, reflecting a general view of squatters as a pariah group. The squatters did make some efforts to forge links with the local community and to emphasise that they were not seeking to deny housing to others. 'We are not queue jumping', read an open letter to residents, 'we will move into another house if any of the houses we occupy is allocated to those members of the Glebe Estate who were here before us'. The squatters also made a contribution in preventing, for the time being, further deterioration of property in the area. It is generally the case that an area with lots of vacant housing quickly becomes run down; but squatters generally try and bring it up to at least minimal standards for habitation. The bottom line remained one of property rights. Interviewed about the squatters, the President of the Real Estate Institute of NSW replied that: 'The Institute sees its role as the defender of the rights of the property owner. Therefore no squatter can ever be a good squatter' (Scott, 1985).

Relationships with the state were even more problematic. The squatters made the federal government increasingly eager to relinquish its ownership of the Estate and the eventual agreed price of $28 million (payable over ten years) for property with an estimated value at the time of between $40 million and $70 million was probably a partial reflection of this. The State government was concerned to maintain its first priority as the orderly public housing of needy people through the Housing Commission and could not condone squatting to the extent that it was seen to undermine this policy. Notices were distributed to the occupied houses, requesting the squatters to return 'from whence they came'. Most stayed put.

At 7 am on 1 March 1985 the police and hired demolition workers arrived to evict the squatters. Violent scenes ensued as barricaded doors were smashed down. Squatters were dragged out. Sixteen were arrested. Many of the police were not wearing identification badges. The media was present in significant numbers: yes, this was the newsworthy action they had been awaiting for months. One journalist reported imaginatively on 'unwashed bodies' emerging from the squats; and prominence was given in the next day's newspaper to one particular photograph of youths with punk haircuts. By the end of the day the occupied houses had been thoroughly smashed up, doors removed, floorboards, fireplaces and stairways destroyed, furniture ejected. There was no possibility of moving back in. The occupation was over.

How are these events associated with the Glebe Estate squatters to be interpreted? Again, our five-fold characterisation of urban social movements can provide some guidelines.

Certainly there was a focus on *urban space/place*: the issue of access to adequate housing for low-income groups in the inner city area was paramount. Equally, the provision of *collective consumption* was an obvious feature: public housing provision, whether by the federal or State government, was the source of the confrontation. The squatters' struggle also focused on the issue of *social reproduction*, both in relation to capital accumulation and legitimation. In bringing the housing crisis sharply into focus, it illuminated a growing contradiction between the need for an adequately housed workforce to ensure continued capital accumulation and the difficulty of the system in satisfying that condition. Although capitalist employers do not need unemployed people, students, pensioners and other welfare recipients to be adequately housed, homelessness of those groups tends to undermine the general legitimacy of the existing economic and social order. Confrontation with *the state* was all too obvious, eventually bringing forth its full coercive powers. As usual it was the state, rather than capitalist employers, which assumed the task of maintaining legitimacy of the existing socio-economic structures. This was particularly pertinent in the Glebe case, of course, because of the unusually large degree of public ownership involved.

Finally, and partly as a result of this centrality of the state, the issue was highly *politicised*. Questions about the proper role of federal and State governments in the provision of public housing were central. Issues of a party factional character were also raised: the Glebe Estate had long been the stronghold of the ALP right wing (reflected in the composition of the Residents' Advisory Committee and the local Glebe ALP branch) whereas the State housing minister was a major figure in the party's left wing, albeit one who was anxious to avoid a conflict with the dominant right-wing faction over this issue. More fundamentally, the squatting issue revealed the political difference between libertarian and authoritarian views: public housing allocated on 'help yourself' basis or through the established bureaucratic procedures? Finally, there was the issue of the legitimacy of using the police as a means of resolving the conflict of interests. These are all aspects of a resource-allocation process which is manifestly political.

In these various respects the squatters had the characteristics of a potentially radical urban social movement: their *urban* struggle involved the provision of a *collective consumption good* which is of a considerable general significance to social *reproduction*, and it focused on the *role of the state* in a way which generated an intense *politicisation*. However, one other aspect — the lack of a clear relationship between the squatters' actions, the labour movement and class struggle — suggests a contrary conclusion. The squatters were in partial conflict with local working-class residents. Alliances with trade unions were notably absent. An offer by unionists to make representations to government, seeking a commitment to urgently develop areas for low cost housing and seek advice on unused government housing that could be occupied by the squatters, was declined by the squatters. The unionists maintained the view that they could not support the squatters' queue-jumping ahead of people on the official public housing waiting list. Thus, the alliance of resident action groups and trade unions which had given such strength and solidarity to the Green Bans was totally absent here.

Looked at in retrospect, it appears that the dominant impact of the Glebe Estate squatters was *reformist*. This was not the principal intent. As we have seen, their goals ranged from the immediate and practical concern for cheap accommodation to a broader political concern with highlighting the severity of the housing crisis. However, the dominant effect of the publicity given to the issue was to accelerate the transfer of the property from the federal to the State government and to reduce the purchase price. The squatting episode also seemed to accelerate the rate of renovation, the State government presumably wishing to avoid the political embarrassment of having evicted the squatters only to leave the houses vacant. Certainly, renovations went ahead more rapidly than in the period before the squatting, although it took some years before all the housing stock was inhabited by public housing tenants. So, the beneficiaries of the squatting were those on the waiting list for public housing, albeit only in terms of a marginal acceleration in their prospects of being allocated a house.

The experience with the squatters on the Glebe Estate clearly shows the tensions associated with urban rehabilitation. The original DURD conception of the Estate involved a commitment of public funding which was not sustained, leading to an under-utilisation of the housing stock at a time when the excess demand for housing, particularly inner-city housing, was steadily increasing. The squatters' actions drew attention to the irrationality of this situation and precipitated a solution, albeit one from which the squatters themselves were not the principal beneficiaries.

CONCLUSIONS

It would be inappropriate to generalise too much from the two case studies of urban protest examined in this chapter. It is the *diversity* of urban protest groups — in composition, organisation, methods, ideology, objectives and durability — which is their most obvious characteristic (Pickvance 1985). There is also a diversity in their effects, both tangible (the realisation of immediate goals such as preventing demolition for urban redevelopment and securing public housing) and ideological (establishing the legitimacy of direct action or of pressure group activity to influence the policies of corporate capital and/or the state). The political consequences are correspondingly varied — reactionary, reformist or revolutionary.

Contemporary capitalism has proved able to accommodate urban protests — whether by concessions and reforms or by direct repression using coercive state power. Capital accumulation may be interrupted — as in the case of the Green Bans stopping profitable urban redevelopment schemes. Legitimation may be under challenge for a while — as in the case of the Glebe squatters exposing the incapacity of the state to mobilise its vacant housing stock in a period of housing crisis. But to impede the overall reproduction of the socio-economic system of capitalism is another matter. Few would claim that a fundamental reshaping of Australian cities is likely to arise from these sources in the foreseeable future.

What is evidently changed as a result of the proliferation of urban protest groups are certain characteristics of the political process. It would be an exaggeration to claim that the 'politics of turf' (Cox 1989) has taken over from the 'politics of class'; but it augments it and modifies it in various ways. Living-places are elevated on a par with workplaces as influences on political identification and practices. The gender imbalance in political activity is redressed to the extent that women are better represented and more active in urban protest groups than in trade unions and political parties based on more traditional class allegiances. The politics of turf also involves a frequent emphasis on *self-help*, especially in housing struggles, which makes it particularly attractive from an anarchist perspective. So too does the recurrent challenge by urban protest groups to the state's claim to be the sole source of legitimate authority in urban management. The overall effect is a diversification of the avenues through which people struggle for a better world — or at least for a better place within it.

FURTHER READING

Lowe (1986): an exposition and critique of Castells' evolving views on urban social movements.

Jakubowicz (1984) and Stilwell (1987): for further details on the two Australian case studies discussed in this chapter.

Mullins (1979) and Rundell (1985): accounts of urban social movements organising around urban freeway developments in Brisbane and Melbourne.

15

Reshaping Australia?

Cities and regions are landscapes of capital, class and state. Their structure affects the availability of jobs, the adequacy of housing, access to transport facilities and the quality of the urban environment. The patterns of urban and regional development shape the quality of our lives, for better or worse.

The distinctive features of Australian cities, including the high degree of metropolitan primacy coupled with low urban population density, interact with other elements of the socio-economic system such as class and gender inequalities, imbalance between public and private sectors and inadequate mechanisms for environmental regulation. The resulting problems are obvious enough—concentrations of unemployment, a continuing crisis of housing affordability, land speculation, inadequate public transport, growing urban social inequality and environmental decay.

These problems have been the focus for remedial public policies ranging from decentralisation to urban consolidation. The disappointing results have fuelled the concerns of diverse urban protest groups. Meanwhile, gentrification proceeds apace in the inner city areas while the suburban sprawl continues on the metropolitan outskirts and beyond. The restructuring of our cities in practice is more market-driven than moulded by enlightened public policy.

Previous chapters in this book have analysed the dimensions and causes of these problems of unbalanced urban and regional development. Some of the limits to the various policy solutions have also been considered. In moving to a conclusion it is appropriate to ask about the potential for future changes to the prevailing patterns of Australian cities. What are the prospects for reshaping Australia?

This issue cannot be resolved independently of a more general consideration of alternative approaches to economic and social policy. Such alternatives embody particular political philosophies. In other words, the resolution of urban and regional problems cannot be a purely technical matter of finding the right mix of policy instruments. It must also be a matter of choice between competing value-systems, between competing visions of what consitutes a good society. The resolution of urban and regional problems must necessarily be part of a broader programme of socio-economic change.

But what direction of change? This concluding chapter considers two broad policy options. One embodies the market-oriented economic values of 'economic rationalism' which have been so dominant in recent years. The other reflects a broader range of concerns about efficiency, equity, ecological sustainability and democracy, coming together in policies which, for want of a better label, we call 'radical interventionism'. By considering these alternatives, urban and regional issues are reinterpreted in terms of a broader debate about the appropriate direction of economic and social change.

These are two starkly constrasting options for reshaping Australia.

ECONOMIC RATIONALISM, CITIES AND REGIONS

'Economic rationalism' is an appealing label. Urban planners and regional development practitioners, just as much as national economic managers, seek rationality and effectiveness in their use of funds and choice of policy instruments. However, the term 'economic rationalism' has come to have a more specific meaning. It rests on the twin beliefs: (i) that economic issues have priority over other social goals, whose achievement in the long run depends on improved economic performance; and (ii) that the market economy generally produces more efficient outcomes than government 'intervention' and planning. These views, with

varying degrees of sophistication, have come to be very influential among politicians, media commentators and among senior
public servants in Canberra, as Michael Pusey (1991) has
demonstrated.

Deregulation, privatisation, user-pays pricing policies, tariff
cuts and flatter ('less distorting') taxes are the most obvious
expressions of 'economic rationalism' in public policy. These
elements are evident in the programmes of both major political
parties. Certainly, the ALP federal government has blended
them with other aspects of economic policy: a continuing
(through wavering) commitment to regulation of labour markets
through the Accord, some selective industry plans, other institutional arrangements for export promotion, and attempts at
macro management through discretionary fiscal and monetary
policy. In effect, there has been an ongoing and uneasy juxtaposition of 'economic rationalist' and more 'interventionist'
elements in policy. However, to take one example, the reluctance
of the Hawke and Keating governments to implement urban
and regional policy on the scale of the Whitlam government is
indicative of the increased reliance on market-induced changes
rather than economic planning. The 'Building Better Cities'
programme shows that the interventionist element survives,
albeit in a tentative form. But to have initiated major structural
economic change without a coherent regional policy is illustrative of the acceptance of market adjustment processes as
paramount.

An understanding of the practical policy aspects of 'economic
rationalism'—including its implications for urban and regional
development—requires an understanding of its theoretical
underpinnings. This is because the policies are based directly on
a particular theoretical vision. Even the terminology is indicative
of this connection. 'Economic rationalism' is rationalist in the
sense of being derived from *a priori* reasoning. Certainly, it
is a stance on economic issues which is buttressed by selective
observations about the experience of policy failures, but its basic
tenets are the product of a distinctive theoretical construction.
This has its roots clearly in neoclassical economics, a theory to
which many of the proponents of 'economic rationalism' were

directly exposed as students. It is a theory which has had a remarkable resurgence in academic economics in the last couple of decades following the partial disillusionment with Keynesian policies of demand management.

Neoclassical economics emphasises the role of markets in achieving efficient allocation of resources, given the pattern of consumer preferences and the state of technology. Its more explicitly political application, in the hands of economists like Milton Friedman, also stresses the posited link between market economic freedoms and more general individual and political freedoms. However, the neoclassical theorists themselves concede five qualifications to the case for giving free rein to market forces. These concern public goods, externalities, monopoly and other market imperfections, economic stability and equity. Each is particularly pertinent to the relationship of market processes (and hence 'economic rationalism') to urban and regional development. The five concerns provide us with a useful framework for examining the impact of 'economic rationalist' policies — both current and projected — on cities and regions.

First, there is the matter of *public goods*. These are goods which will not be provided at all in a free-market economy, since they must be collectively financed and provided. Such basic infrastructure is a key ingredient in urban and regional development. However, the provision of public goods is subject to a deteriorating quality as a result of the dominant expenditure-cutting response to the fiscal crisis of the state. J.K. Galbraith's distinction between 'private affluence and public squalor' becomes more glaring in these circumstances. Existing spatial patterns become more locked in. Historically, the key role of infrastructure provision by the state has been very significant in shaping the pattern of Australian urban and regional development. Some social scientists have regarded this (rather misleadingly) as part of a process of 'colonial socialism'. Downgrading this aspect of the role of the state undermines possible initiatives for new patterns of regional development and decentralisation. Of course, this may be offset if infrastructure expenditure comes to be used more extensively as a means of macroeconomic stimulus, but that goes against the fundamentals of 'economic rationalist' policy. Meanwhile, pressure for more intense use of existing public goods in the cities enhances the drive to applications of the 'user pays' principle and for urban consolidation. As noted in chapter 12, the latter policy has the oh-so elusive potential to generate various economic, social and environmental benefits, creating more compact cities which can be better served by public transport. However, consequential rises in market prices for land are likely to have adverse effects on distributional equity unless urban consolidation is linked with policies for more progressive redistribution of income and access to social services.

Externality problems are a second aspect of market failure. Neoclassical economists concede that where private costs are out of line with social costs the market does not result in optimal allocation of resources. Congestion, pollution and environmental decay are predictable outcomes, as noted in chapters 3 and 5. Such problems become more acute as a result of 'economic rationalist' policies. They also have distinctive urban and regional impacts. For example, the interacting problems of urban congestion and pollution can be expected to increase as a result of cuts in prices of imported cars as tariffs are further scaled down. Urban transport and urban environmental problems are not readily soluble in this way. The case for decentralisation reasserts itself, but therein lies a paradox. Since decentralisation has typically rested on arguments about urban externalities it should become *more* relevant in an era when externality problems are intensifying. However, decentralisation is simultaneously *less* likely to be implemented in these circumstances because of the fundamental conflict between such an 'interventionist' approach to regional policy and the 'economic rationalist' doctrines. This is the paradox — that the case for decentralisation becomes stronger as the result of a policy orientation which undermines the possibility of official support for a vigorous decentralisation programme.

Other 'market imperfections', such as the influence of *monopoly* and *oligopoly* in various industries, are also important in generating increased regional dependency. Orthodox economists recognise that these imperfections can distort market outcomes in inefficient ways. The prevalence of monopolistic and oligopolistic rather than competitive markets is a case in point, as are the effects of resource immobility and imperfect information. The smaller the relevant spatial area, the more likely are regional market characteristics to diverge from perfectly competitive conditions. This is important in the context of the structural economic changes being promoted by 'economic rationalism' since they are tending to increase the concentration of capital. Regional economic prosperity becomes more dependent on transnational corporations whose decisions, including location decisions, are typically undertaken in the light of their global strategic objectives. The result is increased economic vulnerability in local regional economies. All the problems of 'branch plant' regions and localised concentrations of unemployment become more acute in these conditions.

Problems of regional economic *instability* have a yet more difficult character under a regime of 'economic rationalism'. Economic instability is commonplace in market situations. Dynamic adjustment processes may be quite traumatic in their effects, while the tendency towards macroeconomic equilibrium at less than full employment is pervasive. The dismantling of regulations on industry and of tariff protection makes some regions particularly vulnerable to these problems, as we have seen in chapters 1 and 9. In current Australian conditions this suggests that the persistence of intense regional unemployment problems is a long-run structural phenomenon rather than just a short-run problem of cyclical recession. In circumstances of intensified spatial competition for mobile investment beggar-thy-neighbour tendencies become accentuated. Eeven the more successful regions find difficulty in capturing locally generated economic surpluses for balanced regional development.

Spatial *equity* also becomes more threatened by these effects of 'economic rationalism'. In general, the latter doctrine emphasises efficiency goals as prior to equity considerations — structural efficiency first, redistribution later. The underlying neoclassical theory makes no claim that market efficiency is synonymous with social equity or distributional fairness. Indeed, markets recurrently generate economic inequality as a normal feature of

a system based on material incentives. There are always winners
and losers in the marketplace. In the Australian case the forces of
economic polarisation in the 1980s and early 1990s have been
quite pronounced (Raskall 1993; Stilwell 1993b). That these
distributional inequalities translate into greater spatial inequalities comes as no surprise to regional analysts. The long-
established tendency to social-spatial differentiation in cities
widens inexorably, leading to secondary effects generating
multiple deprivation for the relatively disadvantaged, as discussed in chapter 6. André Gorz's (1985) phrase about 'slum
dwellers in the shadows of skyscrapers' returns to mind in this
context, although the multiple deprivation problems tend to be
more skewed towards the urban fringes in the Australian case.

All in all, this is not an attractive scenario. It sees our cities and
regions becoming characterised by striking deficiencies in the
provision of public goods, deteriorating environmental quality,
greater dependency on transnational capital, unstable employment conditions and social polarisation. These are specific urban
and regional dimensions of the more general social costs arising
from the pursuit of 'economic rationalist' policies, as documented
in numerous recent studies (e.g. Pusey 1991, Horne 1992, Carroll
& Manne 1992, Vintilla, Phillimore & Newman 1992, Rees,
Rodley & Stilwell 1993).

Is there an alternative?

RADICAL INTERVENTIONISM

The economic *status quo* is a disappearing option. Some restructuring of the Australian economy and its constituent regions
is necessary to deal with problems of foreign debt, balance of
payments deficit, outdated capital stock, inadequate productive
investment and persistent unemployment. This requires more
effective public policies at all levels. Of course, state 'intervention'
offers no general panacea for market failures. It can be ineffective
relative to its costs. Indeed, regional policy is commonly cited as
an example of this by the proponents of 'economic rationalism'
(Sorensen 1985). Certainly, the extreme associated with the
'command-administrative' economic system offers no solution.
The demise of the bureaucratic state communist regimes in the

former Soviet Union and Eastern Europe is illustrative, among other things, of the unsustainability of that particular model of centralised economic planning, especially where it is insensitive to regionalist aspirations. Evidently, some careful blending of market processes and the planning of long-run development is needed.

Building a 'third way' between the failed models of free market capitalism and bureaucratic state communism is the great challenge for the next decade. It is in this context that progressive urban and regional policies need to be located. Australia has tremendous potential to show the way. Its abundant resources provide an unusual potential for the development of a diversified, even quite self-reliant, economy. Its heritage of institutions experienced in the promotion and regulation of economic development is also impressive. For all their deficiencies, institutions as diverse as the Industrial Relations Commission, the Commonwealth Grants Commission, agricultural marketing boards, the Australian Manufacturing Council, Austrade and state planning departments have a wealth of experience. These institutions are better adapted than swept aside as 'impediments to market forces'. There are also certain Australian cultural characteristics, such as the subtle blend of individualism and collectivism, of anti-authoritarianism and egalitarianism, however constrained, that pervades many aspects of society. This is a social-cultural legacy which should also help in developing a more effective economic system.

The urban and regional focus is an important part of such a progressive alternative. Indeed, this has the capacity to consti-tute a key component of an economic 'third way'. Of course, localism and regionalism are not inherently progressive. They recurrently degenerate into parochialism. 'Kicking the Canberra can' is a tendency which seems to be embedded in the Australian federal structure. Beggar-thy-neighbour tendencies are per-sistent, to say the least. However, localism and regionalism may also generate sensitivity to local concerns, providing a means of securing that elusive goal of 'power to the people'. Space and place are fundamentally important to us as social beings, and this needs to be reflected in economic structures if economic cooperation is to be promoted and the principle of participatory democracy to be extended.

An antidote to both a rapacious free-market capitalism and to centralised state communism is a lot to ask of political-economic reform infused by progressive regionalism. A more local urban and regional focus provides no panacea. Economic cooperation on the basis of common regional interests can be frustrated by other cleavages according to class, gender and ethnicity. Even if achieved, such cooperation may involve subordination to the interests of capital. Local applications of Keynesian approaches to economic policy involve particular contradictions in conditions where 'economic rationalism' dominates nationally (Eisenschitz & Gough 1993). The more well-developed regions are normally better able to implement effective policies for regional economic growth, with the result that the overall extent of regional economic inequality intensifies. A simple regionalisation of economic life does not overcome the basic tendencies of capitalist economies towards inequality and instability. Moreover, it may readily be conceded that the principle of internationalism also has its progressive features. The essential unity of humankind irrespective of accidents of geography is a noble ideal. Evidently, the issue is not purely one of scale: it is a matter of relative autonomy and control.

If nothing else, a 'radical interventionist' stance embracing progressive regionalism can challenge the assertion by 'economic rationalists' of the inevitability of intensifying regional competition in a market economy. That 'tyranny of the macro' which leads inexorably to a social Darwinist outcome can be resisted, even reversed. Localism and regionalism have an important role in this process, helping to counter the tendencies generated by a spatially homogenising capital (Harvey 1989a).

Policies compatible with this approach can be illustrated according to the five categories previously considered as limits to the 'economic rationalist' approach: public goods, externalities, equity, instability and imperfect competition. How can 'radical interventionist' policies embrace these concerns and integrate them with the solution of urban and regional problems?

The provision of *public goods* is an obvious starting point for the reassertion of collective community concerns. Equally, their provision can be an engine for new directions in urban and regional economic development. Increased infrastructure investment is job creating, and can be more effectively targeted to regions of greatest need while helping to lay the foundations for higher productivity and a better quality of life. Of course, it is quite bizarre to have unemployed resources coexisting with unfulfilled social needs: that is the ultimate in economic irrationality! Dealing with these issues through a more interventionist approach provides a context in which urban and regional policy has a potentially progressive role to play. Of course, the *financing* of infrastructure projects and, more generally, a better range and quality of public goods is an important issue. Such financing may require more progressive income tax scales or additional taxation on wealth. To put the issue in perspective, it should be noted that the overall level of government taxes and expenditures in Australia is relatively low by comparative international standards. This suggests considerable scope for a rebalancing of the private and public sectors.

Redressing *externality* effects also requires a more radical interventionist approach in which issues of urban and regional policy are at the fore. The problems of urban congestion and pollution are obvious cases in point. Their redress requires more vigorous policies to promote a shift from private to public transport and to control the degradation of the urban environment. Pricing policy can play an important role here in imposing the full social costs of environmentally degrading activities on their perpetrators. However, this is not enough because, concurrently, attractive ecologically sustainable alternatives have to be provided. Indeed, the rather narrow conception of externalities as a special case of 'market failure' needs now to be replaced by the broader conception of ecologically sustainable development. As noted in chapter 5, this puts housing policy and energy policy on the agenda alongside transport policy and the control of pollution.

The design of new cities embodying environmentally appropriate policies in all these areas becomes, on this reasoning, a priority issue. Decentralisation policy has a reinvigorated rationale in this context. So too does the partial restructuring of existing cities embracing, for example, the policies advocated by Newman, and Robinson Kenworthy (1992) for 'urban villages', traffic calming and light rail. Concurrently, the development of industries producing the necessary ecologically sustainable technologies (e.g. solar power equipment) has the potential to give a considerable boost to the national economy, including export performance. It is an example of where 'thinking globally and acting locally' makes both ecological and economic sense.

Third, there is the recurrent issue of *equity*. The forces generating growing economic inequalities, both nationally and within particular metropolitan areas, have already been much discussed. The spatial dimension is partly derivative of the more general structural-social inequalities. As such, policies addressed at the latter aspects can be expected to produce less spatially divided urban social forms. Such policies include more broadly based incomes policy, more progressive tax policies and an improved social wage (as more fully discussed in Rees, Rodley & Stilwell 1993: ch. 14). This would mean a change from past practices under the Accord whereby wages are the only income source targeted for restraint, while incomes from rent, interest profits and professional fees remain free of any equivalent regulation. It would mean more progressive tax scales, fewer tax exemptions from which high income groups are the principal beneficiaries, and possibly new forms of inheritance and wealth taxation. Policies with a more explicit spatial dimension can be a component in such reforms, such as redistribution of local government revenues in order to improve the capacity of local governments in poorer areas to finance a higher standard of social services.

Fourth, there is a need for policies to address economic *stabilisation* and, more generally, to establish the conditions for more adequate employment opportunities. Again, the urban and regional aspects are partly derivative of the macroeconomic. What is at issue is an integrated set of fiscal, monetary, trade and industry development policies, as discussed more fully in proposals for an alternative economic strategy (e.g. Flew 1991, Green *et al* 1992, Stilwell 1993a). Particularly important in the economic conditions of the 1990s are interventionist and regionally targeted industry policies and a more expansionary and regionally targeted fiscal policy. These can generate a more diversified, balanced economic structure which is less vulnerable to the volatility of the international economy. The pursuit of these policies can also contribute to creating more diversified industrial bases for urban and regional economies. This diversification would help to alleviate problems associated with the concentration of capital and economic dependence on a small number of large corporate enterprises.

These problems are very fundamental. In a world of international competition, a small range of giant corporations tend to be promoted as 'national champions', with consequent problems of over-dependence in the regions where they are located and imbalance between these regions and the others. These are manifestations of the regional problems arising from multi-national domination (as noted by Hymer 1972 and Holland 1976, and discussed in Stilwell 1992: ch. 7). While no general antidote exists within the context of a capitalist economy, policies towards competition, international investment and trade can play a role in ameliorating and regulating the impacts on national and regional economies. This requires a more vigorous role for the Trade Practices Commission. It requires interventionist industry policy that focuses more on import-substitution than the export-promotion which has been the dominant concern to date. It requires policies for the mobilisation of domestic savings and their systematic channelling into productive investment, thereby reducing reliance on overseas capital. The burgeoning superannuation funds can be brought under more public control to ensure they are used for these purposes. Yes, all of this invokes the case for greater self-sufficiency or self-reliance at the regional and national scales, but not to the exclusion of international economic relations. It echoes the case made by Boris Frankel (1987) in support of semi-autarky.

Evidently, discussion of how to resolve socio-economic and environmental problems in Australian cities and regions must embrace questions of broad political philosophy and strategy. As the nation moves towards its centenary and as the movement for becoming a republic gathers strength, it is also appropriate to raise questions of corresponding *constitutional change*. The abolition of State governments in a case in point, as discussed in chapter 9. The States are hangovers from a colonial era, standing as obstacles to progressive contemporary regionalism. A two-tier system, based on local government amalgamations and a partial devolution of existing State and federal functions to those new regional governments, could provide a more effective basis for progressive regionalism. Metropolitan government would have an obvious niche within such a structure, alongside regional governments responsible for other urban areas and their rural hinterlands. Of course, the geographical delineation of the most appropriate regions and the distribution of powers between the two tiers would need to be a matter of extended consideration. A political reorganisation of such magnitude would require comprehensive analysis, consultation, public participation and democratic determination. Whether it is worth the bother is necessarily a matter of political judgement. However, at a time when constitutional change is on the agenda, it seems appropriate to seriously consider a change like this which has the potential to streamline bureaucratic processes, stimulate local democratic impulses and generate more momentum for the implementation of effective urban and regional policies.

Needless to say, many problems need to be confronted in this 'radical interventionist' scenario. Politically, the balance between 'top down' interventionist economic policies and 'bottom up' regionalism is a recurrent difficulty. The reorientation to an ecologically sustainable economy is a huge task. The appropriate mix and timing of the economic policies remains, as ever, a matter of delicate judgement. So too is the linking of urban and regional policies to the broader political-economic restructurings. The issues of economic policy, institutional and constitutional reform necessarily involve political judgements and action as well as academic research. They take us far beyond the scope of this book. What has been attempted here is merely the establishment of some principles for integrating urban and regional concerns with a more radical approach to Australian public policy. It is a scenario in which there is a role for the reassertion of space and place, not just as a passive dimension in which market forces work themselves out, but as an active basis for taking control over our own political-economic destinies.

FURTHER READING

Harvey (1992): a provocative blend of theory, observation of the contemporary city and principles for progress.

Greenpeace Australia (1993): on the practical steps to linking urban change with ecological sustainability.

Rees, Rodley & Stilwell (1993): a compendium of views about alternatives to economic rationalism.

Elkin, McLaren & Hillman (1991): a contribution by Friends of the Earth to the debate on sustainable urban development.

Bibliography

ACTU/TDC (1987) *Australia Reconstructed*, AGPS, Canberra.

ALFORD, R.R. & FRIEDLAND, R. (1985) *Powers of Theory: The State, Capitalism and Democracy*, Cambridge University Press, Cambs.

ALONSO, W. (1989) 'Deindustrialization and Regional Policy' in Rodwin, L. & Sazanami, H. (Eds) *Deindustrialization and Regional Economic Transformation: The Experience of the U.S.*, Unwin Hyman, Boston.

ANDERSON, A./KINHILL (1989) *Multifunction Polis Joint Feasibility Study*, Anderson Consulting, Canberra.

ANDERSON, K. (1987) 'Tariffs and the Manufacturing Sector' in Maddock, R. & McLean, I.W. (Eds) *The Australian Economy in the Long Run*, Cambridge University Press, Cambs.

AUSTRALIAN INSTITUTE OF URBAN STUDIES (1980) *Urban Strategies for Australia: Managing the Eighties*, AIUS Publication No 88, Canberra.

BADCOCK, B. (1984) *Unfairly Structured Cities*, Basil Blackwell, Oxford.

BADCOCK, B. (1989) 'An Australian View of the Rent Gap Hypothesis', *Annals of the Association of American Geographers*, Vol 79.

BALL, M. (1986) 'The Built Environment and the Urban Question', *Environment and Planning D: Society and Space*, Vol 4.

BANFIELD, E.C. (1974) *The Unheavenly City Revisited*, Little Brown and Co., Boston.

BASSETT, K. & SHORT, J. (1980) *Housing and Residential Structure: Alternative Approaches*, Routledge and Kegan Paul, London.

BEAUREGARD, R.A. (1986) 'The Chaos and Complexity of Gentrification' in Smith, N. & Williams, P. (Eds) *Gentrification of the City*, Allen & Unwin, Boston.

BEDER, S. (1989) *Toxic Fish and Sewer Surfing*, Allen & Unwin, North Sydney.

BEED, C.S. (1981) *Melbourne's Development & Planning*, Clewara Press, Melbourne.

BEED, C. & MORIARTY, P. (1988a) 'Urban Transport Policy', *Journal of Australian Political Economy*, No 22, February.

BEED, C. & MORIARTY, P. (1988b) 'Transport Characteristics and Policy Implications for Four Australian Cities', *Urban Policy and Research*, Vol 6, No 4.

BEED, C. & MORIARTY, P. (1992) 'The Car in its Second Century', *Journal of Australian Political Economy*, No 29, May.

BERRY, B.J.L. (1974) *Land Use, Urban Form and Environmental Quality*, University of Chicago Press, Chicago.

BERRY, M. (1983) 'Posing the Housing Question in Australia: Elements of a Theoretical Framework for a Marxist Analysis of Housing' in Sandercock, L. & Berry, M. (Eds) *Urban Political Economy: the Australian Case*, George Allen & Unwin, Sydney.

BERRY, M. (1986) 'Innovation in Planning and Housing: Theoretical Musings', Forum, *Urban Policy and Research*, Vol 4, No 4, December.

BERRY, M. (1990) 'The Politics of Australian Cities', *Arena*, No 91, Winter.

BHAVE, V. (1974) 'God is for Decentralisation', *Resurgence*, Vol 5, No 2 May-June.

BIRRELL, R., HILL, D., & STANLEY, J. (Eds) (1982) *Quarry Australia?*, Oxford University Press, Melbourne.

BLACK, J. (1977) *Public Inconvenience: Access and Travel in Seven Sydney Suburbs*, Urban Research Unit, ANU Canberra.

BLUESTONE, B. & HARRISON, B. (1982) *The Deindustrialization of America: Plant Closing, Community Abandonment, and the Dismantling of Basic Industry*, Basic Books, New York.

BLUNDEN, R.W. & BLACK, J.A. (1984) *Land Use/Transport Systems*, 2nd edition, Pergamon Press, Sydney.

BODDY, M. (1982) 'Planning, Landownership and the State', in Paris C. (Ed), *Critical Readings in Planning Theory*, Pergamon Press, Oxford.

BOOKCHIN, M. (1980) *Towards an Ecological Society*, Black Rose Books, Montreal.

BOULDING, K. (1970) *Economics as a Science*, McGraw Hill, Sydney.

BOURASSA, S.C. (1992) *The Rent Gap Debunked*, Urban Research Program Working Paper No 32, ANU, Canberra.

BOURASSA, S.C. & HENDERSHOTT, P.H. (1992) *Over-Investment in Australian Housing?* The National Housing Strategy, AGPS, Canberra.

BOURASSA, S.C. & HENDERSHOTT, P.H. (1993) *Australian Real Housing Costs*, Urban Research Program Working Paper No 36, ANU, Canberra.

BREITBART, M.M. (1981) 'Peter Kropotkin, the Anarchist Geographer' in Stoddart, D.R. (Ed.) *Geography, Ideology and Social Concern*, Blackwell, Oxford.

BROWN, K. (1990) 'The Great Waste of a Clean Sea', *The Financial Times*, London, 7th September.

BROWN, L. (1977) 'Slowing Urban Growth', *Dialogue*, Vol 10, No 2.

BROWN, L. (1978) 'The Coming Transition', *Dialogue*, Vol 11, No 3.

BRUEGEL, I. (1975) 'The Marxist Theory of Rent and the Contemporary City: A Critique of Harvey', *Political Economy of Housing Workshop*, Conference of Socialist Economists, London.

BRYSON, L. & THOMPSON, F. (1972) *An Australian Newtown: Life and Leadership in a New Housing Suburb*, Penguin, Harmondsworth.

BUNKER, R. (1986) 'Heroic Measures: Urban Consolidation in Australia' in McLoughlin, J.B. & Huxley, M. (Eds) *Urban Planning in Australia: Critical Readings*, Longman Cheshire, Melbourne.

BURDEKIN, B. (1989) *Our Homeless Children: Report of the National Inquiry into Homeless Children*, Human Rights and Equal Opportunity Commission, AGPS, Canberra.

BUREAU OF INDUSTRY ECONOMICS (1985) *The Regional Impact of Structural Change — An Assessment of Regional Policies in Australia*, BIER Research Report No 18, Canberra.

BUREAU OF INDUSTRY ECONOMICS (1990) *Economic Evaluation of the Multi Function Polis*, AGPS, Canberra.

BURGESS J. & McDONALD, D. (1990) 'The Labour Flexibility Imperative', *Journal of Australian Political Economy*, No 27, November.

BURNLEY, I.H. (1980) *The Australian Urban System: Growth, Change and Differentiation*, Longman Cheshire, Melbourne.

BURNLEY, I. & FORREST, J. (Eds) (1985) *Living in Cities: Urbanism and Society in Metropolitan Australia*, Allen & Unwin, Sydney.

BUTLER, G.J. (1983) 'Alternatives to Jobs: Claims to Personal Incomes During the Rest of the Century', *The Australian Quarterly*, Summer.

CAMINA, M. (1975) 'Public Participation — An Australian Dimension', *The Planner*, June.

CARROLL, J. & MANNE, R. (1992) *Shutdown: The Failure of Economic Rationalism*, Text, Melbourne.

CARTER, R. (1983) 'Policy for Non-Metropolitan Regions: the Case for A Re-assessment', *The Australian Quarterly*, Spring.

CARTER, R. (1987) 'Where Will the Money Come From' in Housing: What Happened to the Great Australian Dream, supplement to *Australian Society*, October.

CASTELLS, M. (1977) *The Urban Question: A Marxist Approach*, Edward Arnold, London.

CASTELLS, M. (1978) *City, Class and Power*, Macmillan, London.

CASTELLS, M. (1983) *The City and the Grassroots*, Edward Arnold, London.

CATLEY, R. & McFARLANE, B. (1974) *From Tweedledum to Tweedledee: The New Labor Government in Australia*, Australia & New Zealand Book Co., Sydney.

CHAMBERLAIN, C. & MACKENZIE, D. (1992) 'Understanding Contemporary Homelessness: Issues of Definition and Meaning', *Australian Journal of Social Issues*, Vol 27, No 4,. November.

CHAMPION, A.G. (Ed.) (1989) *Counterurbanisation: The Changing Pace and Nature of Population Deconcentration*, Edward Arnold, London.

CHESTERTON, G.K. (1926) *William Cobbett*, Hodder & Stoughton, London.

CHISHOLM, M. (1983) 'City, Region and—What Kind of Problem? in Patten, J. (Ed.) *The Expanding City*, Academic Press, London.

CLARK, G.L. & DEAR, M. (1984) *State Apparatus*, Allen & Unwin, Boston.

CLARK, M. (1991) 'Two New Boys in Melbourne' in Daniel, A. (Ed.) *Social Democracy and Social Science: Essays in Honour of Sol Encel*, Longman Cheshire, Melbourne.

COCKBURN, C. (1978) *The Local State: Management of Cities and People*, Pluto Press, London.

COLLINS, J.H. (1988) *Migrant Hands in a Distant Land: Australia's Post-War Immigration*, Pluto Press, Sydney.

COMMITTEE OF COMMONWEALTH/STATE OFFICIALS ON DECENTRALISATION (1972) *Report*, Australian Government Printing Service, Canberra, 1972.

CONGALTON, A.A. (1969) *Status and Prestige in Australia*, Cheshire, Melbourne.

COOMBS, H.C. (1981) *Trial Balance*, Macmillan, Melbourne.

COWLEY, J. (et al) (1977) *Community or Class Struggle?*, Stage 1, London.

COX, K.R. (1989) 'The Politics of Turf & the Question of Class' in Welch, J. & Dear, M. (Eds) *The Power of Geography*, Unwin Hyman, Boston.

CROUGH, G.J. & WHEELWRIGHT, E.L. (1982) *Australia: A Client State*, Penguin Books, Ringwood, Vic.

CUMBERLAND COUNTY COUNCIL (1948) *The Planning Scheme for the County of Cumberland*, NSW Government Printer, Sydney.

DALY, M.T. (1982) *Sydney Boom, Sydney Bust: The City and Its Property Market 1850–1981*, Allen and Unwin, Sydney.

DAVID, A. & WHEELRIGHT, T. (1989) *The Third Wave: Australia and Asian Capitalism*, Left Book Club Co-operative Ltd., Sutherland, NSW.

DAVIES, J.G. (1982) 'The Oppression of Progress', in Paris, C. (Ed.) *Critical Readings in Planning Theory*, Pergamon Press, Oxford.

DAVISON, G. (1993) *The Past and Future of the Australian Suburb*, Urban Research Program Working Paper No 33, Australian National University, Canberra.

DEPARTMENT OF ENVIRONMENT AND PLANNING (1988) *Sydney Into Its Third Century: Metropolitan Strategy for the Sydney Region*, Department of Environment and Planning, Sydney.

DIETER, H. (1991) 'Aspects of Australia's Foreign Liabilities: A Mortgage for Future Generations?', *The Australian Quarterly*, Winter.

DONNISON, D. (1974) Radicalism in a Rich Land, *New Society*, October.

ECONOMIC PLANNING ADVISORY COUNCIL (1991) *Urban and Regional Trends and Issues*, Council Paper No 46, AGPS, Canberra.

EDEL, M. (1976) 'Marx's Theory of Rent: Urban Applications', *Political Economy of Housing Workshop* No 2, Conference of Socialist Economists, London.

EISENSCHITZ, A. & GOUGH, J. (1993) *The Politics of Local Economic Policy*, Macmillan, London.

ELKIN, T., MCLAREN, D. & HILLMAN, M. (1991) *Reviving the City: Towards Sustainable Urban Development*, Friends of the Earth, London.

ELLWOOD, W. (1989) 'Car Chaos', *New Internationalist*, May.

ENGELS, F. (1873) *The Housing Question*, Progress Publishers, Moscow (1975 edition).

ENGWICHT, D. (1992) *Towards An Eco-City: Calming the Traffic*, Envirobook, Sydney.

FERRIS, P. (1990) 'A Flawed Project: Filling a National Void' in James, P. (Ed.) (1990) *Technocratic Dreaming*, Left Book Club, Sydney.

FINCHER, R. (1989a) 'Class and Gender Relations in the Local Labour Market and the Local State' in Wolch, J. & Dear, M. (Eds) *The Power of Geography: How Territory Shapes Social Life*, Unwin Hyman, Boston.

FINCHER, R. (1989b) 'The Political Economy of the Local State' in Peet, R. & Thrift, N. (Eds) *New Models in Geography*, Vol 1, Unwin Hyman, London.

FISHMAN, R. (1977) *Urban Utopias in the Twentieth Century: Ebenezer Howard, Frank Lloyd Wright, Le Corbusier*, Basic Books, New York.

FLEW, T. (Ed.) (1991) *Australia Can Work* Left Book Club, Sydney.

FLOOD, J. & YATES, J. (1987) *Housing Subsidies Study*, AHRC Project Series No 160, AGPS.

FORREST, J. (1985) 'Suburbia—the Myth of Homogeneity' in Burnley, I. & Forrest, J. (Eds) *Living in Cities*, George Allen & Unwin, North Sydney.

FORSTER, C. (1988) 'Urban Geography', *Australian Geographical Studies*, Vol 26, No 1, April.

FRANCE, G.H. & HUGHES, C.A. (1972) 'The Role of Government' in Parker, R.W. & Troy, P.N. (Eds) *The Politics of Urban Growth*, ANU Press, Canberra.

FRANKEL, B. (1987) *The Post-Industrial Utopians*, Polity Press, Cambs.

FREESTONE, R. (1989) *Model Communities: The Garden City Movement in Australia*, Thomas Nelson, Melbourne.

FRIEDMAN, M. & FRIEDMAN, R. (1980) *Free to Choose*, Penguin, Harmondsworth, Middlesex.

FROEBEL, F., HEINRICHS, J., & KREYE, O. (1980) *The New International Division of Labour*, Cambridge University Press, Cambridge.

GALBRAITH, J.K. (1974) *Economics and the Public Purpose*, Andre Deutsch, London.

GALBRAITH, J.K. (1977) *The Age of Uncertainty*, Houghton Mifflin, Boston.

GAME, A. & PRINGLE, R. (1979) 'Sexuality and the Suburban Dream', *Australian and New Zealand Journal of Sociology*, Vol 15, No 2.

GAPPERT, G. (1989) 'A Management Perspective on Cities in a Changing Global Environment', in Knight, R.V. & Gappert, G. (Eds) *Cities in a Global Society*, Sage, Newbury Park, California.

GARDINER, W. (1987) 'How the West Was Lost: Urban Development in Western Sydney', *The Australian Quarterly*, Winter, Vol 59, No 2.

GARLICK, S. (1991), *Future Directions in Regional Development Policy*, Pacific Regional Science Association Conference, Cairns (mimeo).

GEORGE, H. (1879) *Progress and Poverty*, New York, Robert Schalkenback.

GLAZEBROOK, G. (1992) *Sydney at the Crossroads: New Land Use and Transport Options*, Planning Research Centre, University of Sydney.

GLYNN, S. (1970) *Urbanisation in Australian History*, Nelson, Melbourne.

GORDON, D.M. (Ed.) (1977) *Problems in Political Economy: An Urban Perspective*, 2nd edition, D.C. Heath, Lexington, Mass.

GORE, C. (1984) *Regions in Question: Space, Development Theory & Regional Policy*, Methuen, London.

GORZ, A. (1985) *Paths to Paradise*, Pluto Press, London.

GREEN, R., MITCHELL, W. & WATTS, M. (1992) *Economic Policy in Crisis: A Proposal for Jobs and Growth*, Evatt Foundation, Sydney.

GREENPEACE AUSTRALIA (1993) *Solutions for Clean Healthy Cities*, Greenpeace, Balmain.

GREGORY, R.G. (1992) *Aspects of Australian Labour Force Living Standards: the Disappointing Decades 1970–1990*, The Copland Oration, 21st Conference of Economists, University of Melbourne, July.

GROENWOLD, N. (1991) 'Regional Unemployment Disparities and Cyclical Sensitivities', *The Australian Journal of Regional Studies*, No 6, December.

GURR, T.R. & KING, D.S. (1987) *The State and the City*, Macmillan, Basingstoke.

HALL, C. & SCHOU, K. (1980) 'Urban Transport Policy and Energy Conservation', *Social Alternatives*, Vol 8.

HALL, P. (1983) 'Decentralization without End? A Re-evaluation' in Patten, J. (Ed.) *The Expanding City*, Academic Press, London.

HALLIGAN, J. & PARIS, C. (Eds) (1984) *Australian Urban Politics: Critical Perspectives*, Longman Cheshire, Melbourne.

HANSEN, N.M. (1976) 'Are Regional Development Policies Needed' *The Review of Regional Studies*, Vol 5.

HARMAN, E.J. (1983) 'Capitalism, Patriarchy and the City' in Baldock, C.V. & Cass, B. (Eds) *Women, Social Welfare and the State*, George Allen & Unwin, Sydney.

HARMAN, E. & HEAD, B. (1982) (Eds) *State, Capital and Resources in the North and West of Australia*, University of Western Australia Press, Nedlands.

HARVEY, D. (1973) *Social Justice and the City*, Edward Arnold, London.

HARVEY, D. (1974) 'Class Monopoly Rent, Finance Capital and the Urban Revolution', *Regional Studies*, Vol 8.

HARVEY, D. (1982) *The Limits to Capital*, Basil Blackwell, Oxford.

HARVEY, D. (1987), 'Urban Housing' in Eastwell, J., Milgate, M. and Newman, P. (Eds) *The New Palgrave Dictionary of Economics*, Macmillan, London.

HARVEY, D. (1989a) *The Urban Experience*, Basil Blackwell, Oxford.

HARVEY, D. (1989b) *The Condition of Postmodernity*, Basil Blackwell, Oxford.

HARVEY, D. (1990) 'Between Space and Time: Reflections on the

Geographical Imagination', *Annals of the Association of American Geographers*, Vol 80, No 3, September.

HARVEY, D. (1992) 'Social Justice, Postmodernism and the City', *International Journal of Urban and Regional Research*, Vol 16, No 4.

HAUGHTON, G. (1990) 'Manufacturing Recession: BHP and the Recession in Wollongong', *International Journal of Urban and Regional Research*, Vol 14, No 1.

HEAD, B.W. (1983) (Ed.) *State and Economy in Australia*, Oxford University Press, Melbourne.

HEAD, B.W. (1986) (Ed.) *The Politics of Development in Australia*, Allen and Unwin, Sydney.

HENDERSON, J. & CASTELLS, M. (1987) *Global Restructuring and Territorial Development*, Sage, London.

HENDERSON, R.F. (Chair) (1975) 'Australian Government Commission of Inquiry into Poverty, First Main Report', *Poverty in Australia*, AGPS, Canberra.

HERBERT, D.T. & SMITH, D.M. (Eds) (1989) *Social Problems and the City: New Perspectives*, Oxford University Press, Oxford.

HEYWOOD, K. & TAMASCHKE, R. (1991) 'Australian Financial Deregulation and the Growth of the Foreign Debt', *Journal of Australian Political Economy*, No 28, September.

HILLS, B. (1992) 'The $2 Billion Creature On A Black Lagoon', *The Sydney Morning Herald: Good Weekend*, June 27.

HIRSCH, W.Z. (1973) *Urban Economic Analysis*, McGraw-Hill, New York.

HIRSCH, W.Z. & GOODMAN, P. (1967) 'Is There an Optimum Size for a City?' in *Urban America: Goals and Problems, Hearings of the Subcommittee on Urban Affairs*, Joint Economic Committee, US Congress, August.

HOLLAND, S. (1976) *The Regional Problem*, MacMillan, London.

HOMEL, R. & BURNS, A. (1985) 'Through a Child's Eyes: Quality of Neighbourhood and Quality of Life in Burnley, I. & Forrest, J. (Eds), *Living in Cities*, George Allen & Unwin, North Sydney.

HORNE, D. (Ed.) (1992) *The Trouble With Economic Rationalism*, Scribe, Newham, Vic.

HORVATH, R.J. & ENGELS, B. (1985) 'The Residential Restructuring of Inner Sydney' in Burnley, I. & Forrest, J. (Eds) *Living in Cities*, George Allen & Unwin, Sydney.

HORVATH, R.J., HARRISON, G.E. & DOWLING, R.M. (1989) *Sydney: A Social Atlas*, Sydney University Press, Sydney.

HOUSING WORKSHOP (1975) *Political Economy and the Housing Question*, Conference of Socialist Economists, London.

HOWARD, E. (1902) *Garden Cities of Tomorrow*, Faber and Faber, London.

HOWE, B. (1991) *Building Better Cities: A Commonwealth-State Partnership*, Address to Australian Institute of Urban Studies and Planning Research Centre, University of Sydney, September.

HOWE, B. & STAPLES, P. (1991) *Rebuilding the Foundations: Budget 1991-92*, Australian Government, Portfolio of Health, Housing and Community Services, AGPS, Canberra.

HUXLEY, M. (1990) 'The Multifunction Polis: the Issues', *Arena* No 90.

HUXLEY, M. & BERRY, M. (1990) 'Capital's Cities: Polarising Social Life' in James, P. (Ed.) *Technocratic Dreaming*, Left Book Club, Sydney.

HYMER, S. (1972) 'The Multinational Corporation and the Law of Uneven Development' in Radice, H. (Ed.) *International Firms and Modern Imperialism*, Penguin, Ringwood, Victoria.

JACOBS, J. (1961) *The Death and Life of Great American Cities*, Random House, New York.

JACOBS, M. (1991) *The Green Economy: Environment, Sustainable Development and the Politics of the Future*, Pluto Press, London.

JAGER, M. (1986) 'Class Definitions and the Aesthetics of Gentrification' in Smith N. & Williams P. (Eds) *Gentrification of the City*, Allen & Unwin, Boston.

JAKUBOWICZ, A. (1984) 'The Green Ban Movement: Urban Struggle and Class Politics' in Halligan, J. and Paris, C. (Eds) *Australian Urban Politics*, Longman Cheshire, Melbourne.

JAMES, P. (Ed.) (1990) *Technocratic Dreaming: of Very Fast Trains and Japanese Designer Cities*, Left Book Club, Melbourne.

JAY, C. (1978) *Towards Urban Strategies for Australia*, Australian Institute of Urban Studies, Canberra.

JOHNSTON, R.J. (1982) *Geography and the State*, Macmillan, London.

JOHNSTON, R.J. (1989) 'The State, Political Geography & Geography' in Peet, R. & Thrift, N. (Eds) *New Models in Geography*, Vol 1, Unwin Hyman, London.

JONES, E. (1989) 'Australia's Balance of Payments: Recent Trends', *Journal of Australian Political Economy*, No 24, March.

JUPP, J., McROBBIE, A. & YORK, B. (1990), *Metropolitan Ghettoes and Ethnic Concentrations*, Centre for Multicultural Studies, University of Wollongong.

KATZ, S. & MAYER, M. (1985) 'Gimme Shelter: Self-Help Housing Struggles Within and Against the State in New York City and West Berlin', *International Journal of Urban and Regional Research*, Vol 9, No 1, March.

KEMENY, J. (1981) *The Myth of Home Ownership: Private Versus Public Choices in Housing Tenure*, Routledge and Kegan Paul, London.

KEMENY, J. (1983) *The Great Australian Nightmare: A Critique of the Home Ownership Ideology*, Georgian House, Melbourne.

KENDIG, H. (1979) *New Life for Old Suburbs: Post War Land Use and Housing in the Australian Inner City*, Allen and Unwin, Sydney.

KENDIG, H. (1981) *Buying and Renting: Household Moves in Adelaide*, Australian Institute of Urban Studies, Canberra.

KILMARTIN, L. & THORNS, D. (1978) *Cities Unlimited*, Allen and Unwin, Sydney.

KNOX, P. (1987) *Urban Social Geography*, Longman, Harlow.

KNOX, P. & AGNEW, J. (1989) *The Geography of the World Economy*, Edward Arnold, London.

LAWRENCE, G. (1987) *Capitalism and the Countryside: The Rural Crisis in Australia*, Pluto Press, Sydney.

LE CORBUSIER (1935) *La Ville Radieuse*, d'Aujourdhui, Boulogne.

LEITNER, H. & SHEPHERD, E. (1989) 'The City as Locus of Production', in Peet, R. & Thrift, N. (Eds) *New Models in Geography*, Vol 2, Unwin Hyman, London.

LEY, D. (1980) 'Liberal Ideology and the Postindustrial City', *Annals of the Association of American Geographers*, Vol 70.

LLOYD, C.J. & TROY, P.N. (1981) *Innovation and Reaction: The Life and Death of the Federal Department of Urban and Regional Development*, Allen and Unwin, Sydney.

LOGAN, M. (1978) 'Regional Policy' in Scott, P. (Ed.) *Australian Cities and Public Policy*, Georgian House, Melbourne.

LOGAN, M., MAHER, C., McKAY, J. & HUMPHREYS, J. (1975) *Urban and Regional Australia: Analysis and Policy Issues*, Sorrett Social Sciences, Malvern, Victoria.

LOGAN, T. (1979) 'Recent Directions of Regional Policy in Australia', *Regional Studies*, Vol 13, No 2.

LOWE, S. (1986) *Urban Social Movements: The City After Castells*, Macmillan, London.

LYBRAND, COOPER & SCOTT (1984) *Homelessness and Inadequate Housing*, Report prepared for the Department of Housing and Construction, AGPS, Canberra.

MANN, M. (1984) 'The Autonomous Power of the State: Its Origins, Mechanisms and Results', *European Journal of Sociology*, Vol 25.

MANNING, I. (1991) *The Open Street*, Transit Australia Publishing, Sydney.

MANNING, P. & HARDMAN, M. (1975) *Green Bans*, Australian Conservation Foundation, Melbourne.

MARKUSEN, A.R. (1980) 'City Spatial Structure, Women's Household Work and National Urban Policy', *Signs: Journal of Women in Culture and Society*, Vol 5, No 3, Spring.

MARX, K. and ENGELS, F. (1848) *Manifesto of the Communist Party*, Foreign Languages Publishing House, Moscow (1960 edition).

MASSER, I. (1990) 'Technology and Regional Development Policy: A Review of Japan's Technopolis Programme', *Regional Studies*, Vol 24, No 1, February.

MASSEY, D. and CATALANO, A. (1978) *Capital and Land: Land Ownership by Capital in Great Britain*, Edward Arnold, London.

MASSEY, D. and MEEGAN, R. (1982) *The Anatomy of Job Loss: The How, Why and Where of Employment Decline*, Methuen, London.

MAY, R.J. (1971) *Financing the Small States in Australian Federalism*, Oxford University Press, London.

McCARTY, J.W. (1970) 'Australian Capital Cities in the Nineteenth Century', *Australian Economic History Review*, September.

McCORMACK, G. (1989) 'Multifunction Polis: Japan-Australia Co-Prosperity', *Arena*, No 86.

McCORMACK, G. (1990a) 'Multifunction Polis: A Change of Tack', *Australian Society*, May.

McCORMACK, G. (1990b) 'Metamorphosis of the MFP', *Australian Society*, September.

McLOUGHLIN, J.B. (1991) Urban Consolidation and Urban Sprawl: a Question of Density, *Urban Policy & Research*, Volume 9, No 9, September.

McLOUGHLIN, J.B. (1992) *Shaping Melbourne's Future? Town Planning, The State and Civil Society*, Cambridge University Press, Cambs.

McLOUGHLIN, J.B. & HUXLEY, M. (Eds) (1986) *Urban Planning in Australia: Critical Readings*, Longman Cheshire, Melbourne.

MEADOWS, D.H., MEADOWS, D.L., RANDERS, J. & BEHRENS III, W.W. (1972) *The Limits to Growth*, Earth Island Limited, London.

MELMAN, S. (1983) *Profits Without Production*, AA Knopf, New York.

MILIBAND, R. (1973) *The State in Capitalist Society*, Quartet Books, London.

MILIBAND, R. (1991) *Divided Societies: Class Struggle in Contemporary Capitalism*, Oxford University Press, Oxford.

MILLER, L. & FUHR, R. (1983) 'The Real Sydney', *Australian Society*, Vol 2, No 3, April.

MINGIONE, E. (1984) *Social Conflict and the City*, Basil Blackwell, Oxford.

MINISTRY OF INTERNATIONAL TRADE & INDUSTRY (1987)

MFP Planning Committee, *A Multifunction Polis Scheme for the 21st Century — Basic Concept*, Tokyo, September.

MINNERY, J.R. (1992) *Urban Form and Development Strategies: Equity, Environmental and Economic Implications*, Report for the National Housing Strategy, AGPS, Canberra.

MISHAN, E.J. (1967) *The Costs of Economic Growth*, Penguin, Ringwood.

MOWBRAY, M. (1982) 'Rates, Roads, Rubbish and Redistribution: The Politics of Local Taxation', *Journal of Australian Political Economy*, No 11, January.

MULLINS, P. (1979) 'The Struggle Against Brisbane's Freeways', *International Journal of Urban and Regional Research*, Vol 13, December.

MULLINS, P. (1982) 'The Middle Class and the Inner City', *Journal of Australian Political Economy*, No 11, January.

MUMFORD, L. (1964) *The Highway and the City*, Secker & Warburg, London.

MURPHY, P,. (1990) Levels of Economic Opportunity in NSW Regions, *Urban Policy and Research*, Vol 8, No 1, March.

MURPHY, P. & BURNLEY, I.H. (1990), 'Regional Issues Affecting the Financing of Urban Infrastructure in NSW', *Urban Policy and Research*, Vol 8, No 4, December.

NATIONAL HOUSING STRATEGY (1991a) *Australian Housing: the Demographic, Economic and Social Environment*, AGPS, Canberra.

NATIONAL HOUSING STRATEGY (1991b) *The Affordability of Australian Housing*, AGPS, Canberra.

NATIONAL HOUSING STRATEGY (1992) *National Housing Strategy: Summary of Papers*, AGPS, Canberra.

NEUTZE, G.M. (1965) *Economic Policy and the Size of Cities*, ANU, Canberra.

NEUTZE, G.M. (1977) *Urban Development in Australia: A Descriptive Analysis*, Allen and Unwin, Sydney.

NEUTZE, G.M. (1978) *Australian Urban Policy*, Allen and Unwin, Sydney.

NEVILE, J., VIPOND, J. & WARREN, N. (1984) *Sydney's Costly Housing: A Comparison with Melbourne*, Centre for Applied Economic Research, paper No 21, University of New South Wales.

NEWMAN, P. & KENWORTHY, J. (1989) *Cities and Automobile Dependence: An International Sourcebook*, Gower, Aldershot.

NEWMAN, P., KENWORTHY, J. & ROBINSON, L. (1992) *Winning Back the Cities*, Australian Consumers Association and Pluto Press, Sydney.

NICOLADES, J. (1989) 'Urban Consolidation: A Solution to Housing Need?', *Shelter* No 45, February.

NSW DEPARTMENT OF ENVIRONMENT & PLANNING (1988), *Sydney Into Its Third Century: Metropolitan Planning for the Sydney Region*, DEP, Sydney.

NSW GOVERNMENT, PLANNING & ENVIRONMENT COMMISSION (1978) *Social Indicators*, Government Printing Office, Sydney.

OFFICE OF LOCAL GOVERNMENT (1991) *Regional Economic Strength, Resilience and Vulnerability*, Working Paper, Department of Immigration, Local Government and Ethnic Affairs, Canberra.

OHLSSON, L. (1984) *International and Regional Specialisation of Australian Manufacturing: Historical Developments and Implications for National and Regional Adjustment Policies*, Bureau of Industry Economics, Contributed Paper 1, AGPS, Canberra.

ORTNER, J. & WACHS, M. (1979) 'The Cost Revenue Squeeze in American Public Transport', *Journal of American Planning Association*, January.

OWEN, W. (1989) 'Mobility and the Metropolis' in Knight, R.V. & Gappert, G. (Eds) *Cities in a Global Study*, Sage, London.

OWENS, S. (1984) 'Spatial Structure and Energy Demand' in Cope, D.R., Hills, P. & James, P. (Eds) *Energy Policy and Land-Use Planning*, Pergamon, Oxford.

PAINTER, M. (1979) 'Urban Government, Public Policies and the Fabrication of Urban Issues: the Impossibility of Urban Policy', *Australian Journal of Public Administration*, Vol 38, No 4, December, reprinted in Halligan, J. & Paris, C. (Eds) (1984) *Australian Urban Cities*, Longman Cheshire, Sydney.

PARIS, C. (Ed) (1982) *Critical Readings in Planning Theory*, Pergamon Press, Oxford.

PARIS, C. (1984) *Affordable and Available Housing: the Role of the Private Rental Sector*, Australian Institute of Urban Studies, Canberra.

PARIS, C. (1987) 'Housing under Hawke: Promise and Performance', *Journal of Australian Political Economy*, No 21, May.

PARIS, C. (1992) 'The Slow Death of A Very Fast Train', *International Journal of Urban and Regional Research*, Vol 16, No 4.

PARK, R.E. (1967) 'The City: Suggestions for the Investigation of Human Behaviour in the Urban Environment' in Park, R.E., Burgess, E.W. & McKenzie, R.D., *The City*, University of Chicago Press, Chicago.

PARKIN, F. (1972) *Class Inequality and Political Order*, Paladin, London.

PEARCE, D., MARKANDYA, A. & BARBER, E.G. (1989) *Blueprint for a Green Economy*, Earthscan Publications, London.

PEEL, M. (1992) *Planning the Good City in Australia: Elizabeth as a New Town*, Working Paper No 30, Urban Research Program, Australian National University, Canberra.

PETTY, B. (1976) *Petty's Australia — and How it Works*, Penguin, Harmondsworth.

PICKVANCE, C. (1982) 'Physical Planning and Market Forces in Urban Development' in Paris, C. (Ed.) *Critical Readings in Planning Theory*, Pergamon Press, Oxford.

PICKVANCE, C. (1985) 'The Rise and Fall of Urban Movements and the Role of Comparative Analysis', *Environment and Planning D: Society and Space*, Vol 3.

PINCUS, J.J. (1987) 'Government' in Maddock, R. and McLean, I.W. (Eds) *The Australian Economy in the Long Run*, Cambridge University Press, Cambs.

PLOTKIN, S. (1987) 'Property, Policy and Politics: Towards a Theory of Urban Land-Use Conflict', *International Journal of Urban and Regional Research*, Vol 11, No 3.

POWELL, S. (1987) 'Temporary, Insecure and Expensive in Housing: Whatever Happened to the Great Australian Dream?', Supplement to *Australian Society*, October.

PUSEY, M. (1991) *Economic Rationalism in Canberra*, Cambridge University Press, Melbourne.

RAE, J.B. (1971) *The Road and the Car in American Life*, MIT Press, Cambridge.

RASKALL, P. (1993) 'Widening Income Disparities in Australia' in Rees, S., Rodley, G., & Stilwell, F., (Eds) (below).

REES, S., RODLEY, G. & STILWELL, F. (Eds) (1993) *Beyond the Market: Alternatives to Economic Rationalism*, Plugo Press, Sydney.

REX, J. & MOORE, R. (1967) *Race, Community and Conflict*, Oxford University Press, Oxford.

RICH, D.C. (1986) *The Industrial Geography of Australia*, Methuen, North Ryde, NSW.

RICHARDSON, H.W. (1973) *The Economics of Urban Size*, Saxon House, Farnborough.

RICHARDSON, H.W. (1978) *Regional and Urban Economics*, Penguin, Harmondsworth.

RIMMER, P.J. (1988a) 'Transport Geography', *Australian Geographical Studies*, 26:1 April.

RIMMER, P.J. (1988b) 'Japanese Construction Contractors and the

Australian States: Another Round of Interstate Rivalry', *International Journal of Urban and Regional Research*, Vol 12, No 3.

ROBINS, P.A. (1981) 'The Regional Impact of Structural Change in Australian Manufacturing Industry: the Case of South Australia' in Linge, G.J.R. & McKay, J. (Eds) *Structural Change in Australia: Some Spatial and Organisational Perspectives*, ANU, Canberra.

RODDEWIG, R.J. (1978) *Green Bans: The Birth of Australian Environmental Politics*, Hale & Iremonger, Sydney.

ROSE, D. (1984) 'Rethinking Gentrification: Beyond the Uneven Development of Marxist Urban Theory', *Environment and Planning D: Society and Space*, No 2.

RUNDELL, G. (1985) 'Melbourne Anti-Freeway Protests', *Urban Policy and Research*, Vol 3, No 4, December.

SANDERCOCK, L. (1975) *Cities for Sale: Property, Politics and Planning in Australia*, Melbourne University Press, Melbourne.

SANDERCOCK, L. (1979) *The Land Racket: The Real Costs of Property Speculation*, Silverfish, Canberra.

SANDERCOCK, L. & BERRY, M. (Eds) (1983) *Urban Political Economy: The Australian Case*, Allen and Unwin, Sydney.

SAUNDERS, P. (1984) 'Beyond Housing Classes: the Sociological Significance of Private Property Rights in Means of Consumption', *International Journal of Urban and Regional Research*, Vol 8, No 2, June.

SCHULTZ, J. (1985) *Steel City Blues: The Human Cost of Industrial Crisis*, Penguin, Ringwood.

SCHUMACHER, E.F. (1979) *Good Work*, Harper Colophon Books, Sydney.

SCOTT, C. (1985) Quoted in the *Sydney Morning Herald* 27/9.

SEARLE, G.H. (1981) 'The Role of the State in Regional Development: The Example of Non-Metropolitan New South Wales', *Antipode*, Vol 13, No 1.

SELF, P. (1975) *Econocrats and the Policy Process: The Politics and Philosophy of Cost-Benefit Analysis*, Macmillan, London.

SHEPPARD, E. & BARNES, T.J. (1986) 'Instabilities in the Geography of Capitalist Production', *Annals of the Association of American Geographers*, Vol 76.

SINGH, S. (1989) *Banking on the Margin*, Report prepared for the Australian Financial Counselling and Credit Reform Association, Melbourne.

SMITH, D.M. (1979) *Where the Grass is Greener: Living in an Unequal World*, Penguin, Harmondsworth.

SMITH, J. (1992) *Fiscal Federalism in Australia: a Twentieth Century*

Chronology, Federalism Research Centre Discussion Paper No 23, Australian National University, Canberra.

SMITH J.W. (1990) *MFP—Adelaide, Economic Irrationality and the Open Veins of Australia*, Flinders University of South Australia, (Mimeo).

SMITH, N. (1979) 'Towards a Theory of Gentrification: A Back to the City Movement by Capital Not People', *Journal of the American Planning Association*, Vol 45.

SMITH, N. (1987a) 'Of Yuppies and Housing: Gentrification, Social Restructuring and the Urban Dream', *Environment and Planning D: Society and Space*, Vol 5.

SMITH, N. (1987b) 'Gentrification and the Rent Gap', *Annals of the Association of American Geographers*, Vol 77.

SMITH, N. & WILLIAMS, P. (Eds) (1986) *Gentrification of the City*, Allen and Unwin, Boston.

SNELL, B.C. (1974) *American Ground Transport: A Proposal for Restructuring the Automobile, Truck, Bus and Rail Industries*, Subcommittee on Antitrust and Monopoly, Committee on the Judiciary, United States Senate, Washington D.C.

SOCIALIST ALTERNATIVE MELBOURNE COLLECTIVE (1985) *Make Melbourne Marvellous*, Communist Party of Australia, Melbourne.

SORENSEN, T. (1985) 'On Corpses and Ghosts: A Surrealistic Approach to Regional Policy', *Urban Policy and Research*, Vol 3, No 4, December.

SOUTH AUSTRALIA: UNITED TRADES & LABOR COUNCIL (1991) *MFP: A Strategy for Change: A Union Perspective*, Submission to MFP-Adelaide Community Consultation Panel, January.

SPEARRITT, P. (1978) *Sydney Since the Twenties*, Hale & Iremonger, Sydney.

SPEARRITT, P. & DE MARCO, C. (1988) *Planning Sydney's Future*, Allen and Unwin, Sydney.

STEVENSON, G. (1977) *Mineral Resources and Australian Federalism*, ANU, Canberra.

STILWELL, F.J.B. (1972) *Regional Economic Policy*, Macmillan, Basingstoke.

STILWELL, F.J.B. (1974) *Australian Urban and Regional Development*, Australia and New Zealand Book Co. Pty. Ltd., Sydney.

STILWELL, F.J.B. (1980) *Economic Crises, Cities and Regions: An Analysis of Current Urban and Regional Problems in Australia*, Pergamon Press, Sydney.

STILWELL, F.J.B. (1983) 'State and Capital in Urban and Regional

Develpoment' in Head, B. (Ed.) *State and Economy in Australia*, Oxford University Press, Melbourne.

STILWELL, F.J.B. (1986) *The Accord and Beyond: The Political Economy of the Labor Government*, Pluto Press, Sydney.

STILWELL, F.J.B. (1987) 'The Housing Crisis, Squatters and the State: The Glebe Estate Experience, *Urban Policy & Research*, Vol 5, No 2, June.

STILWELL, F.J.B. (1988) 'Speculation Versus Productive Investment', *Journal of Australian Political Economy*, No 23, August.

STILWELL, F.J.B. (1989) 'Structural Change and Spatial Equity in Sydney', *Urban Policy and Research*, Vol 7, No 1.

STILWELL, F.J.B. (1990) 'VFT Plus MFP: an Economics of Desperation' in James, P. (Ed.) *Technocratic Dreaming*, Left Book Club, Melbourne.

STILWELL, F.J.B. (1991) Economic Aspects of Immigration in Smith, J.W. (Ed.) *Immigration, Population and Sustainable Environments: the Limits to Australia's Growth*, Flinders Press, Adelaide.

STILWELL, F.J.B. (1992) *Understanding Cities and Regions: Landscapes of Capital and Class*, Pluto Press, Sydney.

STILWELL, F.J.B. (1993a) From Fightback and One Nation to an Alternative Economic Strategy, in Rees, S., Rodley, G. & Stilwell, F. (Eds), *Beyond the Market: Alternatives to Economic Rationalism*, Pluto Press, Sydney.

STILWELL, F.J.B. (1993b) *Economic Inequality: Who Gets What in Australia*, Pluto Press, Sydney.

STILWELL, F.J.B. & HARDWICK, J.M. (1973) 'Social Inequality in Australian Cities', *The Australian Quarterly*, December.

STILWELL, F. & JOHNSON, M. (1991) *Metropolitan and Non-Metropolitan Areas: Comparative Economies*, Report commissioned by the Department of Employment, Education and Training, Public Sector Research Centre, University of NSW, Sydney.

STIMSON, R.J. (1982) *The Australian City: A Welfare Geography*, Longman Cheshire, Melbourne.

STONE, C. (1985) 'Urban Consolidation: Problems and Prospects' in Burnley, I. & Forrest, J. (Eds) *Living in Cities*, Allen and Unwin, Sydney.

STORPER, M. & WALKER, R. (1989) *The Capitalist Imperative: Territory, Technology and Industrial Growth*, Basil Blackwell, New York.

STRANGE, S. (1986) *Casino Capitalism*, Basil Blackwell, Oxford.

STRETTON, H. (1970) *Ideas for Australian Cities*, Hugh Stretton, Adelaide.

STRETTON, H. (1974) *Housing and Government*, 1974 Boyer Lectures, Australian Broadcasting Commission, Sydney.

STRETTON, H. (1987) *Political Essays*, Georgian House, Melbourne.

SUGIMOTO, Y. (1990) 'High Tech City for Lonely Technocrats', *Arena*, No 90.

TANAKA, Y. (1990) 'The Japanese Political-Construction Complex' in James, P. (Ed.) *Technocratic Dreaming*, Left Book Club, Sydney.

TAYLOR, M.J. & THRIFT, N. (1980) 'Large Corporations and Concentrations of Capital in Australia: A Geographical Analysis', *Economic Geography*, Vol 56.

THORNS, D.C. (1972) *Suburbia*, MacGibbon and Kee, London.

THUROW, L. (1989) 'Regional Transformation and the Service Activities' in Rodwin, L. & Sazanami, H. (Eds) *Deindustrialisation and Regional Economic Transformation*, Unwin Hyman, Boston.

TIMMS, D. (1971) *The Urban Mosaic: Towards a Theory of Residential Differentiation*, Cambridge University Press, Cambridge.

TROY, P.N. (Ed.) (1981) *Equity in the City*, Allen and Unwin, Sydney.

TROY, P.N. (1989) *Metropolitan Planning and Urban Consolidation*, Working Paper No 11, Urban Research Unit, Australian National University, Canberra.

TROY, P.N. (1991) *The Benefits of Owner-Occupation*, Urban Research Program Working Paper No 29, Australian National University.

TROY, P.N. (1993) 'Australian Housing Policy', *Urban Research Program Newsletter*, No 14, April.

UREN, T. (1973) Paper presented to the Second National Congress of Urban Developers, reported in *The Australian*, 13.3.73.

UREN, T. (1974) Second Reading Speech in the Glebe Lands (Appropriation) Bill in the House of Representatives, *Department of Urban and Regional Development Press Release*, 11.7.74.

VINTILLA, P., PHILLIMORE, J. & NEWMAN, P. (1992) *Markets, Morals and Manifestos*, Institute for Science and Technology Policy, Murdoch, W.A.

VIPOND, J. (1985) 'Unemployment – a Current Issue in Intra-Urban Inequalities' in Burnley I. & Forrest J. (Eds) *Living in Cities*, George Allen & Unwin, North Sydney.

VFT CONSORTIUM (1989) *VFT: Focus on the Future*, A Progress Report, October.

WALKER, R. (1974) 'Urban Ground Rent: Building a New Conceptual Framework', *Antipode*, Vol 6, No 1, April.

WALKER, R. (1981) 'A Theory of Suburbanisation: Capitalism and the Construction of Urban Space in the United States' in Dear, M. &

Scott, A.J. (Eds) *Urbanisation and Urban Planning in Capitalist Society*, Methuen, Andover.

WALSH, C. (1992) *Fiscal Federalism: an Overview of Issues and a Discussion of their Relevance to the European Community*, Discussion Paper No 12, Federalism Research Centre, Australian National University, Canberra.

WATSON, S. (1988) *Accommodating Inequality: Gender and Housing*, Allen & Unwin, Sydney.

WHEELWRIGHT, E.L. (1974) *Radical Political Economy*, Australia and New Zealand Book Company, Brookvale.

WHEELWRIGHT, E.L. (1991) 'The Great Depression in the 1990s', *Arena*, 94.

WHITLAM, E.G. (1985) *The Whitlam Government 1972–75*, Viking Press, Melbourne.

WILDE, P.D. (1981) 'Industrial Change, Structural Adjustment and the Periphery: the Case of Tasmania' in Linge, G.J.R. & McKay, J. (Eds) *Structural Change in Australia: Some Spatial and Organisational Perspectives*, ANU, Canberra.

WILDE, P.D. & FAGAN, R.H. (1988) 'Industrial Geography: Restructuring in Theory and Practice', *Australian Geographical Studies*, Vol 26, No 1, April.

WILLIAMS, P. (1986) 'Class Constitution through Spatial Reconstruction? A Re-Evaluation of Gentrification in Australia, Britain and the United States' in Smith, N. & Williams, P. (Eds) *Gentrification of the City*, Allen and Unwin, Boston.

WILLIAMS, R. (1975) *The Country and the City*, Paladin, St. Albans, Herts.

WILMOTH, D. (1989) Book Review: Planning Sydney's Future, *Urban Policy and Research*, Vol 7, No 4, December.

WRIGHT, E.O. (1978) *Class, Crisis and the State*, New Left Books, London.

WRIGHT, E.O. (1985) *Classes*, Verso, London.

WRIGHT, F.L. (1958) *The Living City*, Horizon Press, New York.

YATES, J. (1988) 'Housing in the 1980s: Dream or Nightmare', *Current Affairs Bulletin*, Vol 65, No 1, June.

YATES, J. (1989) *Home Ownership: Who Misses Out in the Private Sector and Why*, Background Paper, National Housing Policy Review, Department of Community Services and Health, Canberra.

YATES, J. (1990) Income and Access to Home Ownership, Economic & Social Policy Group, *Income Distribution Seminar: Papers and Proceedings*, Sydney, February.

YATES, J. & VIPOND, J. (1991) 'Housing and Urban Inequalities', in Social Justice Collective (Ed.) *Inequality in Australia*, William Heinemann, Port Melbourne.

ZIPF, G.K. (1941) *National Unity and Disunity*, Principia Press, Bloomington.

Index